The
De Sacramento Altaris
of William of Ockham

Edited by

T. BRUCE BIRCH, Ph.D., D.D.

(Former Harrison Fellow, University of Pennsylvania)

Professor of Philosophy in
Wittenberg College

English Translation

WIPF & STOCK · Eugene, Oregon

Wipf and Stock Publishers
199 W 8th Ave, Suite 3
Eugene, OR 97401

The De Sacramento Altaris of William of Ockham
By Birch, T. Bruce
ISBN 13: 978-1-60608-377-2
Publication date 01/22/2009
Previously published by The Lutheran Literary Board, 1930

To
My Esteemed Professors

JOHN C. ROLFE and WALTON BROOKS MCDANIEL

of the University of Pennsylvania, who, by
their encouragement and assistance, have
helped to make this book possible

TABLE OF CONTENTS

	PAGE
Preface	vii
Introduction	xi
Plates	
I. Facsimile Copy of Inscription	xvii
II. Facsimile Copy of Balliol Coll. MS. 299	xx
III. Facsimile Copy of Strassburg Text, 1491	xxi
Table of Titles and Chapters	xxxviii
Text of the De Sacramento Altaris	11
Bibliography	252

PREFACE

The object of this edition is to provide a text of the De Sacramento Altaris of William of Ockham based on the examination of three manuscripts and three text editions. It is hoped that this most important work, which is now easily accessible to scholars, may lead to a re-examination of the philosophical, psychological, theological, and ecclesiastical problems of the stirring times of Ockham and his immediate successors. It is also hoped that this work may give rise to a renewed and careful study of Nominalism—its vitality, its influence in re-shaping philosophical systems, in developing new psychological procedures and theological doctrines, and in modifying ecclesiastical policies and political theories.

Literary style and finish have been made secondary to accuracy of translation. A rather literal translation may be expected to aid the reader to obtain the precise thought of the Latin text and to carry along important shades of meaning of words and of expressions.

The critical apparatus contains the various readings which may give rise to modifications of the meaning of a passage.

With few exceptions, for the sake of brevity, the notes on the text are limited to the citation of various writers and to the places where references are found. I am under obligation to Professor John C. Rolfe, Ph.D., Lit.D., of the University of Pennsylvania, for

vii

PREFACE

instruction and direction in the study of Palaeography and Epigraphy, which have held me to a continued interest in these subjects.

For assistance and criticism in the preparation of the Latin text and the English translation, I am indebted to Professor Walton Brooks McDaniel, Ph.D., of the University of Pennsylvania, whose comprehensive knowledge of Latin was placed at my service; to Dr. Edwin F. Keever, while a graduate student of Harvard University, who shared with me his knowledge of the philosophy of the period of Ockham and acquaintance with the Latin abbreviations; and to my wife, Sarah Caroline Birch, for her knowledge of Latin abbreviations and of the Latin structure of the period, and for the untiring service rendered by her during the entire period of preparation of the text. For his critical examination of the Latin text, for many discerning and scholarly suggestions relative to it, and for his keen, painstaking reading of the proof of the Latin text, I am indebted to my colleague, Jens Anderson Ness, Ph.D., Professor of Latin.

For many valuable suggestions and assistance in the preparation of the bibliography, I am indebted to my colleague, John O. Evjen, Ph.D., D.D., Professor of Church History.

For the original suggestion of the need of a readily accessible and critical edition of Ockham's De Sacramento Altaris and for continued encouragement to complete the task, I am indebted to Professor Frank P. Manhart, D.D., LL.D., Dean of the Theological Seminary of Susquehanna University.

PREFACE

Miss Grace Prince, A.M., the librarian of Wittenberg College, and William H. Allen, bookseller, Philadelphia, have given valued assistance in locating and securing important books and material.

Acknowledgment should be made here of the uniform courtesy and assistance in securing access to the works of Ockham, rendered by the librarians of many institutions, including: Balliol College, Merton College; the Universities of Paris, Rouen, Columbia, Johns Hopkins, Harvard, Minnesota, Nebraska, Pennsylvania and Yale; Gettysburg Seminary; and the public libraries of Boston, New York, and Philadelphia.

The librarians of the Universities of Munich and Venice, and of the Congressional Library of Washington, D. C., have at various times supplied valuable data.

Scholars interested in this text will join me in appreciation of the courage, taste, skill manifested by the Lutheran Literary Board in publishing this work, and in appreciation of the singular accuracy and care of its readers and compositors.

For valuable information about the birthplace of Ockham, the origin of his name, details of his life and activities, I am greatly indebted to The Rt. Hon. Mary, Countess of Lovelace, who is the present owner of Ockham Park.

To President Rees Edgar Tulloss, Ph.D., D.D., LL.D., of Wittenberg College, my thanks are due for encouragement, many necessary and valuable suggestions, and the leisure secured by release from full-time teaching and various extra-curricular activities.

PREFACE

As Harrison Scholar, at the University of Pennsylvania, 1905-1906, and as Harrison Fellow, 1906-1908, I shared in the benefits made possible by the generosity of the late Dr. Charles C. Harrison, former provost of the university, who established the George Leib Harrison Foundation in order to encourage scientific study and research.

A Latin text and an English translation based upon the text edition, Strassburg, 1491, were submitted in 1908 as a thesis in partial fulfillment of the requirements for the degree of Ph.D., at the University of Pennsylvania.

T. BRUCE BIRCH.

Wittenberg College,
Springfield, Ohio,
November 30, 1929.

INTRODUCTION

I. THE AUTHOR, WILLIAM OF OCKHAM

William of Ockham was born late in the thirteenth century in the village of Ockham in the county of Surrey. His name, which is spelled in various ways, was taken from the name of his birthplace which is spelled Bocheham in Doomsday book. It is, however, spelled Ockham in an inscription of the year 1483, which is on an urn in the church at Ockham. Nothing is known of his parents or his early life.

Ockham's attention was early turned to Merton College which developed out of the "Domus Scolarium de Merton," which was established near Ockham at Malden in Surrey in 1264 "to support twenty scholars living at Oxford or wherever else a university may chance to flourish." In 1274 it was "moved from Malden to Oxford."

Ockham was a student at Merton College, Oxford, most probably from about 1312 to 1320. It is likely that he then became a member of the Franciscan order; for he was a Friar Minor.

Ockham received the degree of B.D. at Oxford after the completion of his thesis on the Sentences of Peter Lombard. He taught as a bachelor at Oxford until about 1323. There is no certain proof that he was a pupil of Duns Scotus, or that he was a student or a professor at the University of Paris.

It is not certain that he ever received the degree of

master or of doctor, for he is generally spoken of as the "Venerable Inceptor" (an inceptor at Oxford was one who did not go on to a Master's degree). However, the terms, inceptor, expositor, indagator, magister, professor, and doctor are associated with the name of Ockham. Ockham is also called: Venerable Preceptor, Doctor Subtilissimus, Unparalleled Doctor, Doctor Invincible, Singular Doctor, Author of Nominalism, and Father of the Nominals.

The academic advancement of Ockham may have been stopped by his engaging in the controversy concerning evangelical poverty. He was no doubt present at the chapter of the Franciscans at Perugia in 1322; though, perhaps, not as Provincial of England, as is frequently stated. He heard there the famous speech of Michael de Cesena, the General Minister of the Franciscan order, which set forth the position of the order relative to evangelical poverty and developed the bitter controversy between Cesena and Pope John XXII. This was the beginning of the revolt of the whole order, as distinguished from the Spirituals. In 1323, Bonagratia wrote a book against Pope John XXII, which supported the position of Cesena; but it was not until 1327 that he stated that Ockham was present when Cesena spoke against Pope John XXII in a convention of Friars Minor. But in a letter in 1323, Pope John instructed the Bishops of Ferrara and Bologna to inquire about the report that in a sermon at Bologna Ockham had upheld his conception of evangelical poverty in opposition to that of the Pope. If the report was correct, the Bishops were to

INTRODUCTION xiii

send Ockham "to Avignon within a month." Sullivan believes that Ockham would never "have opposed the Pope had that question of evangelical poverty not been raised."

In 1327, Pope John XXII issued a bull charging Ockham with having uttered "many erroneous and heretical opinions." DeWulf cites Ehrle as asserting that the Pope issued this statement relative to Ockham in 1329 and that "the process had nothing to do with the case of the Spirituals and the quarrel over evangelical poverty."

Ockham, Cesena, and Bonagratia did not feel safe in captivity at Avignon; therefore, on May 25th, 1328, they fled from Avignon. Ockham arrived at Pisa, where Louis IV of Bavaria received him. He accompanied Louis to his court at Munich in Bavaria. According to Trithemius, Ockham presented himself before Louis with these words: "O imperator, defende me gladio et ego defendam te verbo." Townsend cites these words: "Tu me defendas gladio, ego te defendam calamo." On May 28th, Pope John XXII sent a letter to all the princes and the bishops instructing them to seize Ockham and to return him for trial. On June 6th, he issued a bull telling of Ockham's escape, cited the heresies of Ockham and excommunicated him. On June 20th, the Pope issued a bull informing the archbishop of Milan and his associate bishops that Ockham had been excommunicated. In 1328 or 1329, the Pope sent letters containing like information to the archbishops in Germany, and the letter to the archibishop of Cologne was publicly read in the cathedral on June 30th. On April 21st, 1329, the Pope published a bull similar to that of June 6th, 1328.

About June 11th, 1329, Ockham was condemned by the Minorite General Ode and the members of his order were instructed not to assist him. On April 1st, 1330, the Pope issued a bull instructing all ecclesiastics in Germany to seize Ockham. In a letter of July 31st, the Pope again charged Ockham with heresy, and submitted the writings of Ockham to certain doctors who found many heresies in them. On January 4th, 1331, John again issued a bull forbidding anyone to aid Ockham; for he was said to uphold the error of Marsiglio of Padua, who had been condemned for stating that "the emperor can depose the pope." Ockham and others were summoned to a general council to be held on May 10th. The bull and the summons were to be nailed to the door of the church at Avignon, and the heresies were to be reviewed even if the heretics were absent. In 1331, the Minorite General Geraldus opposed the errors of Ockham.

During 1331 and 1332, Ockham and his associates took advantage of the unpopularity of the view of Pope John XXII relative to the Beatific Vision. The controversy waxed warm. The Pope's view produced "a profound sensation in the Church, for it had been denied. Princes, clergymen, laity urged John to retract. He retracted." Ockham declared that John was "wholly ignorant in theology."

After the death of Pope John XXII, on December 4th, 1334, Ockham continued the controversy relative

INTRODUCTION xv

to the imperial and the papal authority with Pope Benedict XII and Pope Clement VI. Both popes confirmed the excommunication of Emperor Louis. Pope Benedict confirmed the excommunication of Ockham. Ockham, however, continued to support Louis until the death of Louis on October 11th, 1347.

For about twenty years Ockham lived in the house of his order in Munich under the protection of Louis, in whose service Ockham and Marsiglio advocated political theories which anticipated those of the present.

When the crisis in the affairs of Louis IV arose in 1338, Ockham more earnestly continued his controversial writings. In July, the electors at Rense stated that Louis did not need confirmation of his election as emperor by the Pope. On August 8th, Louis declared that the action taken by the Pope was null and he appealed "from the Pope to a general council." Ockham wrote a defense of the claims of Louis and entered into a discussion of the nature of the authority of the emperor and the Pope.

In 1339, students were warned against the writings of Ockham, which had become popular. On December 29th, 1340, the University of Paris prohibited his teachings, and in a letter of May 10th, 1346, Clement refused to permit the masters and the scholars of the University of Paris to study the doctrines of Ockham. In 1348, the general chapter of the Augustinian order prohibited the reading of the works of Ockham under threat of excommunication.

Before Cesena died in 1342, he is said to have transferred the seal of his order and his claims to leadership to Ockham, who became the nominal head of the order, and after the death of Bonagratia in 1347 he became the undisputed chief of a powerful minority.

As early as 1343, Clement VI sought a reconciliation with Ockham and his followers; but Ockham continued his opposition to the Pope, although Emperor Charles had made peace with the Pope. It is said that not until 1349 did he send "back the seal of the order to the orthodox General Minister" and profess a desire to become reconciled to the church. Sullivan states that in letters of November 29th, 1347, and June 8th, 1349, Clement again sought a reconciliation with Ockham on several conditions. Ockham "was to promise to believe as the Holy Catholic Church believed, was to declare heretical the statements that the Emperor could select, create and depose the pope, to obey the present pope and his successors, to renounce the heretical opinions of Louis of Bavaria and Michael of Cesena and to promise not to give help to the enemies of the Church. . . . Ockham rejected them at first and was cited to appear before the papal court. It is uncertain whether he ever agreed to them or not. . . . In 1348, he had already rejected almost the same demands." There is no documentary evidence that Ockham ever accepted the proposal and was absolved. Some writers insist that "he remained an excommunicated heretic." It is not generally believed that he became reconciled to the church before his death.

There are various opinions regarding the year of

INTRODUCTION xvii

his death and even the place of his burial. It is reasonably safe to believe that Ockham died in the convent of his order at Munich and was buried there. Earlier writers, and in particular Volumes I and II of the Analecta Franciscana, state that Ockham died on April 10, 1347, and was buried in Munich as the inscription on the tombstone in the Franciscan chapel at Munich indicates. Leidinger, of the Department of Manuscripts, Bayerische Staats-Bibliothek, Munich, states that the St. Francis Church of Munich, in which

Ockham was buried, was pulled down in 1803 and that the tombstone no longer exists. He has, however, supplied a photographic copy of the inscription cited which was on the cover of the grave. The copy of the inscription is preserved in Cod. lat. 1755 I, page 34. (Monumenta ecclesiae Fratrum Minorum Monachii.)

In view of the document of Clement VI and the tract of Ockham treating of the election of Charles IV, recent conclusions lead to the belief that Ockham died April 10th, 1349, or at least not before the year 1349. Seeberg says that "some believe that the date of his death is as late as April, 1350, but 1349 is the most probable date."

II. The New Text

The new text is based upon the Balliol College, the Merton College, and the University of Rouen manuscripts, and the text editions of c. 1490, Paris; 1491, Strassburg; 1504, Venice.

The new text is based chiefly upon the Balliol manuscript and the 1491 text of Strassburg.

The Balliol College MS. 299 contains the entire text of the De Corpore Christi.

The Merton College MS. 137 is incomplete, ending with the words: "et per concilia," of Chapter XXXVI. It is much similar to the Balliol College MS.

The Rouen MS. 561 is quite unlike the other MSS., though the substance is much the same. It is a manuscript of the fifteenth century.

The text printed at Paris about 1490 contains the entire text of the De Sacramento Altaris. This text is found in the library of the University of Minnesota.

The text printed at Strassburg in 1491 contains the entire text of the De Sacramento Altaris. This text is found in the libraries of the following institutions: the Universities of Columbia, Harvard, Johns Hopkins, Pennsylvania, and Yale; and the libraries of the Andover-Harvard and the Gettysburg Theological Seminaries.

The text printed at Venice in 1504 contains the entire text of the De Sacramento Altaris. The text is found in the library of the University of Nebraska.

Many earlier writers looked for this treatise under two different titles: De Coena Domini and De Corpore Christi; but the problem of the title is now settled by this text.

The original text was based upon the lectures of Ockham, which were delivered at the University of Oxford. It was finished after the Epiphany of our Lord, as stated in the Colophon. No date fixes the year of its composition.

In preparing the present text, the 1514 edition of the Corpus Juris Canonici of Gratian was of the utmost service. This Corpus and the glosses made it possible to indicate the passages quoted by Ockham. The 1505 and the 1513 editions of the Sextus Liber Decretalium of Boniface VIII were also of assistance.

The manuscripts and the previous texts are full of Latin abbreviations, and for this reason this work has not been easily accessible to scholars. (Brampton has just recently published a full Latin text of the De Imperatorum et Pontificum Potestate of Ockham.) How

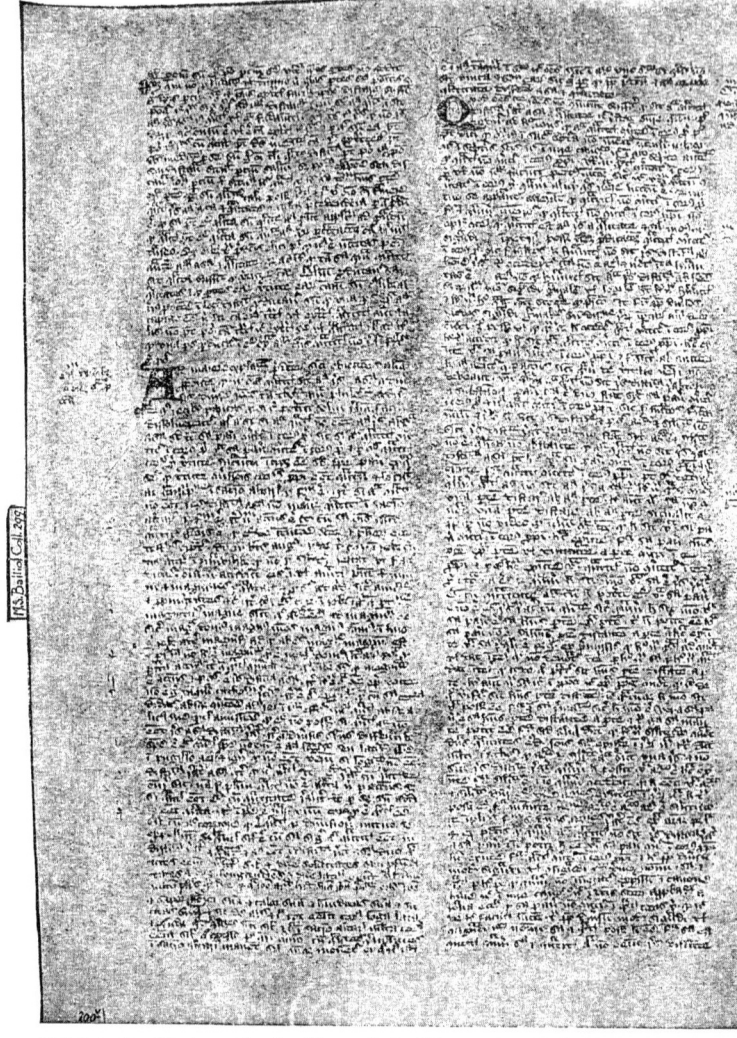

Reprint of a Photograph of a Page of the Manuscript of the De Corpore Christi of William of Ockham Which Is Used by the Courtesy of Dr. W. A. Pickard-Cambridge, Librarian of Balliol College, Oxford, England.

The reprint is a page of the Balliol College MS. 299, Oxford University, England. The Librarian of Balliol College provided the following quotation from the report of the examination of the manuscript by Dr. H. H. E. Craster of the Bodleian Literary: "Balliol MS. 299 is written in two hands which I should date on palæographic grounds about 1340-60. A note on an end fly-leaf gives evidence that the MS. was certainly written before 1368 and was then in Oxford, where it has ever since remained. The MS. was certainly written in England, and the presumption is that it was written at Oxford. An early reader has entered a few English sentences in the margins. On my dating it is almost if not quite contemporary with the Author, who died about 1349."

"The fly-leaves of the MS. contain four inscriptions recording the name of the former owner, William De Wilton, who was Chancellor in 1373-5. I fancy that the date of his death is not known."

The reprint shows some of the standard forms of Latin abbreviations in current use during the middle of the fourteenth century. It also shows the Latin word-order of the period.

ſposa ſuiua ⁊ ſuiuſum. ⁊ ipſe comedens ⁊ qui comedit. Itē beat⁹ Grego. ⁊ habet. ſ.q.j.multi. Polluit͂ inquit pane.i. corp⁹ rp̄i quādo indigne accedim⁹ altare.   Et bis aliſq⁢ pluribꝰ auctoritatibꝰ euidenter oſtendif̄ corp⁹ rp̄i ſub ſpecie panis realiter ꝯtineri ⁊ quia illud a pmordio fidei rp̄iāe oībus fidelibꝰ erat pſpicuū ideo circa ciuſ ꝯfirmatōȝ nolo diutꝰ immorari.
Capitulū. iij.
Q̊ ſubſtantia panis conuertif̄ in corp⁹ chꝛiſti.

Quamuis in ſcriptura canonica expreſſe tradaf̄. q̄ corpus rp̄i ſub ſpecie panis eſt fidelibꝰ porrigendū. tamē q̄ ſubſtātia panis in corpus rp̄i realiter ꝯuertif̄ vel trāſ ſubſtātiaf̄. in canone biblie nō inuenif̄ expreſſum. ſed hoc ſanctis patribꝰ credif̄ diuinitus reuelatū vl auctoritatibꝰ biblie diligenti ⁊ ſolerti inquiſitōr̄. ꝓ iſtā ⁊ ideo ad iſtā veritatē ꝓbandā auctoritates ſanctoꝝ parȝ adducā.   Un̄ dicit Euſeb⁹emiſſenus. ⁊ habet de ꝯſe. diſ. ij. q̄ corp⁹. Inuiſibilis ſacerdos viſibiles creaturas in ſubſtantiā corporis ſui ſanguinis verbo ſuo ſecreta poteſtate ꝯuertit. Et ſubdif̄. quāta itaq̄ȝ q̄ celebranda bn̄ficia vis diuine benedictionis operef̄. ⁊ q̄ꝰ tibi nouū ⁊ impoſſibile eſſe nō debeat q̄ in rp̄i ſubſtātiā terrena ⁊ mortalis ꝯuertif̄   Itē Amb. ⁊ habetur de ꝯſe. diſ. ij. panis. Si tanta inquit vis eſt in ſermone dn̄i. vt incipet eſſe q̄ nō erat. quanto magis operatius eſt vt ſint q̄ erant. ⁊ in aliud ꝯmutenf̄ȝ ſic q̄ erat pa͂is ante pſecratōȝ. iam eſt corp⁹ rp̄i poſt conſecrationē.   Item extra de ſūma tri. ⁊ fi. catholica. firmiter. vbi dicit Inno. iij. in cōcilio generali Una eſt fidelių vniuerſal̄ eccleſia. extra quā null⁹ omīno ſaluaf̄. In q̄ ipſe ide͂ ſacerdos eſt ⁊ ſacrificiū ibus rp̄us cuiꝰ corpus ⁊ ſanguis in ſacrame͂to altarꝭ ſub ſpecie panis ⁊ vini veraciter ꝯtinetur. trāſſubſtātiatis pane in corp⁹ ⁊ vino in ſanguinē. diuina poteſtate.   Itē extra de cele͂. miſſaꝝ. Lū marthe.Si tunc d’ oculos leuauit ad patre͂ cū ad corp⁹ exanime animaȝ lazari reuocans. ꝓbabilit⁰ eſſe videf̄ q̄ tunc oculos leuauit ad patre͂ in cela͂ cum pane͂ ⁊ vinū in corp⁹ ⁊ ſanguinē ꝓprie ꝯmutauit. Et quibꝰ aliſq̄ Ꝗpluriimis ſanctoꝝ ⁊ doctoꝝ auctoritatibꝰ ꝯſtat q̄ ſubſtātia panis virtute diuina realit̄ ⁊ veraciter i ſubſtantiā corpis rp̄i trāſſubſtātiaf̄ ꝯuertitur ſeu ꝯmutaf̄. ſine cn̄ augme͂to vl trāſmutati one ſubſtātiali corpis rp̄i.
Capitulū. iiij.
Q̊ ſubſtātia panis ꝯuertif̄ in corp⁹ rp̄i nō in diuinitate. nec i anima͂. nec i ſanguinē. nec in aliq̄ accidēs ſubſtātie.

Redicta conuerſio ſeu trāſſubſtātiatio panis ꝓp̄e accipiendo vocabula nō fit i ani ma͂ rp̄i. nec in diuinitate. nec in aliq̄ accidens ſubſtantie corpis rp̄i. nec in ſanguinem. ſed tn̄ in corpus chꝛiſti. Q̇uis impro pr̄et large ſumendo hoc vocabulū couerſio vel trāſſubſtātiatio. poſſet ꝯcedi q̄ panis tranſſubſtantiaf̄ in anima͂ vel accidēs corporis chꝛiſti vel ſanguine͂. Q̊ enim ſubſtantia panis in anima͂ rp̄i vel diuinitate͂ nō ꝯuertaf̄ doc. auctoritatibꝰ pſuadetur. vnde dicit gloſa de conſe. diſ. ij. ſuper caplo. Quid ē rp̄ȝ māducare In ſola carne͂ panis conuertitz̄ vinū in ſanguine͂.   Itē magiſter ſentē. in libro. iiij. diſ. xj. licet inquit ſub vtraq̄ ſpecie totus rp̄us ſumitur. tame͂ nō fit couerſio panis niſi in carnem. nec vini niſi in ſanguine͂. Et quibꝰ auctoritatibꝰ claret q̄ ſubſtantia panis erq̄ in ſola carne conuertif̄. nō in diuinitate vl anima͂ rōnale͂ vel ſanguine͂ trāſſubſtātiaf̄. nec per ꝯſeques in accidēs carnis nec anime. Sed hoc quide͂ verꝭ eſt ꝓprie ſumendo hoc vocabulū ꝯuertif̄.   Unde ſcienduȝ q̄ in illud ꝯuertif̄ vel trāſſubſtātiaf̄ ſubſtātia panis . qd nō quia cōiunctū eſt alteri. ſȝ etiam ſi ab aliīs eſſet ſeparatū ad prolationem verboꝝ ſacrame͂taliū a ſacerdote ſuper materia ꝯueniente cum intentione debita poteſtate diuina incipit eſſe ſub ſpecie panis. Huiuſmōi aūt eſt caro rp̄i ⁊ nō a͂ia nec ſanguis nec aliud accidens inherens carni vel anime. nā ſi eſſet anīa ſeparata a carne. quātūcunq̄ ſacerdos cū intētiōe ꝓferr̄ȝ verba ſacrame͂talia ſuper materia ꝯueniēte. nō ibi inciperet eſſe a͂ia chꝛiſti ſȝ caro tn̄. Similit̄ ſi ſanguis eſſet ſeparatus a carne. nō ibi inciperet eſſe ſanguis ſed caro tn̄. Et ide͂ iudiciū eſt de aliīs accidētibꝰ

Reprint of a Photograph of a Page of the Text Entitled "Tractatus Venerabilis Inceptoris Guilhelmi Ockham de Sacramento Altaris," Which Is Used by the Courtesy of the University of Pennsylvania and of Professor Walton Brooks McDaniel, Ph.D., of the Latin Department of the University.

The reprint is a page of the edition which was published with the Quotlibeta Septem of Ockham at Agrigentum in 1491.

The reprint shows some of the standard forms of Latin abbreviations in current use during the late fifteenth century. It also shows the Latin word-order of the period.

This page was selected because it contains the shortest chapter of the book and therefore shows the captions of two chapters.

difficult it has been to study the works of Ockham is seen from the statements which follow.

W. J. Townsend, in *The Great Schoolmen of the Middle Ages*, states that "the works of Ockham have never been collected and published in an uniform edition. They are very scarce, and are carefully preserved in some of the great libraries of Europe. So difficult are they of access that Brucker, when he wrote his *History of Philosophy*, had not seen them, and even one so widely read as Sir James Mackintosh had not been able to consult them."

A. E. Taylor, Edinburgh, *Present Day Thinkers and the New Scholasticism*, p. 67, says: "How hard it is, for example, even to have copies of Duns Scotus or Ockham at hand. I know very little about Ockham for this reason. His works are simply not accessible to me, as I am too busy to go where I could get at them."

Martin Grabmann, Munich, *Present Day Thinkers and the New Scholasticism*, p. 145, says: "It is a very welcome fact that historical research is now turning with greater briskness to the history of Nominalism and is beginning to draw a faithful picture of this powerful intellectual movement from the laborious study of manuscripts difficult to decipher. . . . The philosophy of Nominalism contains much philosophic acumen and propounds difficulties which still agitate philosophic thought."

III. The Latin Problems

The treatise presents many items of interest to the teachers of Latin: orthography, peculiarities of syn-

INTRODUCTION

tax, and the contributions of Scholastic Latin to the Latin vocabulary, especially to Latin and English philosophical and theological terminology. The Latin word-order of the first part of the text is that of the text of 1491. The Latin word-order of the second part of the text, the De Corpore Christi, is that of the Balliol MS. of 1340-1360. Differences in the word-order of the two centuries are quite apparent.

IV. *The Influence of Ockham upon Luther*

The influence of Ockham upon Luther was most profound. While in the University of Erfurt, Luther used Ockham's works as textbooks in philosophy. Melanchthon, in his Vita Lutheri, states that Luther "read Occam much and long and preferred his acumen to that of Thomas and Scotus."

In his *Table Talk* Luther states that "the Terminists is the name of a school in the universities to which I belong. They oppose Thomists, Scotists, and Albertinists, and are called also Occamists, from Occam their founder. . . . Occam is a wise and sensible man, who endeavored earnestly to amplify and explain the subject."

Luther, however, criticizes Ockham "as one who had no knowledge of spiritual temptations."

Luther refers to him as "Mein Meister Occam" and "Mein Lieber Meister Occam."

In the *Bekenntniss vom Abendmahl* Luther classes Ockham among the Sophists because of his views, but states that "he was correct in this matter."

Luther says that "they have condemned not only me, but Occam."

But in a most significant passage in the De Captivitate Babylonica Ecclesiae, Luther refers to a discussion of the doctrine of the Real Presence of D'Ailly, whose view was similar to that of his teacher, Ockham. Luther states that "formerly, while I was gulping down the Scholastic theology, the Cardinal of Cambry (D'Ailly), in Book IV of his Sentences, gave me occasion to reflect, by contending very acutely that it would be far more probable, and fewer superfluous miracles would be required, if it were understood that true bread and true wine, and not their accidents alone, were on the altar."

A footnote in the present volume cites a long quotation from the original which shows what Luther read, and indicates that Ockham and his pupil, D'Ailly, were in full agreement upon many points. Erdmann, *History of Philosophy*, states that D'Ailly set forth "pure Occamistic teaching."

These few external proofs of Luther's indebtedness to Ockham do not compare in value with the internal evidence as seen in the writings of each. In *Young Luther*, Professor Fife has recently shown Luther's dependence upon Ockham.

A careful comparison of the *Bekenntniss vom Abendmahl*, 1528, with this treatise shows that many passages are similar in each treatise and that many of the conclusions of both authors are identical in meaning. The present text makes it possible for the first time for scholars in general to make a careful esti-

INTRODUCTION xxv

mate of the psychological, philosophical and theological indebtedness of Luther to Ockham.

Professor R. Seeberg, Berlin, *History of Dogma,* states that this tract influenced Luther very greatly, for it is the theoretical foundation of his doctrine of the Real Presence.

This new Latin text indicates very clearly that this tract had the most direct bearing and influence upon Luther's views of the doctrine of the Real Presence and the defense of his position as supported by psychology and philosophy. No other tract more ably, simply and practically applies psychology and philosophy to the formulation of theology than this tract of Ockham, upon which Luther draws so often.

Harnack, *History of Dogma,* states that Luther "called in the aid of Occam's Scholasticism . . . in order to establish the Christian faith in respect to the Doctrine of the Real Presence." There are many passages of the tract that deal with the doctrines of the Communicatio Idiomatum and of the Ubiquity of the body of Christ, and with circumscriptive and definitive presence in a place, as advocated by Luther.

A study of the present text aids in showing why Luther was a Nominalist, and how profoundly the philosophy of Ockham shaped the views of the Reformers and of the later philosophers.

Ockham was called the greatest Modernist of his day. Luther studied Ockham's writings, saw his strength and his weakness, and was thus assisted in developing his own constructive program which sufficiently blended progress and conservatism.

INTRODUCTION

V. *The Psychology and Philosophy of Ockham*

Ockham was an important contributor to the Reformation and a forerunner of later philosophies of England and of Protestant Germany. This treatise provides abundant evidence of his theories.

1. Here is applied his theory of the sign, sense cognition, intuitive intellectual cognition, and abstract intellectual cognition, and his dualistic psychology of sense and of intellect.

2. Here is also seen applied his terministic philosophy, which influenced Luther and other Reformers in their conceptions of individuality, democracy, and the functions of faith and reason. They were thus led to contend against Aristotelian realism, and the ideas of solidarity and absolutism.

This text makes clear Ockham's use of vox, nomen, terminus, intentio, suppositio, substance, subject, quantity, quality, accidents, continuum, time, space, etc.

3. In this treatise Ockham applies the law of Parcimony—"Frustra fit per plura, quod potest fieri per pauciora." Ockham did not believe in multiplying entities needlessly. This text supports the conclusion of Thorburn, as found in The Myth of Occam's Razor.

4. This treatise sets forth Ockham's view of the failure of reason, and the need and function of faith. He shows the relation between reason and faith, but insists that "God can act according to His arbitrary pleasure and can do that for good against reason and experience."

Sorley, *A History of English Philosophy*, p. 7, states

INTRODUCTION

that at the hands of Ockham "the separation between theology and philosophy, faith and reason, was made complete. He admitted that there are probably arguments for the existence of God but maintained the final thesis that whatever transcends experience belongs to faith. In this way he broke with Scotism as well as with Thomism on a fundamental question."

5. Here is shown Ockham's exaltation of the Scriptures over the authority of the church. Taylor, *The Medieval Mind*, Vol. II, states that "Occam asserted the verity of the Scriptures unqualifiedly."

6. Ockham here advocates absolute voluntarism, "for the will intervenes in the discursive operation of the understanding." He "also teaches the most entire self-determinism of volition." He "makes the Free Will of God the sovereign arbiter of moral good and evil. But if nothing is of itself morally good or evil, the study of nature can teach us nothing about morality; intelligence is powerless to instruct us on the requirements of the Divine Law."

Human reason of itself can not establish the spirituality or immortality of the soul.

7. Here he sets forth his philosophical views concerning point, line, surface, substance, subject, quantity, continuum, quality, accident, etc., as he uses these conceptions to justify the various doctrines brought out in the discussion of the Lord's Supper.

VI. The Influence of Ockham upon English and German Philosophy

1. The repeated uses of Ockham's Law of Parcimony, or of Ockham's Razor.

2. He influenced the subsequent political theories, as seen in the development of the social contract theory of government, popular sovereignty, and the inalienable and indestructible right of freedom.

3. He influenced the development of all subsequent philosophical and theological thought and is profoundly influencing present-day thought.

Townsend, *The Great Schoolmen of the Middle Ages*, quotes John Selden (born 1584) as stating "that his works were the best that had been written in former ages on the Ecclesiastical Power."

Kuno Fischer, *History of Modern Philosophy*, states that Ockham's philosophy was a "fore-runner of that empiricism and sensualism with which modern philosophy began its course in the native country of Occam."

Townsend affirms that "Occam and Locke join hands in the adoption of a principle which must lead to a philosophy of pure sensationalism. . . . He anticipated the teaching of Hobbes, Berkeley, Hume, Hartley, and Condillac." He opened "the way for the extreme idealism of Berkeley on the one hand and for the scepticism of Hume on the other. . . . He taught a doctrine similar to Locke's, which defined sense and reflection as the sources of all knowledge."

Townsend also states that Ockham "was either the originator of the celebrated maxim, or enforced it more than any other Schoolman:—'There is nothing in the understanding that was not previously in the senses.' . . . Occam's view combined elements which were mediæval, and elements which were adopted by the Reformation and modern philosophy. . . All metaphysicians are agreed that William of Occam, by denying the existence of the species which had been taught by Aristotle as the direct object of perception, and which he said interposed between the object and subject, took the same ground which has conferred immortality upon Reid and the Scotch school of Philosophy. There is also remarkable similarity, if not identity of view, between the theory of William of Occam—that substances can be known only through their attributes and that therefore substans can never be known by the understanding, but only by faith, and the celebrated doctrine of Locke upon the same subject."

R. L. Poole, *Illustrations of the History of Mediæval Thought and Learning,* states that "Ockham, in virtue of his greater conformity to the spirit of his day, not to speak of his eminence as a philosopher, unequalled among contemporaries and hardly surpassed by Thomas Aquinas or John Duns Scotus, handed down a light which was never suffered to be extinguished, and which served as a beacon to pioneers of reform like Wycliffe and Huss. In politics, as well as in some points of doctrine, Ockham may be greatly claimed as a precursor of the German reformers of the sixteenth century." He "left an unbroken line of successors until the enduring elements of his aim found a partial realism in the religious revolution of the sixteenth century."

Bishop Turner, the Catholic philosopher, says that Ockham "has been described as the first Protestant.

And, indeed, he defended in his controversial writings the principles subsequently invoked by the first reformers to justify the encroachments of the secular power. In philosophy, too, his whole attitude is one of protest against the prevailing realism, and against the belief that the study of philosophy can be of material aid to theological sciences. In an age when theism and spiritualism were universally taught as philosophical tenets, he protested, in the name of human reason, that belief in God and in the spirituality of the human soul has no foundation except in revelation."

Numerous references show that Ockham influenced the philosophy of Locke, Reid, Hamilton, and the Scotch philosophers.

Michalski, Cracow, asserts that Ockham wrote the De Sacramento Altaris in order to set forth and defend his new philosophy. Ockham realized that the then much discussed Lord's Supper provided the best opportunity for a pragmatic application of his Nominalistic philosophy in opposition to the Realism of the day. This treatise clearly states Ockham's reason for writing this text.

The pragmatism of C. S. Pierce and the Nominalistic pragmatism of William James are based upon Ockham's philosophy. The latter states that the discussion of the Lord's Supper afforded "the only pragmatic application of the substance-idea with which I am acquainted," and that in this discussion "the substance-notion breaks into life, then, with tremendous effect."

C. Delisle Burns, *Aristotelian Society,* Vol. XIV, and *Mind,* Oct. 1916, states that Ockham "seems to have had in his philosophy all the prestige of tradition and all the promise of a new beginning"; "for the difficulties which were once faced by William of Ockham still need discussion." He sees "obvious likeness between Ockham and Hume." He also says that "there are interesting parallels to be found between the ideas of Ockham and Mr. Bertrand Russell; sometimes there is even a close likeness between the actual sentences of the ninth question in the first book of Ockham's *Quotlibeta* and those in Mr. Russell's *Our Knowledge of the External World.* . . . This question . . . has a close connection with his treatment of 'magnitude' in the De Sacramento Altaris."

James Lindsay, *The Monist,* states that "Occam had the merit to anticipate Kant" and "Descartes," and the "tendencies of modern empiricism," as well as "modern idealism."

W. M. Thorburn, *Mind,* July, 1918, states that Ockham "denies the reality of an Instant of Time, showing some anticipation of the doctrines associated with the names of Bergson and William James. . . . Few or no competent critics will question Mansel's judgment of Ockham, on page 4 of his Introduction to the *Rudiments of Aldrich:* 'The ablest writer on Logic whom the Schools have produced. . . . The Summa Totius Logicae of Occam is the most valuable contribution of the Middle Ages to the Logica Docens. His editor, Mark of Beneventum, said that if the gods used Logic, it would be the Logic of Occam.' "

M. Grabmann says: "Indeed, the basic researches of P. Duhem confront us with the fact that the Nominalist school of Ockham . . . is most intimately connected with the amazing anticipation of the scientific world-picture of a Copernicus and a Galileo. . . . The Medieval period has given us no scientific discussion and appraisal of William of Ockham, one of the most influential thinkers of the Middle Ages. . . . Great schools were formed: . . . that of Ockham, which is a prelude to modern Empiricism."

Pres. J. H. Ryan says: "The student of the history of mediæval philosophy, too, is well aware of the analysis of the inductive method made by Ockham and the disciples of his school. Without such preparatory studies the advance of science would certainly have been delayed for a long period."

J. S. Zybura says: "The precursors of modern natural science were philosophers of the School of Ockham."

Dr. Maréchal says: "The modern philosophers who preceded Kant and followed Duns Scotus and Ockham." (Quoted by Zybura.)

Ockham's discussion of "quantum" and "quanta" is well worth reading by the advocates of the modern "quanta theory." Equally interesting to the Neo-Realists is Ockham's discussion of realities and qualities.

All of the philosophical views stated above are developed in the De Sacramento Altaris. Many other views are likewise discussed in practical fashion; for all of his subtle skill and wealth of psychological,

INTRODUCTION xxxiii

philosophical, and theological knowledge is shown in this work as he defends himself from widespread criticism and the charge of heresy. In this work he sets forth and defends philosophical views which were to influence the thinking of the entire world and to change theological, philosophical, political, social, and other views of life.

VII. Ockham's Irony

This treatise has much light to throw upon this mooted question.

Rettberg, Baur, Lindsay, et al., have expressed their opinion that Ockham meant to be ironical when he refers to his belief in the Dogmas of the church. Rashdall, Erdmann, and Harnack agree with Geisler when he states "that Occam was really sincere in all his professions of respect for the Doctrines of the church."

R. Seeberg says that "the reader can not escape a painful impression when the talented author apologizes for his bold conclusions as harmless intellectual exercises."

Erdmann states that "this may seem strange to the Protestant, but to assert that no one could be in earnest in making such statements is to brand as rascals the most honest men of the various ages, who have made like declarations."

Rashdall asserts that Ockham was "unimpeachably orthodox on all questions except the authority of the Papacy and its relation to the Civil Power."

This treatise, more than any other work of Ockham,

dispells the charge of irony, for there is at the time he writes this treatise a ring of sincerity in all of his declarations of belief in the fundamental doctrines of the church.

VIII. Ockham and Marsiglio of Padua

It is apparent that a close relationship existed between Ockham and Marsiglio and that they mutually influenced the writings of each other. Pope Clement VI asserts that Ockham profoundly influenced Marsiglio in formulating many of his theories relative to the power and authority of the Pope. If they were not fellow teachers at the University of Paris, they were both at the court of Louis IV in Bavaria and were united in their efforts to defend the emperor during his controversy with Pope John XXII. Each in common aided in developing the political ideas which in dominant fashion shaped the political theories for the next two hundred years and are still vital in current political theories. Emerton states that "the distinction between them is that Ockham was primarily a philosopher trying to apply his general principles to human institutions, while Marsiglio was a trained physician and theologian without, so far as we can see, a definite philosophical system."

Previté-Orton, The Defensor Pacis of Marsilius, page xxiii, 1928, states: "Whereas supporters of the Papacy, and even opponents like Ockham, made principal use of the Canon Law, i.e. chiefly, though not wholly, papal decretals, in proving their case, Marsilius, far more explicitly than Dante before him, expressly

INTRODUCTION xxxv

declines to consider the Canon Law as of any weight or as providing any evidence whatever, and indeed he denounces it as a chief abuse contrary to the nature of the State."

(Note: Quotations from various sources have been used rather than subjectively derived conclusions.)

IX. Works of Ockham in This Country

(Known to the author of this text)

1. Centiloquium theologicum M. Guilhelmi de Ockam; Lugduni, 1495: Univ. of Penna., Harvard, Andover-Harvard Theol. Seminary, Boston Public Library, Peabody Institute Library, Baltimore.
2. Compendium errorum Iohannis Papae XXII; Lugduni, 1494: Harvard, Andover-Harvard, Boston Public Library, Univ. of Penna., Yale, Nebraska, N. Y. Public Library, Episcopal Divinity School, Phila.
3. Dialogus inter clericum et militem super dignitate papali et regia, etc.; Lugduni, 1491: Univ. of Penna., Harvard, Columbia. 1494: Univ. of Penna., Yale, Harvard, Andover-Harvard, Boston Public Library; c. 1500: Nebraska.
4. A Dialogue betwene a knyght and a clerke concernynge the power spiritual and temporall; Thomas Berthelet, London, 1559: Harvard.
5. Defensorium (a paupertate Christi) contra Iohannem XXII; Venice, 1513: Boston Public Library, N. Y. Public Library.

INTRODUCTION

6. Disputatio inter clericum et militem super potestate praelatis ecclesiae atque principibus terrarum commissa sub forma Dialogi; London, Thomas Berthelet, 15??: Johns Hopkins, Harvard.

7. Expositio aurea et admodum utilis super totam artem veterem edita per venerabilem inceptorem fratrem Guilhelmum de Occham cum quaestionibus Alberti parmi de Saxonia. Impressis prudentisimi uiri Benedicti Hectoris bononiensis artis impressoriae solertissimi Bononiaeque Impressa anno domini, 1496: Widener Branch of the Phila. Public Library.

8. Scriptum in primum librum sententiarum; Argenti, 1483: Univ. of Penna., Johns Hopkins, Yale.

9. Letterae F. Michaelis de Cezenae; 1331: Univ. of Penna., Harvard, Andover-Harvard, Boston Public Library.

10. Opus XC dierum; Lugduni, 1495: Univ. of Penna., Yale, Harvard, Andover-Harvard, Boston Public Library.

11. Philosophia naturalis Guilhelmi Occham; Romae, 1637: Univ. of Penna.

12. Quaestiones et decisiones in IV libros sententiarum; Lugduni, 1495: Univ. of Penna, Yale, Harvard, Johns Hopkins, Andover-Harvard, Boston Public Library, Peabody Institute Library, Baltimore.

13. Quotlibeta septem; Argenti, 1491: Univ. of Penna., Gettysburg Theological Seminary, Yale, Harvard, Columbia, Johns Hopkins, Andover-Harvard; c. 1487: Nebraska.
14. Summaria seu epitomata CXXXIII Capitulorum operis; Lugduni, 1495: Harvard, Nebraska, Andover-Harvard.
15. Summulae in lib. physicorum adsunt; Svardis, Venice, 1506: Univ. of Penna., Nebraska.
16. Tabulae ad diversas huius operis magistri Guilhelmi de Ockam super quattuor libros sententiarum; Lugduni, 1495: Univ. of Penna., Harvard, Nebraska, Boston Public Library.
17. Tractatus logicae: Dudum me frater et amicae . . . Omnes loycae tractatores . . . Explicit loici Magistri Guilhelmi Ocham. MS. at the Univ. of Penna. Text; Paris, 1488: Harvard Atheneum Library.

Summa totius logicae nuper correcta; Venetizis, per Lazarum de Svardis, 1508: Harvard Atheneum Library.

The Table of Titles and Chapters of the Tract of Venerable Ockham concerning the Body of Christ

QUESTION	PAGE
I. Whether a point is an absolute thing really distinct from a quantity	4
II. Whether a line and a surface are really distinguished from one another and from a body . .	42
III. Whether a body, which is a quantity, is an absolute thing really distinct from a substance . .	47
Prologue	80

CHAPTER	PAGE
I. What the Catholic doctors discerned by the senses concerning the reality of the Eucharist	82
II. That the body of Christ is really contained under the species of bread . .	84
III. That the substance of the bread is converted into the body of Christ	87
IV. That the substance of the bread is converted into the body of Christ, not into the divinity, or the rational soul, or the blood, or some accident of the substance	89
V. That the substance of the bread does not remain after consecration	92
VI. That the body of Christ is not circumscribed in a place in the sacrament of the altar	95
VII. That the body of Christ in the sacrament of the altar is not seen by us with the bodily eye	100
VIII. That the accidents remaining after consecration are not subjectively[1] in the body of Christ	102

TABLE OF TITLES AND CHAPTERS xxxix

CHAPTER		PAGE
IX.	That the quantity, which was before in the substance of the bread, remains	104
X.	That the sensible qualities remain	106
XI.	That every extended material substance is composed of substantial parts really distinct	107
XII.	That an absolute thing can be prior by divine power without a posterior	110
XIII.	That the omnipotence of God can make a substance without any absolute accident formally inhering in it	112
XIV.	That a substance, which is extended, can be preserved locally unmoved, although all of its absolute accidents may be destroyed through divine power	115
XV.	That a material substance through its intrinsic parts is present in the place in which it is circumscribed	118
XVI.	In which certain arguments are advanced to prove that the quantity remaining in the sacrament of the altar is not really distinct from the qualities remaining	121
XVII.	That any quantity is not an absolute thing really distinct from substance and that any quantity is not an absolute thing really distinct from quality	124
XVIII.	That all the qualities in the sacrament of the altar are not one subject of one quantity	127
XIX.	That not any quality may be the immediate subject of a quantity	130

TABLE OF TITLES AND CHAPTERS

CHAPTER		PAGE
XX.	That the quantity remaining is not subjectively in one quality and not in another	132
XXI.	In which it is proved by the testimony of the Catholic doctors that qualities are not subjectively in a quantity other than a substance	134
XXII.	That a quantity really distinct from a substance may not be a subject of qualities in the sacrament of the altar, is also confirmed through the statements of the philosophers	141
XXIII.	That the quantity remaining in the sacrament of the altar is not an absolute thing really distinct from the qualities remaining in the same sacrament	143
XXIV.	That before consecration there was one quantity, which was not an absolute thing really distinct from the substance of the bread	144
XXV.	That a substance can be a quantum without any absolute thing really distinct added to it	146
XXVI.	In which other reasons[2] are adduced to prove the same conclusion, which was stated before; namely, that a substance can be a quantum without a distinct quantity added to it	151
XXVII.	That the same conclusion, which was stated before, seems to follow from the statements of adversaries	157
XXVIII.	That a substance may be a quantum through its substantial parts without every quantity which is called a thing really distinct from substance and quality	160

TABLE OF TITLES AND CHAPTERS xli

CHAPTER		PAGE
XXIX.	The same conclusion, which was stated before, is proved through arguments taken from the statements of Catholic doctors	166
XXX.	Concerning objections contrary to the previous statements	178
XXXI.	In which replies are posited to the previous objections	181
XXXII.	In which it is shown that both propositions stand at the same time: some quantity is not another thing really distinct from substance and quantity is an accident	193
XXXIII.	It declares how quantity is an accident, and how it obtains with this, that some quantity is not a thing distinct from substance	202
XXXIV.	In what way it must be replied to the passages of Augustine, introduced before in Chapter XXX., in the fourth and the fifth arguments	210
XXXV.	How quantity is a category distinct from quality and substance; notwithstanding that no quantity may be distinct from part of a thing, from substance and quality. In which there is a reply to the sixth argument showing that categories are signs predicable of things	215
XXXVI.	That the previous opinion ought not to be rejected as heretical, contrary to certain writers who condemn that opinion as heretical; and through this the seventh reason, adduced before in Chapter XXX, is explained	219

TABLE OF TITLES AND CHAPTERS

CHAPTER		PAGE
XXXVII.	That the previous opinion is not contrary to experience, and the eighth reason, cited before in Chapter XXX, is explained	227
XXXVIII.	How all lengths are of the same species, and how some differ in species; and the ninth reason, adduced in Chapter XXX, is explained	231
XXXIX.	Concerning a diverse mode of predicating quantity according to diverse categories; explaining the tenth reason posited before in Chapter XXX	233
XL.	In what manner diverse quantities can be subjectively in a substance, since two bodies may not be able to be naturally at the same time; and the last reason is explained	237
XLI.	Concerning the explanation of certain arguments contrary to the previous statement	242

---

[1] Seeberg, *Hist. of Doctrines*, trans. E. G. Hay, Vol. II., p. 191: "Subjective-substantively, or objectively: objective-imaginatively. The meaning of the terms is now just the reverse." Fleming, *The Vocabulary of Philosophy*, p. 354: "Subjective is used by Will. Occam to denote that which exists independent of mind."
Burns, *William of Ockham on Universals*, Proceedings of the Aristotelean Society, New Series, Vol. XIV., 1913-1914, note p. 76: "It is sufficiently well known that what we call objective was in the mediæval philosophy called subjective."

[2] Ratio is sometimes translated reason or ground, as seems best, in order to convey a very definite meaning.

THE TRACT OF THE VENERABLE INCEPTOR, WILLIAM OF OCKHAM, CONCERNING THE SACRAMENT OF THE ALTAR

2 THE SACRAMENT OF THE ALTAR

The very renowned tract of the Venerable Inceptor, William of Ockham, of England, a very famous teacher of sacred theology, a most discriminating investigator of realities, of the order of Friars Minor, concerning the sacrament of the altar and with special reference to the distinction of point, line, surface, body, quantity, quality, and substance. It begins auspiciously.

Concerning the conversion of the bread into the body of Christ, as says a certain gloss on the De Consecratione, Distinction II., Chapter, 'In sacramentorum.' "There are various opinions. One opinion asserts that that substance, which was bread at first, afterwards is the flesh and the blood of Christ. It is argued later in the Chapter, 'Panis est in altari,' and in the Chapter, 'Quia corpus.' The second opinion holds that the substance of the bread and of the wine ceases to be there, and only the accidents remain; namely, taste, color, and weight, and similar accidents; and under those accidents the body of Christ begins to be there. The third opinion holds that the substance of the bread and of the wine remains there, and that the body of Christ is in the same place and under the same species. It is argued later in the Chapter, 'Ego.' Each opinion, however, acknowledges that the body of Christ is there. The second opinion is more true, as in the margin of the De Summa Trinitate, Chapter, 'Firmiter,' Una." These are the words of the gloss.

From this it appears that the substance of the bread is converted into the body of Christ, so that the substance of the bread does not remain but only the accidents remain which were before in the substance

THE SACRAMENT OF THE ALTAR 3

of the bread. And in confirmation of this truth it is said in the margin of the De Summa Trinitate, 'Firmiter,' as the previous gloss asserts: "There is one universal church of all the faithful, outside of which no one at all is saved; in which the priest and the sacrifice are the very same, Jesus Christ, whose body and blood are truly contained in the sacrament of the altar under the species of bread and of wine, since the bread is transubstantiated into body and the wine into blood by divine power."

With a view to the exposition of this truth, some questions must be asked about two points principally, as is obvious; first, about the entity and the distinction of those accidents; secondly, concerning the separation of them from a subject.

Moreover, since it is commonly conceded by all that color, taste, and sensible qualities of such a kind, are really distinguished from each other and also from substance; therefore, since this is conceded, some questions must be raised about the distinction of these qualities from quantity, figure, rectitude, and the like; concerning which there is great doubt as to how they may be distinguished.

And because this consideration pertains not only to theology but also to philosophy, since it may be the province of philosophy to come to know the natures of things and their distinctions; therefore, it is necessary to investigate what the philosophers have thought of this matter; and especially the prince of philosophers, Aristotle, and also what the theologians may say. But that I may proceed with more regard for logical order, I shall inquire first concerning the distinction of point, line, surface, and body; and afterwards of other matters.

4 THE SACRAMENT OF THE ALTAR

QUESTION I

Therefore, I ask, first, whether a point is an absolute thing really distinct from quantity. Which is answered affirmatively; for the terminus of every single thing is distinguished from that of which it is a terminus. But a point is a terminus of a line; therefore, it is really distinguished from a line, and consequently it is for the same reason really distinguished from any quantity.

On the contrary, every positive thing is substance or quantity or quality or relation, and so of the other categories. But a point is not a substance distinct from quantity, nor a quality distinct from quantity, nor a relation distinct from quantity, and so of other respective genera; therefore, a point is not a thing other than quantity.

Before answering this question and all following concerning this matter, I make in advance one statement; namely, that whatever I shall say under whatever form of words, which can in any mode be regarded as contrary to whatever has been said in Sacred Scripture or in the writings of the Saints, or contrary to the determination and the doctrine of the Roman Church, or contrary to the opinion of the Doctors approved by the church, I shall not say by affirming but by quoting precisely in the person of those who also hold the opinion to be discussed; whether that opinion be true or false, or Catholic, or heretical, or erroneous. Whence, if I shall use such words as "I say," "It must be said," and the like; I desire those words to be understood not as used by me personally but as used by those who hold such opinions.

THE SACRAMENT OF THE ALTAR 5

With this understood, I shall proceed thus with respect to the question proposed. First, I shall show that a point is not some positive and absolute thing really distinct from any quantity and especially from a line. In the second place, I shall posit some reasons and passages to prove that a point is another thing. In the third place, I shall reply to these.

First, therefore, I prove that a point is not a thing other than a line, or any quantity; and in the first place, through philosophical reasons; in the second place, through passages of the philosophers; in the third place, through theological reasons.

According to the first way; I, first, argue ostensively thus: if a point be a thing other than quantity, it is either substance or accident; but a point is not substance distinct from quantity nor accident distinct from quantity; therefore, a point is not a thing other than quantity.

The major premise is known; the minor premise I prove. And, first, I prove the first part; namely, that a point is not a substance distinct from quantity; for every substance is either matter or form or a composite or substance abstracted from matter. But it is manifest that a point is not matter or form or a composite; nor is it form abstracted from matter, if a point be indivisible and in no way a quantum, as is posited by the opponents; therefore, et cetera.

I prove the second part thus; namely, that a point may not be an indivisible accident distinct from quantity. In the first place thus: every absolute accident is placed in any subject adequate to it, so that that accident is either a whole in a whole subject and in each part, or a whole in a whole and a part in a part or is an indivisible accident having an indivisible subject, as a spiritual accident is in the rational soul as if in its primary and adequate subject. But a point in none of these three modes has or can have any primary and adequate subject; therefore, the major premise of that syllogism is obvious through induction as regards any absolute accident.

The first part of the minor premise is obvious; namely, that a point does not have any adequate subject so that there may be a whole in a whole and in each part. For I take a point terminating the line A, and let that be called B; and I take another corresponding point, and let it be called C; then I ask whether B is in A, as if in its adequate subject or in the subject of itself; and it follows in either way, that C will be in the same adequate subject for the same reason.

Then I argue thus: whatever things are in the same adequate subject, they do not differ either in situation or in place; but B and C are distinguished or separate in place and in situation; therefore, they are not in the same adequate subject. If it be said that B is not in the whole line A, nor in the subject of the same line A, but in a part of the same line or in part of the subject (of the line); on the contrary, if B be not in the whole line as if in an adequate subject nor in the whole subject of the same line; then it is in a part as if in an adequate subject. Let that part be D; then I argue, B is in D as if in an adequate subject; therefore, for the same reason another point corresponding to the same B, at which D is terminated out of another part, will be in the same D as if in an adequate subject, and let that point be

THE SACRAMENT OF THE ALTAR

called E. From which it follows that B and E are in the same adequate subject; and consequently they are not separate in place and in situation, which is most manifestly false. So, therefore, there can not be any point in any divisible quantum, and as if in its adequate subject, so that a whole may be in a whole and a whole in each part; not only because two points of that divisible would not then be separate in situation, which is false; but also because a point the same numerically would then be in two situations, which is false.

If it be said that a point is in some divisible part but another point does not correspond actually to that part, it can not correspond to it, because that part can not be existent per se, but only non-existent to another.

On the contrary; whatever part is designated, God can of His absolute power separate it from another part and can preserve it existent per se; therefore, this part, which is the primary and adequate subject of a point, God can preserve without another. Therefore, let it be posited in being, then it will actually have another point, which will be for the same reason in that subject as if in its primary subject; for there is no greater reason that one point terminating a line may be in that whole line or in that whole subject of that line than for another point terminating the same line; and consequently these two points will not be separate in situation; for those accidents, which are in the same adequate subject, are not separate in situation. Moreover, a corresponding point is not merely potentially in whatever way it is about to be potentially; therefore, it is in the nature of things and consequently has another primary subject, and this can not be granted unless a line or a subject of a line terminating at another point; therefore, these two points are in the same primary subject and consequently are not separate in situation, which is false. Moreover, if it were in some divisible subject, as if in a primary subject, then they would not be separate in situation from another part, nor could it be more separate from one part than from another.

The second principal part of the minor premise is thus proved; namely, that a point is not a whole in a whole subject and a part in a part; for a point would then be a quantum, and the thesis is established.

The third part of that minor premise; namely, that it is not in some indivisible as if in its primary and adequate subject, is obvious; because that indivisible would be either substance or accident. It is not accident; for I ask in what genus? And it is obvious that it can not be conceded to be in a genus other than the genus 'substance'.

Similarly, inquiry must be made concerning the subject of that accident, as about the subject of the point. Nor is that indivisible a substance; for, if it be a substance, it is either matter or form or a composite or a substance abstracted from matter; but it is not matter, since all matter is divisible; nor is it form; for, if it be form, it is either form extended and consequently is divisible or it is form non-extended and consequently is a rational soul; for the rational soul alone is non-extended; but it is manifest that it is not a rational soul; therefore, it is manifest that it is not form which is one part of a composite, nor is it a composite; and it is manifest that it is not form abstracted from matter; therefore, it is not some in-

THE SACRAMENT OF THE ALTAR

divisible substance, which may be able to be the primary and adequate subject of a point.

Moreover, if there be in a stone some indivisible substance which may be able to be the primary and adequate subject of a point; then I take this substance, and I ask whether or not it makes one per se with the matter and the form of the stone. If so, there would, therefore, be some indivisible substance in a stone which would be matter or form with respect to the matter of the stone; for whenever some making one per se are of diverse grounds in the genus 'substance,' one of these is act, the rest indeed power; and consequently one is matter and the rest form.

But it is impossible that that indivisible is primary matter, for primary matter is extended. But if this indivisible substance does not make one per se with the matter and the form of the stone, it is surely not part of the stone and consequently can not be part of the stone; and consequently can not be part of any substance.

But every substance, which can not be part of some substance, is subsistent per se and per se in a genus and in a species; and consequently this substance would be subsistent per se and per se in a genus and in a species, which is false; therefore, it remains that there is no substance in a stone except matter or form or a composite; but every such is divisible and possessed of parts really distinct; therefore, none of them is indivisible. So, therefore, it is obvious that neither any indivisible nor any divisible can be a primary and adequate subject of the same point, if a point be a certain absolute thing really distinct from every divisible.

If it be said as regards the principle reason, that the major premise is false; now there are many accidents which are not wholes in a whole and in each part, nor wholes in wholes and parts in parts, nor are they indivisible accidents having indivisible subjects but indivisible accidents having divisible subjects; and yet they are not in any part but a whole in a whole, as time is in the whole movement of the whole heaven, and yet it is not in any part of the movement of any part of heaven. Similarly, doubleness is a whole in a whole double, and neither doubleness nor any part of it is in a part of a double with respect to the same half. And it seems so of many other accidents, that they are in a whole; and yet neither they themselves nor a part of them are in any part of the whole.

But this reply does not suffice. First, because it accepts the fallacy that there are some indivisible accidents existing at first in some divisible and yet in no part of it; whence, time is not some absolute accident really distinct from motion and from permanent things, existing subjectively in a whole motion and in no part.

In the second place, this reply does not suffice; for, if this is granted, the argument still obtains; for a point is not such an accident. First; because it is obvious, that no accident existing in any adequate subject, whether it be a whole in a whole and a whole in each part or a whole in a whole and yet in no part, is separate in place and in situation from any accident existing in the same subject adequate to it; for color is not separate from the color of the same subject. Similarly, time, if it be another accident, is not separate in situation from some accident in the same

THE SACRAMENT OF THE ALTAR 11

subject adequate to it. Similarly, doubleness is not separate in situation from some accident existing in the same subject, as if adequate to it; and so in general of every accident. It is obvious, that it is not separate in situation from some accident existing in the same subject adequate to it. But a point is separate in situation from each point of that quantum, of which it is a point; therefore, two points can not be in the same primary and adequate subject, which however would be necessary if a point were an indivisible accident having some divisible for an adequate subject.

In the third place, no accident is separate in situation from each part of its primary and adequate subject; as the whiteness of that part A is not separate in situation from each part of the same A, although it is separate in situation from another part joining with A.

Similarly, if time or doubleness be an accident really distinct from a double or motion, it is manifest that time is not separate in situation from some part of motion, nor is doubleness separate in situation from some part of a double; and so of every other accident. But if each divisible is designated on the ground that it ought to be considered the primary subject of that point, it is manifest that this is separate in situation from another part of this divisible; therefore, that divisible is not the primary and adequate subject of the same point.

This reason is confirmed; for, when any accident is in some primary and adequate subject, it is obvious by induction that that accident is not more separate in situation from one part of this subject than from another. But it is manifest that that point is more separate in situation from one part of that divisible, whatever divisible is designated, than from another; therefore, that divisible is not the primary subject of this point.

From which it is obvious, that a point is not some absolute accident really distinct from every divisible, having some divisible for a primary and adequate subject; namely, that which is a subject in itself or per se and not through its own part.

Moreover, it can not be conceded that a point connecting two halves, in which it is subjectively, is in one half more than in the other, or, therefore, in both; and then an accident the same numerically would be in subjects several numerically, which is impossible, or in neither; and consequently in none subjectively.

If it be said that a point may be in some indivisible subject, as was mentioned before, this does not obtain, as was proved before.

And I shall prove it again; since some indivisible would be in a divisible subject, say, in a stone. Let that stone be divided in correspondence with that indivisible, and I ask, whether that indivisible remains or does not remain. If it remains; I ask, where it remains, whether with each part, or in one and not in the other, or separate from both. The first can not be conceded; for then some substance one numerically would be in distinct places which do not make one, which is impossible naturally. The second can not be conceded; for there is no greater reason that it be in one part than in another. Similarly, the third can not be conceded; since then nothing existing per se or in some other would make one per se; each of which is obviously false and impossible.

THE SACRAMENT OF THE ALTAR 13

In the second place, I argue principally thus. Every positive and absolute thing really distinct from every other thing not making one per se, as if a part with another thing, is per se in a genus. But a point, if it be such an indivisible thing, is not a part of any divisible, nor does it make one per se with any other; therefore, it will be per se in some category; but this is false, for then it would be either substance or quantity or quality or respect, any one of which is false according to those positing such indivisibles.

The major premise of that syllogism is manifest; for when there are some things distinct as regards themselves as wholes, of which neither is part of the other, there is no greater reason that one of them be per se in some category than for the other, as is obvious by induction.

But it is said in reply to this, that a point is not per se in a genus, but only through reduction; for it is not, unless a terminus of quantity.

But that reply does not obtain; first, because a line could not then be per se in the genus 'quantity,' since it may not be unless a terminus of quantity. If it be said that a line is not only a terminus of quantity but even a quantity; it is, therefore, per se in a genus. But a point is not per se a quantity; therefore, it is not per se in the genus 'quantity' but only through reduction. This does not obtain; for, if a point be such an indivisible thing, not only will it be a terminus of quantity, but it will be one absolute thing really distinct as regards itself as a whole from every other thing, and consequently will be per se in some category.

This is confirmed; for every thing absolute and permanent and one per se, not merely one through aggre-

14 THE SACRAMENT OF THE ALTAR

gation or order, is per se in some category or is a part of something existing per se in a category. This is obvious by induction of every thing, unless you insist upon the proposition. It is also obvious; for, if that major premise be denied, every way of proving that some thing is per se in a genus is destroyed; for thus of other things I may say, that something is not per se in a genus because it is the terminus of any substance; as you say, that a point is not per se in a genus, for it is the terminus of something existing per se in a genus; therefore, this is obvious, that everything one per se is per se in some category or is part of something existing in a category; but it is obvious by induction that a point is not a part of something existing per se in a category; therefore, a point is per se in a category; which was proved to be false. From which it follows that a point is not such an indivisible thing.

In the third place, I argue thus. It is impossible that there may be things infinite actually, distinct as regards themselves as wholes, and of which none may be part of another, and which do not make some one. But if a point were such an indivisible thing, such would be infinite actually. For example, I take wood. It is manifest according to those writers that there are here infinite lines; for there are not just so many so that there could not be more, and each of them is terminated actually at some point; for otherwise no line could be terminated actually at some point. And it is manifest that they are distinguished as regards themselves as wholes, if they be indivisibles; nor do they make one per se, since they may not be parts of anything; therefore, such will be infinite actually, which is impossible and contrary to all philosophy. There-

THE SACRAMENT OF THE ALTAR 15

fore, it remains that a point is not any such indivisible thing really distinct from every divisible.

In the fourth place thus: some thing positive and absolute is not caused through division only of a continuum. Let, therefore, wood be divided; and I ask about the terminating points, whether they were before or not. If they were, it is certain that they will not be separate in situation; therefore, a point was immediate to a point; which is false even according to those writers. If they were not before and now are; they are, therefore, generated de novo, and consequently some absolute thing necessarily would be generated through division alone, which is false.

In the fifth place; since they can become continuous through the union only of parts of water or of another, whose parts were separate before, some new absolute thing is not generated nor is an absolute corrupted. But if a point were such an indivisible thing, whenever such parts would become continuous, of necessity some absolute thing would be corrupted; say, these two points which before terminated two lines, and a new thing would be generated; namely, one point connecting those two parts. Indeed, it would follow that infinite, absolute things distinct as regards themselves as wholes would be corrupted, and infinites would be generated; as can be deduced through the third principal reason previously stated; all of which are impossible, and consequently a point is not such an indivisible thing.

I prove this same conclusion through theological reasons. First thus: every absolute thing distinct as regards itself as a whole from another absolute thing, of which it is not subject nor effect, nor conversely, God can create without the second thing.

But if a point be such an indivisible thing, it is manifest that a line as regards itself as a whole is distinguished from a point; for it is manifest that a line is not a part of a point, nor is a point a part of a line, nor again is a line the subject of a point, as was proved before; and conversely a point is not the subject of a line. Moreover, a line is not the cause of a point, nor conversely; as is obvious by a survey of all classes of causes; therefore, God can of His absolute power make a line without any point.

Then I ask, whether that line is finite or infinite. If it be finite and without any point; it is consequently needless to posit a point to terminate a line, and yet it is not posited by virtue of another by those who thus posit it. If, however, that line be not terminated nor finite, and is in the nature of things per casum; it, therefore, is infinite, which obviously is manifestly false; for that line will not by virtue of this be greater, or longer because that point is separated or destroyed; therefore, in no mode will there be that infinite, no matter to what extent all the points may be destroyed. Moreover, if all the points be destroyed by God, and the line is saved; I ask whether or not that line is continuous. If it is, and not through a point, for it is not per casum; there is, therefore, a continuous line without any point, and consequently a point is needlessly posited there. If it be not continuous; I ask whether any part of it be continuous, in which case the preceding argument applies, or else no part is continuous; from which it follows that there is some line which is not composed of continua, which is impossible.

THE SACRAMENT OF THE ALTAR 17

Similarly, that line is continuous or discrete; if continuous, the thesis is established; if discrete, then each part is divided into a quantum infinite as regards all its parts, which is impossible. But this reason proves that a line is sufficiently continuous and finite through its proper nature without any other thing added to it; and consequently, since a point ought not to be posited by virtue of another, a point is needlessly posited to be such an indivisible thing.

If it be said that God can not of His absolute power make a line without a point; on the contrary, when any absolute thing can through nature be made without many things separately so that it may be without any of them singly, that thing can be made through the divine power without all of them joined together so that none of them may be with it; which is especially true, when these things as regards themselves as wholes are really distinct and neither of them is an effect or an accident of the other; as is the case of the point and of the line. If the point be such an indivisible thing, (but this line can through nature be without this point and that point and so of others and so of any,) God can, therefore, make this without any point; and so the thesis is established.

Moreover, if that, which essentially depends on something as an effect depends on a cause and an accident on its subject, can be separated from that through divine power; much more firmly can God make that, which does not depend on another either as a whole on a part or as an accident on its subject or as an effect on another, without that.

But an accident in the sacrament of the altar depends before the separation on a substance as if on a cause and on its subject; and yet through divine power it becomes an accident without a subject; therefore, much more firmly can the line, which does not depend on the point either as if on its part or as if on a subject or as if on its cause, be made without it; and so the first argument obtains.

That reason is confirmed; for, according to the Philosopher in the second book of the Physics, "Quantity is per se finite or infinite." But if a quantity were finite through another thing, as a line is finite through points as if through another thing, it itself would not be finite per se but through another. In the sacrament of the altar a quantity is separated from every substance; therefore, a line is separated from every subject. Then I ask about the point terminating that line, whether or not it is separated from every subject; if so, then that point and the line do not in any mode make one, for they are neither one per se nor one through an accident, since neither may be receptive of the other; and consequently the line can not otherwise be terminated through a point, unless as water is terminated by a solid body; namely, earth or something similar, which can not correspond to a point.

But if a point may not be without a subject, and it is manifest that it is not subjectively in a substance; since it may not be there unless the body of Christ, in which a point can not be posited; that, therefore, is subjectively in a line, but this is impossible as was proved before; for if it were subjectively in a line or in some part of a line, as if in a primary and adequate subject and not only through a part, as this whiteness is said to be in Sortes; for it is in one part of Sortes, a point might be able to be separate in place and in situation

THE SACRAMENT OF THE ALTAR 19

from no part of a subject, say, a line or a part of a line, as was affirmed before; which is manifestly false, as was proved before.

By virtue of the previous statements and many others, which can be adduced, those positing might say that nothing is simply indivisible in things through the creation of all parts really distinct except substances separate from matter and principally the rational soul and its accidents; and that a point is not a thing indivisible, positive and absolute, really distinct from a line and every quantity. But they might say that any thing divisible in itself is formally finite, terminated and continuous; if it be continuous without any other thing added to it, it is causally terminated, finite, and continuous by God and other causes per se placing it in being, whatever may be those causes; whence this line without any other thing added to it. Indeed, if any other thing were destroyed and this line were preserved by God, it would truly be finite, terminated and continuous; and, indeed, since such an indivisible thing may not be posited by virtue of others, it seems as impossible as superfluous to posit that a point is such an indivisible thing.

And if it is asked: What is a point? Whether it is a thing divisible or an indivisible? Which must be answered thus by saying, 'a point is something' or 'a point is a thing' or anything else of the kind. If a point stand for something so that it may have precisely the force of a *name* and may not embrace as an equivalent one compounded of a noun and a verb, or something very similar which can represent a supposition for a verb according to a property of speech; it ought to be conceded that a point is something and that a point is a thing, and this because it ought to be conceded that a point is a line or a point is a quantity; for then this name 'point' will be equivalent to this 'a line of such or such length,' or 'a line not farther lengthened or extended,' or to some whole compounded of a noun and a verb with an intervening conjunction or adverb or this pronoun 'quae'; according to which it is pleasing to give diverse definitions expressing some characteristic of that name 'point.' And indeed, as this predicate 'a divisible thing' is predicated of such a subject and consequently of a composite of an adjective and a substantive, so it is predicated of a point.

Whence, as some say that this name 'privation' is equivalent in significance to this whole 'subjectum privatum'; and by virtue of this, as they concede this, 'subjectum privatum' is matter; so they concede this, 'privation' is matter. So if this name 'point' is equivalent in signification to this whole, 'a line not farther lengthened' or to something similar; of which one part may be a line, and other parts may be some adjectives or a verb connected with line, this pronoun 'quae' intervening, or another similar. As this is conceded, 'a line is divisible,' so this is conceded according to the virtue of signification, 'a point is a line,' 'a point is divisible.' For whatever is true of this name 'line,' when used significatively, is true of this name 'point' when used significatively, and this by speaking according to the virtue of signification; yet this, notwithstanding that one proposition, in which this name 'point' is substituted, could be per se; and another, in which this name 'line' is posited, will not be per se, and conversely.

THE SACRAMENT OF THE ALTAR 21

Just as whatever is predicated of one of the convertibles, when used significatively, is true of the rest when used significatively, and yet one of them per se and not the rest. Whence, this is per se in the first mode, 'every man is an animal,' and not this, 'every risible is an animal.' But if this name 'point' will be equivalent in signification to some composite of a noun or a verb or a conjunction or an adverb and this pronoun 'qui,' or of a composite of an oblique case and a verb, which according to a property of common speech can not express, speaking grammatically, a supposition for a verb; consequently, too, any language, in which it is posited, is not according to a property, but is figurative speech and can be reduced to a figure which is called by the grammarians 'hypallage,' of which they say that hypallage is the conversion of cases or of a construction or sometimes of a whole sentence.

So it ought to be conceded that 'a point is an indivisible thing' and that 'a point does not have parts,' and anything else of the kind. But those propositions and similar ones must not be conceded according to a property of common speech, as proper propositions must not be disposed of through any grammatical figure; and consequently in the investigation of reality it must not be argued from these, unless they are taken according to the sense which they have according to the intention of the authors; but they must be conceded under that sense, which they have from this, that they are disposed of through the aforesaid figure; for this reason, namely, that one expression is posited in place of one form of language or of a composite of many expressions, and at the same time with this it is necessary to convert the language by transposing and even by changing sometimes one part of the language into another, and sometimes one expression into another, and a case into a case, or one grammatical accident into another, or in a similar mode by conversion; that the sense of this proposition, 'a point is indivisible,' may be this, 'a line is not farther lengthened,' of which, however, each part is divisible; or another similar sense according as one is pleased to explain the previous proposition. But the sense of this proposition, 'a point is divisible,' may be that or some similar sense; for whatever part of the line is taken, it is still proper to take the more remote.

And as it is said of these propositions, so it must be said of similar propositions; and not only is this true of this name 'point'; but it is also true of all verbal names and all *names* formed from adverbs, conjunctions, pronouns, prepositions, and in general of all syncategorematics, and in general of all, which do not precisely have the virtue of a *name;* so that they can not be the extremes of a proposition separated by a copula without any figure and a property of common speech. And according to this, all such: 'action is in passion,' 'motion is in the mobile,' 'likeness is in the similar,' 'whiteness is the terminus of motion,' 'every thing is produced through production,' 'fire makes warm by heating,' and innumerable propositions of a similar kind, which are found in the statements of the philosophers and of the Saints and even in Sacred Scriptures, must be figuratively disposed of through some grammatical figure. Nor is it inconsistent to concede that the philosophers and the Saints spoke thus figuratively, since many such may be found in Sacred Scripture; not however by accepting the statements of

THE SACRAMENT OF THE ALTAR 23

Sacred Scripture in a spiritual sense but even in a literal sense.

Indeed, even the popular and common mode of speaking frequently employs such figurative expressions; as can be proved through the statements of the grammarians treating of such. Whence, not only the expression can be transferred from a proper to an improper signification, but even sometimes terms are given which have no proper signification, such as they have when first instituted. And as a translation is made according to the grammarians for a threefold cause: sometimes for the sake of metre as in the poets; sometimes for the sake of ornament as in rhetorical speech; sometimes for the sake of necessity, either brevity or utility, as in philosophy; and in all of these ways a translation is made in theology. So the application of such names, whether they be abstract or concrete, is made for a three-fold cause; namely, for the sake of metre, ornament, and utility or brevity. Although from the previous causes many errors occasionally originate among the simple minded, who wish to accept all the statements of the philosophers and of the Saints according to a property of common speech, when they must be taken figuratively.

The second principal division. But a certain Doctor argues first thus against the previous statements. It follows from that opinion that sudden generation, which is not per se the terminus of a continuum, will be nothing or at least in nothing; for it does not have any other positive measure, and so is it of illumination and of all sudden changes, which are not per se terminations of motion. And although they can escape from the changes, which are the terminations of motions and happen in an instant, as in nothing, or the privation of continuity in the privation of continuity; yet concerning these it seems absurd; for they are not the terminations of the continuity of some continuum; for they are by no means characteristic of any continuum, either positively or privatively.

Moreover, in the first book of the Posteriores, the ground of the line is from points; that is, a point falls within the essential ground of the line, which is called the ground according to line in the first mode of speaking per se; but no privation pertains per se to the essential ground of a positive.

In the third place; it follows from the same, that, if a point is only privation, a line will be only privation and surface and body; for the terminate is always limited through a terminant, and a positive does not essentially include privation.

In the fourth place; Aristotle in the Categories seems to be in opposition to that opinion, where he says that parts of a line are terminated at a point as if at a termination; but the terminus is always other than that which is terminated at itself; therefore, a point is such an indivisible thing.

In the fifth place; the philosopher in the first book of the Physics says that 'an indivisible terminus is not infinite'; according to this he affirms that a point, because it is indivisible, is neither finite nor infinite.

In the sixth place; the philosopher in the fourth book of the Physics, where he proves that place is not body, says that we do not have one difference of point and of place; therefore, according to him a point is something distinct from divisible things.

THE SACRAMENT OF THE ALTAR 25

In the seventh place; according to the philosopher in the second book of the Physics, he says that "they touch each other whose extremes are together"; therefore, the two extremes of two lines touching each other are at the same time; but no two parts of these lines are at the same time, nor are the lines themselves at the same time; therefore, besides the lines and their parts, there are others, which are at the same time, which can not be unless indivisible points.

In the eighth place; in the fifth and the sixth book of the Physics he says that those are continuous of which the extremes are one; therefore, the two extremes of two halves in one line are one; but it is manifest that neither those halves nor any parts of them are one; therefore, besides those there are some which are one.

In the ninth place; the philosopher in the same place posits, that a line is divisible and a point indivisible, and this is proved through this, that a line is not composed of points, nor is any continuum composed of indivisibles; which would be futile unless there could be such indivisibles other than continua.

In the tenth place; the philosopher says in the same place that, since however an impartible is indivisible, it is necessary for a whole to touch, et cetera; from which it is obvious that he posits some such indivisible.

Innumerable statements of such a character might be adduced by virtue of which it seems that it may be in accordance with the intention of the philosopher to posit such indivisible things really distinct from divisible things.

The third principal division responds to the reasons; but because another way of solving could appear from the solution of the previous statements; I, therefore, omit those arguments for the sake of brevity, and I reply to these.

As regards the first; I say that an instant is not such an absolute thing really distinct from every divisible thing, which can be proved in various ways.

First; because it does not have any primary subject in which it may be able to be in a primary and adequate subject as if an accident in its subject, as is obviously inductively.

In the second place; because then God might not be able to make time to exist, unless he could necessarily produce infinite things as regards themselves distinct wholes and corrupt the same.

In the third place; because such things, when produced, would not be able naturally to be destroyed; for they could not be destroyed either through the corruption of their subject or through the absence of their preserving cause, or through the induction of their contrary.

In the fourth place; because, if there were such a thing, it could be in a genus per se, which is manifestly false.

In the fifth place; because God can preserve at the same time in the nature of things all things of the same ground, since they may not repel one another; therefore, God could bring it to pass that all past instants might be now, which however are infinite.

In the sixth place, because God may be able to make an instant apart from any subject of its own, which is impossible.

For the sake of brevity I pass by the presentation

THE SACRAMENT OF THE ALTAR 27

of those reasons; but I say that neither change nor generation is such an indivisible thing. And consequently, therefore, as regards the previous statements that all such expressions are figurative and metaphorical: 'an instant is indivisible,' 'generation is in an instant,' 'sudden change is in an instant,' 'generation is sudden,' 'substantial form is a terminus of generation,' 'to have been changed is a terminus of motion,' and any other of the kind; because in all such formal expressions in place of the other extreme of the proposition, one name is posited which has not only the force of a name in signification, but has the force of a noun and of a verb, or has the force of something composed of diverse terms, which compounded according to a property of common speech can not express a supposition for a verb, nor be the extreme of a proposition distinct from the other extreme and a copula.

Whence, so far as this is concerned; it is similar of such expressions, as it would be if there were one name put in to signify that which signifies 'tunc bene,' say, A; according to a property of common speech it would not be well said, 'tunc bene est.' So it would not be well said, 'A is something'; yet there might be such a saying, 'A is something' to be accepted, as if a metaphorical and figurative expression that might be equivalent to this, 'that, which is tunc bene, is something,' or any other of a like kind. So I say of such, 'generation is sudden,' and of any other of a like kind, that they are not proper expressions but figurative; and it is from this, that this name 'instant' and this name 'generation,' and any other of a like kind, are not finite names having finite signification, as if they signify precisely certain things for which they may have to substitute, according to the mode in which such names as 'angel,' 'whiteness,' 'blackness,' 'heat,' 'cold,' have finite significations; but there are certain derivatives from verbs or other parts of formal speech or similar to such, which are not instituted, unless for the sake of metre, or ornament, or for the sake of brevity of speech.

And, therefore, as many statements in poetry and in an ornate mode of speaking must not be quoted unless they be explained and interpreted; so many statements must not be accepted for the sake of brevity according to a property of common speech, but according to the intention of the authors saying these things, who spoke figuratively by virtue of the cause stated; and this, because such were sufficiently well known in their times, that they were not true according to a property of common speech, although some later writers have ignored this.

Whence, I say that this proposition, 'generation is in an instant,' must not be accepted under the meaning which it signifies, as if one thing may be in another; as through this proposition, 'water is in a vase,' it is denoted that one thing is in another in a distinct thing; whence, in distributing through all the modes in which this proposition 'in' is taken equivocally, of which the philosopher speaks in book four of the Physics, it is obvious that according to none of those can it be said that generation is in an instant; but this proposition, 'generation is in an instant,' ought to be accepted under this meaning, 'when something is generated, a part is not generated before a part, but the whole is generated at the same time'; that this brief proposition, 'generation is in an instant,' may be posited for the

THE SACRAMENT OF THE ALTAR 29

sake of brevity in place of that long formal expression, 'when something is generated, a part is not generated before a part but the whole at the same time.'

Similarly this proposition, 'motion is in time,' ought not to be accepted under that meaning which it signifies according to the form of the proposition; namely, that one thing is in another thing really distinct from it, but it ought to be accepted under this meaning, 'when something is moved, it acquires one part before another, or it acquires one before another without interruption,' or under such a meaning, 'when something is moved, it acquires or loses one thing after another, co-existing at the same time with a movable first acquiring one after another,' or in some such meaning as that brief formal expression, 'motion is in time,' is posited in place of such a long formal expression or of some very similar expression. And when it is said that according to the preceding statements, 'generation would be nothing,' I say that 'generation is something' under this meaning, 'when something is generated, one whole form is acquired at the same time and not a part before a part is added to matter.' And under a meaning opposed to this, this is false, 'generation is nothing.' And if it be said, 'generation is not per se the terminus of a continuum, nor is it something continuous'; then it is nothing. For everything, which is in these inferiors, is a continuum or part of a continuum. It must be said that, according to the virtue of common speech and according to every property of common speech, that that proposition is true, 'everything, which is in these inferiors, is per se one and a continuum or the terminus of a continuum'; for the other part is true; namely, 'everything one per se in these inferiors is a continuum'; for there is nothing in these inferiors except a continuum, unless perchance the rational soul may be included with these inferiors. And, therefore, if this proposition, 'generation is something,' were true according to a property of common speech, this would be true according to a property of common speech, 'generation is continuous'; but neither is true according to a property of common speech; and there is a reason why this is not true according to a property of common speech, 'generation is continuous or the terminus of a continuum.' Nor is it true according to the meaning of the authors; for they understand this, 'when something is generated, one part of the form is acquired mediately before another or before something of the same ground was acquired.' And, therefore, it must not be imagined that generation may be something positive or privative really distinct from every continuum and from every permanent thing.

On the contrary, according to a property of common speech, neither of these is true, 'generation is something,' 'generation is nothing,' whether generation is negation or privation; as any one of these is not true according to a property of common speech, 'man is something,' 'man is nothing,' whether negation or privation; and this by accepting significatively all the terms; for according to a property of common speech such an abstract 'generatio' ought not any more to be formed from this verb 'generari,' than such an abstract 'hominitas' from this accusative case 'hominem.' And, therefore, through a similar mode through which you might reply to such questions raised about an abstract corresponding precisely to this accusative case 'homi-

THE SACRAMENT OF THE ALTAR   31

nem.' What may such humanity be? What is humanity? Is humanity either something or nothing, or is it a thing? I reply to such questions; generation is either something or nothing, and so of others; for thus even such questions are not proper according to a property of common speech; but if they ought to be accepted, they ought to be accepted according to the good sense of those using. So I say of such, whether 'generation may be something,' and of similar questions.

And in general, I say proportionately of all abstracts, which are formed from adverbs, prepositions, verbs, conjunctions, and in general of syncategorematics and of other abstracts for which their concretes stand; not for those for which their concretes stand, as if they might be able to stand for those for which their own concretes stand, unless they may equally include in signification something syncategorematic. Whatever is conceded of a concrete, ought to be conceded according to a property of common speech of an abstract.

And, therefore, as Aristotle concedes this, 'man runs'; so he would concede this, 'humanity runs,' unless humanity may precisely signify form. And so it may be said that whatever is predicated of any abstract, if it be truly predicated, is predicated of that per se in the first mode. It must be said that that proposition is simply false. For if that proposition thus accepted were true, all such would be false: 'deity is seen by the blessed,' 'deity is really distinguished from creatures,' 'deity is omnipotent,' 'humanity is in the nature of things,' 'humanity is unible with a supposition for a verb,' 'humanity is distinguished from angel,' and many such; since they may not be per se in the first mode; and yet it is manifest that they may be true and that many of them fall under faith, so that the opposite are heretical.

Whence, neither among the philosophers nor among the ancient Saints nor among others, is it found that they have posited such a distinction between an abstract and a concrete, as the modernist make. But among the ancient writers there have been many synonyms with their concretes, and many abstracts were not necessarily considered according to a property of common speech; but they could become formed only by virtue of any of the three causes previously mentioned. And, therefore, I do not censure the ancients, because they formed such abstracts for the sake of utility and metre, or the embellishment of common speech, or brevity. And this was sufficiently convenient for them, for it was about a thing sufficiently well known to them; at least to the wise, especially to Aristotle. And indeed Aristotle cared less about a mode of speaking; from which the thing was well known, as is obvious in the first book of the Physics, that he had moderate solicitude about names. And indeed many fall into various errors by virtue of this, that they accept the passages of the ancients as they sound according to the letter and according to a property of common speech, which intent, however, the ancients have not held.

Consequently, it ought to be said according to the previous statements that all such propositions are improper; 'aditas is something,' 'abietas is relation,' 'aquietas is respect,' 'haectitas is distinct from nature,' and so of many such, which are accepted by the modernists. Nor are they to be accepted according to a property of common speech any more than if from these

THE SACRAMENT OF THE ALTAR 33

adverbs: 'dum,' 'cum,' 'tunc,' 'iam,' and from other adverbs; and from such conjunctions: 'si,' 'et,' 'vel,' 'at,' 'quia'; and from others such abstracts may be formed: 'dummitas,' 'cummitas,' 'tunctitas,' 'iammitas,' 'siitas,' 'attitas,' 'etitas,' 'quiitas.' And by virtue of this, such propositions may be formed: 'dummitas is something,' 'siitas is something,' 'velitas is God,' and so of others.

As regards the second point, I say that the philosopher does not intend that a point falls within the definition of a line, as if something of the essence of a line, or as if signifying something of the essence of a line and distinct from a line. But he intends that in a definition expressing something characteristic of the same name 'line,' this name 'point' is posited, and according to the famous definition of a line, whether or not that be a true definition of a line; which however is not a true definition except according to the intention of the one judging correctly of a point and a line. Nor is it, however, to be understood that a point may be any privation totally distinct from a line, as men commonly imagine; which it is impossible to imagine; namely, that a point may be something, either a privative or a positive, distinct as regards itself as a whole, or not the same as a line. On the contrary, according to a property of common speech or of signification, it must not be conceded that it is a positive, nor that it is a privative.

And if it be said that these are contradictories: 'a point is a positive,' 'a point is not a positive'; then, according to a property of common speech, one is true and the other is false. I say that, as according to property, these are not contradictories: 'to see a man is something,' 'to see a man is not something'; nor these: 'it does not have farther extension is something,' 'it does not have farther lengthening is not something,' 'a point is something,' 'a point is not something'; and this by accepting all the terms significatively. And by virtue of these neither of them is to be conceded according to the virtue of common speech. And this with the preceding statements may be said according to that mode of positing of those who say that this name 'point' is equivalent in signification to one aggregate of many expressions, which can not express a supposition for a verb according to grammatical science; and, therefore, no language is proper, in which it is posited, that in speaking grammatically it may be substituted with respect to a verb. But if another mode of positing concerning that, which was stated before, be held; it must be so conceded that a point is something positive, and a point is a quantum, and a line is divisible; for it is equivalent to this: 'so much quantum,' or 'something is of so much extension,' and 'a quantum is divisible,' and so of others.

As regards the third point, I concede proportionately of a line and of a surface as of a point; whence, as according to one mode of speaking this must be conceded, 'a point is divisible,' so this, 'a line is a body.' But according to another mode of speaking, as this is not proper, 'a point is something,' so neither this, 'a line is something,' nor this, 'a surface is something'; but each of them is stated figuratively and must be accepted.

And when it is said that a terminate is defined through a terminant, it must be said that that proposition, as it is formed, is false. Whence, it must not be

THE SACRAMENT OF THE ALTAR

imagined that there may be some terminate there, and by virtue of that terminate there may be another terminant distinct from a terminate, whether a privative or a positive terminating that terminate; but there is there only a mode of expression of names signifying the same things in different grammatical modes, as these two in oblique cases 'hominis' and 'homini' signify the same things, yet in entirely diverse grammatical modes.

And there is no inconsistency concerning such names, if one falls within a definition expressing something characteristic of another name. For thus this name 'entity' falls within a definition expressing some characteristic of that name 'unum,' and of that name 'verum,' and of that name 'bonum'; and yet nothing is signified through one name that may not be signified through the rest, although it is understood through one name in an oblique case as well as in a direct case and through another name not unless in a direct case; whence, we know through this name 'verum,' that there is as much signified in an oblique case as in a direct case; for this that we understand, 'entity is knowable and cognizable by the intellect.' But through this name 'entity' it is not signified except in a direct case only, and indeed in the proposition it might be able to be conceded either properly or figuratively according to a diverse mode of positing that those names 'terminant' and 'terminate' are significative; that 'the same' is 'terminant' and 'the same' is 'terminate,' and 'the same' terminates itself; as 'the same' understands itself, or 'the same' is that which is 'the same' to itself. And when it is said that a positive never includes essentially a privation, it is obvious; for this must not be conceded, 'a point is privation,' 'a surface is privation,' and this according to a property of common speech and according to the fancy of those who imagine that privation may be something apart from a thing in any mode whatever distinct from positive things.

Whence, those arguments are cited or made contrary to that fancy which imagines, that a point may be apart from a thing, a certain privation distinct from a line as regards itself as a whole in every mode imaginable. According to which intent that Doctor seems to reject that opinion in opposition to which he offers the arguments touched upon before.

But that opinion does not thus posit, nor does it posit that a point is privation any more than that it is a positive; although in a definition expressing some characteristic of the same name, one name 'negative' or a concept 'negative' may necessarily be posited. And, therefore, according to the virtue of common speech either it must be conceded that a point may be an absolute thing, a quantum and divisible, or that every formal expression is improper in which this name 'point' is posited for one extreme distinct from the other extreme and from a copula; and no such expression ought to be accepted according to property but as if stated figuratively, and the arguments of the Doctors in no mode proceed contrary to that mode of positing.

As regards the fourth point, which was touched upon after the arguments of the Doctor, it can be said in various modes that the philosopher there as well as in the book of the Physics as also in other places where he speaks of a point, was speaking according to the famous opinion according to his custom; because he adapted himself to the mode of speaking of others,

THE SACRAMENT OF THE ALTAR   37

when he was treating a matter not according to intention. Whence, concerning his passages touching upon any matter which he treated not according to intention, it does not seem that he exercised much care; for he then frequently spoke as many do; and, therefore, where he treated such matters according to intention, he frequently said the opposite; as he says in the book of the Categories that "genera and species are secondary substances." But in the seventh book of the Metaphysics, where he inquires according to intention whether 'genus' and 'species,' generally universals, may be substances, he decides according to intention that no universal is a substance; so is it in the proposition.

Nowhere is it found that Aristotle according to intention thoroughly treated that question, whether a point may be an indivisible thing really distinct from every divisible thing. Therefore, all his passages, which affirm that a point is such another thing, must be explained and interpreted, because either he spoke as many do or according to that famous opinion or for the sake of an example or figuratively; or diverse passages must be explained in different ways, as will be obvious further on of diverse passages.

Whence, the philosopher in the book of the Categories does not intend that one absolute thing really distinct from parts of a line may mutually connect parts of a line, and by virtue of this a line may be called continuous; for then a line would not be continuous through itself or through some of its parts, but through one thing totally distinct from a line; and it might be said with the same facility that two pieces of wood are continuous through one stone. Nor can it any more be said that a point, if there be such a thing, may be the terminus of a line than that a stone is the terminus of wood, since the distinction between a line and a point may be as much or greater than the distinction between stone and wood.

Nor can it any more be said that a point may be an accident of a substance existing in a line than that a stone is in wood. And, therefore, the philosopher understands through this proposition, 'parts of a line are joined at one common terminus,' this proposition, 'nothing is intermediate between parts of a line and they make one per se'; so that two are required for this, that 'a line may be continuous'; namely, that 'nothing may be in situation intermediate between parts of a line.' And by virtue of this when one body is in one situation and another body is in another situation and between those bodies there is in situation another intermediate, those two bodies are not continuous.

A second statement is required; namely, that they make one per se, and by virtue of this the contiguous are not continuous; and so through this proposition, 'parts of a line are joined at a point as if at a common terminus,' and through similar propositions the philosopher understands that copulative, 'nothing is intermediate between parts of a line and they themselves make one line per se.' And when it is said that a terminus is always distinguished from a terminate; it must be said that, if this name 'terminus' is precisely substituted for another thing so that it may have precisely the force of the name 'category' in signification, that it may not be equivalent to any other part of language nor to any composite of such a part; and similarly this name 'terminate'; then it might be able to

THE SACRAMENT OF THE ALTAR 39

be conceded that 'terminus' is really distinguished from 'terminate,' if one be a 'terminus' and another a 'terminate.' But in taking them thus; this is false, 'a point is a terminus,' and 'a line is terminated through a point.' If those names 'terminant' and 'terminate' signify differently; then that proposition can be denied or conceded according as one is pleased to express in various modes the significations of terms.

Yet I say this, that it must not be imagined that a line may be a certain thing distinct from a thing which is a terminus or which may be a terminus; but from this itself, that 'a line is such a thing and is not farther lengthened,' it is said to be terminated there. As when we say that whiteness is the terminus of whitening and substantial form is the terminus of generation, it must not there be imagined that where there is one thing which may be whitening and generation, and afterwards or at the same time one other thing which is whiteness and form; for no contradiction appears but that God might be able to make form without any other thing even in a subject; nor does it appear why that thing ought to be destroyed if it be posited. But through this proposition, 'form is the terminus of generation,' this ought to be understood, 'when something is generated, form is added de novo to pre-existing matter'; and as it is said of this, so it must be said proportionately of many other similar propositions.

As regards the fifth and the following point, it can be said that the philosopher speaks according to the famous opinion which posits that a point is such another thing, not according to a proper opinion.

As regards the seventh point, I say that this term 'simul' is accepted in various ways. Sometimes, 'simul' is equivalent to this whole, 'nothing is intermediate,' so that it may be the sense of such a proposition, 'these are at the same time'; that is, 'nothing is intermediate between them.' And so this must be conceded, 'those touch each other whose extremes are at the same time' under this sense, 'those touch each other between which nothing is intermediate.' Sometimes 'simul' is equivalent in signification to this, 'not to be separate in situation'; and so no two things, which may be touching each other in any mode whatever, are at the same time; nor does the philosopher wish this. But through this proposition, 'those touch each other between which nothing is intermediate,' he understands this, as was said, 'those touch each other between which nothing is intermediate,' and if there could be such indivisibles in these touching, these would be at the same time; and this by taking this term 'simul' in the second mode; for they would not be separate in place nor in situation. And when it is said that no parts of two lines are at the same time; it must be said that in accepting 'simul' in the second mode it is true, and this is not required for this, that some touch each other; yet in accepting 'simul' in the first mode parts of a line are at the same time, for nothing is intermediate between them.

As regards the eighth point; when it is said that those are continuous whose extremes are one, it is manifest that that proposition ought to be explained; for it is false according to the virtue of common speech since it involves a contradiction, as that involves a contradiction, 'more men are one man'; for, if they are extremes, they are more, and consequently are not one. Therefore, I say that the understanding of the philos-

THE SACRAMENT OF THE ALTAR 41

opher is this, 'those are continuous which make one per se,' that is, 'they are not separate,' or 'between which nothing is intermediate.'

As regards the ninth point; when it is said that a point is indivisible, it must be said that the philosopher either was speaking according to the famous opinion or the proposition must be explained, as was stated before.

When it is said for confirmation that the philosopher proves that no quantum is composed of indivisibles, it must be said that it is true; and that, since it may be negative, does not infer any such affirmative, 'something is indivisible.'

And when it is said that it would have been useless to prove so diffusedly that a continuum is not composed of indivisibles unless there were some such indivisibles, it must be said that it is not useless to prove one conclusion through diverse intermediates, although it might be able to be proved sufficiently through one intermediate. Whence, an intermediate was sufficient to prove that there is no indivisible, but however others would not be superfluous, and this especially in that case; for to prove that nothing is indivisible in these inferiors can not be accomplished except through subtle reasons, which mathematicians and others less skilled in metaphysics and logic can not comprehend. But to prove that a continuum is not composed of indivisibles through other intermediates, even if there were such indivisibles, can be accomplished through reasons more apparent to mathematicians and to all others, as will be shown elsewhere; and, therefore, the reasons are not superfluous.

As regards the tenth point; it can be said just as about the preceding; for he was speaking according to the famous opinion.

As regards the principal argument it is obvious, that this, 'a point is the terminus of a line,' is false according to the virtue of common speech, yet it is true according to the sense that it alleges, as has been said.

QUESTION II

In the second place it is asked, whether a line and a surface may really be distinguished from each other and from a body. And it seems that they are; for they are distinct species of quantity according to the philosopher in the Categories; therefore, they are really distinguished from each other and from a body.

As regards the opposite; as is the relation of a point to a line so is the relation of a line to a surface, and a surface to a body; but a point is not really distinct from a line, as was proved in the Categories; therefore, a line is not distinct from a surface nor a surface from a body, and consequently a line and a surface are not distinguished from each other or from a body.

With respect to that question, I say that a line and a surface are not things distinct from each other and from a body. For that a line may not be distinct from a surface can be proved through the first, third, and fourth reasons, and through other theological reasons through which it is proved that a point is not an indivisible thing really distinct from a line; for if a line were such another thing, it would be in some primary and adequate subject. Similarly, there would be infinite lines, none of which would be a part of another.

THE SACRAMENT OF THE ALTAR 43

Similarly, God might not be able to divide one continuum unless He could create more absolute things, and could destroy some absolute things; nor would He be able to unite, unless He could very similarly corrupt and produce new things. Similarly, then it does not seem contradictory that there could be a surface without a line, and consequently there could be a surface not terminated, and yet it would be of finite length.

But that a surface could be distinct from a body can be proved through the first theological reason; for another primary and adequate subject can not be assigned to itself, as is evidently clear. Similarly, this can be proved through the third reason, for there would be surfaces infinite actually but potentially only finite; for the extreme surfaces alone of a body are actually; but the others are not except only potentially.

In opposition to those positing thus; either the parts of the body are joined to a surface, which is in the nature of things and is existent, or to a surface which is not in the nature of things but can be. If the first be granted; then that surface is actually, and consequently there are surfaces infinite actually. If the second be conceded, then those parts of a body are not actually continuous but only potentially; for no parts are actually continuous through that which is not in the nature of things.

And then I ask, how that potentiality may be reduced to actuality; whether when those parts are continuous or when they are not continuous. Not in the first mode, for then according to those writers a continuant surface always is potentially, not actually; nor in the second mode, for then they are not continuous. But it may be said that that surface is not indeed said to

44 THE SACRAMENT OF THE ALTAR

be potentially; for it is not in the nature of things; but because it is not separate from a body; as parts are said to be potentially, not because they are not in the nature of things, but because they are not separate from a whole.

On the contrary, this does not suffice. First, because according to this such an inconsistency follows; namely, that infinites are in the nature of things of the same quantity. In the second place, because everything, which is in the nature of things and is not part of another, is simply actually suitable to itself, but that surface is in the nature of things and is not a part of another; therefore, it simply is actually.

In the third place thus; for, as that intermediate surface is not separate from a body, so neither is the extreme separate from a body; therefore, as the extreme is actually, so that is actually. Thus, therefore, it is obvious that, if a surface be a thing other than a body; this inconsistency follows, that infinites of the same quantity, of which none is part of another, are actually.

However, the principal conclusion can be proved through four and five reasons and through other reasons which follow. For if a surface be a thing as regards itself as a whole distinct from a body, there does not appear any contradiction that God may make it without a body, or conversely; and consequently a body can be without any such surface, and yet it will be finite and continuous; therefore, a surface is needlessly posited.

Similarly, I ask how a surface and a body make one in the sacrament of the altar; whether they make one per se or one through accident or one only by aggre-

THE SACRAMENT OF THE ALTAR 45

gation. The first can not be granted; for then a surface would be part of a body or both would be essential parts of another, which can not be conceded. And if it be said that a surface, although it may not be a quantitative part of a body, is however an essential part of a body; it is not refuted by the philosopher, although it may be refuted, that a surface may be a quidditative part of a body.

On the contrary, whenever something is part of another, either it is of the same ground as another part or it is of another ground. Therefore, if a surface be a part of a body which is per se one, either it is of the same ground as another part of a body or it is of another ground, which also can not be conceded; for, whenever some parts of diverse grounds make one per se, one of them is matter or potentiality, and the other is actuality or form; but potentiality and actuality making one per se are never distinguished in place or situation, as is manifestly obvious; therefore, in no mode are body and surface potentiality and actuality, and consequently they do not make one per se.

The second also can not be granted; namely, that a surface and a body make one by accident; for then one would be the actuality of another, and consequently a surface would be subjectively in a body, or conversely; each of which is false according to the arguments set forth in the preceding question.

Nor can the third be conceded; namely, that they make one by aggregation, since it could not then be affirmed that a surface would otherwise be a terminus of a body than that a vase is a terminus of water. Then also no contradiction appears in the statement that God might be able to make a body in the same

46 THE SACRAMENT OF THE ALTAR

place and situation without a surface, as he can make water in the same place and situation without a vase; and yet a body would then be an infinite continuum without any surface; if this is conceded, it is obvious that such a surface is posited entirely in vain.

Similarly, then before transubstantiation a surface either would be without a substance or would be in another substance, as if in a primary and adequate subject, and not in the same substance in which a body is in a primary and adequate subject; as can be proved through the arguments set forth in the preceding question, and consequently there would be another substance there besides matter and form in which a body is posited, which is a quantity subjectively.

From the preceding statements it is obvious, that a line and a surface are not really distinguished from each other; and because it was proved that a surface is not distinguished from a body; therefore, neither is a line, and consequently they are not really distinguished from each other or from a body.

As regards the principal argument, I say that these concepts 'line' and 'surface' are distinct, and this suffices for a distinction of species; yet notwithstanding this, those, which are signified, are not distinct; for 'place' and 'surface' are thus distinct species, and yet they are not really distinct; but it suffices that they signify the same in diverse modes, as the commentator says in Book IV. of the Metaphysics concerning 'entity' and 'one,' where he states that 'entity' and 'one' signify the same, but in diverse modes.

Whence, as such diversity of modes of signifying the same thing vitiates the predication of one of another, although there may be only two such modes of

THE SACRAMENT OF THE ALTAR 47

signification, namely, 'case' and 'number'; so a diversity of modes of signification suffices for the distinction of species, no matter how frequently one be truly predicated of another.

There are many arguments contrary to these which I pass over for the present; for I have spoken of them elsewhere in diverse places.

QUESTION III

It is asked in the third place whether a body, which is a quantity, may be an absolute thing really distinct from substance. Which is thus proved; for according to the philosopher in the first book of the Posteriores, a negative is immediate in which one category is denied of another, as this is immediate, 'no substance is a quantity,' and consequently a substance is a thing other than a quantity.

As regards the opposite; a substance has of itself parts; therefore, it is of itself a quantum; therefore, it is not a quantum through another thing; and consequently it is not another thing.

Regarding this question; in the first place, I shall declare one opinion through the mode of narration; in the second place, through the mode of demonstration; in the third place, I shall posit the objections against this opinion and I shall refute them.

Regarding the first, I say that quantity is not another absolute thing really distinct from substance and quality. But if this name 'quantity' be substituted for another thing and have precisely the force of the name 'categorematic' in signification, it ought to be conceded that any quantity is not substance but quality, so that quantity is predicated particularly of substance as well as of quality; for any substance is a quantity, and any quality is a quantity.

But the mode of positing is this: some substance is simply not divisible into parts of the same ground, which substance is an angel and a rational soul; but every other substance is composed of some parts of the same ground among themselves, although not all parts may be of the same ground with the whole among themselves; as also in man some parts are of the same ground among themselves, although not all the parts are of the same ground with man; but such as are so constituted out of their own natures without any thing added, that they are more, although they are not more causally out of themselves but through their essential causes, say, efficient and final; so out of their natures are they constituted that they are not in the same place and situation naturally and through created agency, whatever may be of the absolute divine power. And indeed from this, that they are produced by whatever created agency they are produced, they are in a distinct situation so that one part is separate from another in situation and is outside another, no matter how much no other thing may be produced with it; and if there be another place surrounding the same product, that product, no matter how much no other thing might inhere in it, would be circumscriptively in that place, so that the whole would be in a whole place and a part in a part; and consequently by this itself it would be a quantum; since nothing other could be quantity, concerning which there is a question, than a continuous body per se one or a thing having parts or a part outside of a part existing circumscriptively in a place,

THE SACRAMENT OF THE ALTAR 49

if there be a place surrounding it. And so the substance itself through this alone, that it has part outside of part without any thing advening to it, is a quantum; and consequently for this, that it may be a quantum, such another thing is not required. And as it is of substance that something has such parts, so is it of any quality, which would be a quantum without any thing added to it; even if it could be separated from every other thing and could have part outside of part, and consequently this quality would not really differ from this quantity. So, therefore, any quantity is substance, and any quantity is quality; as any substance has part outside of part, and any quality has part outside of part.

In the second place, I prove this conclusion; namely, that any substance is quantity, and in the same mode it can be proved that any quality is quantity; so, namely, that it may not be another distinct thing.

First in this way: God can of His own absolute power preserve every absolute thing prior to another absolute thing, and can destroy a posterior not by changing that prior thing locally or in situation. Therefore, if this substance be quantum, say, that stone, God can of His absolute power preserve that substance and destroy that posterior thing, which is posited as quantity, not by changing the substance of that stone locally or in situation, but with the repose of that substance; for it does not seem necessary, so that the opposite of this may involve a contradiction, if God wills to preserve that absolute thing prior, that He be compelled to change it from place to place.

Therefore, let it be posited that that prior thing may be preserved without local change and that a posterior may be destroyed. Then I ask whether that substance is circumscriptively in a place or is not circumscriptively in a place. If the first is granted, then that substance is quantum; therefore, this is some quantity and this is not another posterior thing; therefore, this, 'some quantity is without quantity,' which is false; if it be not circumscriptively in a place.

On the contrary, I take one part of that substance and I ask, whether or not it is either definitively or circumscriptively in the same place in which there is another part. If so, then it has been changed locally, because it was not before in the same place. If it be not in the same place, then it is in another and consequently a whole is in a whole place and a part in a part; and consequently the whole is circumscriptively in a place, and consequently the whole is a quantum without any other thing added to it.

Whence, it much more restricts the divine power by saying that God can not preserve a thing prior without local change of it and destroy a thing posterior, which however follows according to the contrary opinion, than to posit that some quantity is substance; if it be said that that substance does not have parts except through quantity; and, therefore, when quantity is destroyed, it does not have part and consequently will not be in a place circumscriptively but only definitively.

On the contrary, this proposition does not vitiate a response; for there always follows that inconsistency, that God of His absolute power can not preserve a thing prior without local change by destroying the thing posterior. Moreover, the response embraces a falsehood; namely, that substance does not have parts except through quantity, if quantity be another thing.

THE SACRAMENT OF THE ALTAR 51

First; because, if a whole substance is prior to a whole quantity and the subject of it, so a part of a substance is prior to a part of a quantity and the subject of it; therefore, parts of a substance are prior to parts of a quantity, if quantity is a thing existing subjectively in substance; therefore, substance does not have parts precisely through another thing advening to it. Moreover, that, which remains without another, is before this, but this part of substance is without that quantity; therefore, it is prior to it, and for the same reason is prior to another quantity.

If it be said that substance does not have other parts except parts which are parts of a quantity, so that these are not substances but are quantities, (on the contrary that part of a quantity is in some primary subject; therefore, either in the same primary subject in which there is another part of quantity, or in another; therefore, if in the same, that subject is not extended through quantity more than the rational soul, which is a whole in a whole body and a whole in each part; if it be in another subject, then there are distinct parts of quantity there say, wood may be divided into two parts) it is manifest; that each quantity is in some subject, and not in the same; therefore in distinct, and consequently either a new substance is caused through division or these substances, which are of these quantities, were before division; and the proposition is maintained.

In the second place, I argue thus: it is not more impossible for God to make 'a thing having parts really distinct' to coexist with some whole not informing so that a whole coexists with a whole and a part with a part, than to make this same thing to coexist with such a whole informing. But according to those holding this opinion in common, 'a substance having parts really distinct coexists with a whole quantity informing so that a whole substance is under a whole quantity,' and 'a part of a substance is under part of a quantity'; therefore, it is possible for God to bring it to pass that a whole substance may be coexisting with the same quantity not informing and part with the whole. This having been posited, this substance is truly a quantum; for it truly has part distinct in situation from part, and a substance is not a quantum through some other quantity informing; for it is posited that no quantity of a substance may inform it, but it may only coexist with it; therefore, it is a quantum through itself; therefore, the substance itself is a certain quantity, which is the thesis.

I posit the confirmation of this ground through the statements of those holding opposite views; for according to them, whatever may be of a respect intrinsically advening, is said of a respect extrinsically advening, yet it is true; but God can make extremes without such a respect; for the respect of inherence, by which quantity inheres in a subject, is a respect extrinsically advening according to those writers; therefore, God can make these extremes without such a respect. Therefore, God may preserve this substance of stone and that quantity by destroying precisely that respect of inherence. This having been posited, still this substance will have the respect of presentiality as regards this quantity, so that a whole will be present with a whole and a part with a part; therefore, that substance has part outside of part, and consequently would be a quantum and yet without any quantity informing;

THE SACRAMENT OF THE ALTAR   53

therefore, the substance itself is then quantity. Those two reasons prove that substance is truly quantum through its substantial parts without any other thing advening to itself, and consequently that it itself is quantity.

From which I argue farther that there is not any other quantity except substance or quality; for that is needlessly accomplished through more which can be accomplished through fewer; but all, which can be saved through such a quantity distinct from substance and quality, can be saved without it, as is obvious inductively; therefore, such a quantity distinct from substance and quality must not be posited. It can also be proved through these two reasons, that quality is quantity; since this major premise is assumed, that God for this reason can make quality without quantity, if it be another thing, since it may no more depend on quantity than on substance. Similarly, if God can make such quantity, which they posit, without substance; for the same reason he could make quality without quantity, since quality no more depends on quantity than quality on substance. I confirm the previous arguments.

It is not more inconsistent for a substance having parts through its own self without every other thing informing it to be in a divisible place so that a whole thing may be in a whole place and parts in parts of a place, than it may be inconsistent for an indivisible thing without every thing informing it to be in a whole place and in each part; but an indivisible thing, as an angel and a rational soul, is a whole in a whole place and in each part; therefore, it is not inconsistent for a thing having parts really distinct, of such a kind is

54 THE SACRAMENT OF THE ALTAR

material substance and also many qualities, to be a whole in a whole place and a part in a part without every other thing advening. But if this is posited, such a thing will truly have part outside of part, and consequently will be quantum without any other thing advening to it; whence they seem to detract much from the divine power who say that God of His own absolute power can not bring it to pass that one thing may be separate from another in situation, unless He create one other thing making those things to be separate; and they seem to reject the divine omnipotence more than those who say that a substance having parts is a quantum without any other thing advening to itself and is circumscriptively in a place.

Again, the preceding reasons are confirmed. It is not more inconsistent for a substance composed of some things really distinct and created to be separate in situation to be through itself without a thing added to itself in a place in a mode suitable to itself, than it is inconsistent for an indivisible substance not having parts to be in a place in a mode suitable to itself without a thing added to itself. But an angel without any thing added to itself is in a place definitively; therefore, it is not inconsistent for a substance having parts really distinct to be in a place circumscriptively without any thing added to itself. But nothing is in a place circumscriptively except a quantum; therefore, a substance can be a quantum without any thing really distinct added to it; therefore, such another quantity is needlessly posited.

Again, it is confirmed; for every thing, which is present to another thing locally, is present to itself through itself or through another intrinsic; for it has

THE SACRAMENT OF THE ALTAR 55

not been said that one thing is locally present to another, unless because its *end* is present there locally. If, therefore, the substance of a stone be present in a place, it is present in a place through itself, and consequently for the same reason parts of a substance are present in a place through themselves, and consequently the whole substance is through itself fundamentally and circumscriptively in a place; but every thing, which in itself is circumscriptively in a place, is in itself a quantum; therefore, substance in itself is quantum and consequently is quantity. The same reason can be applied concerning quality.

Again, the previous reasons are confirmed; for when some are created to make one which however can not make one, of such kind are parts of water and of air and of many others; for sometimes the same parts make one per se, sometimes not. If God can make these to be distinct in place and in situation, when they do not make one per se without any thing added to them, God can make these same to be distinct in place and in situation without any thing added to them, although they make one per se; for no reason appears why one more than the rest ought to be denied of the divine omnipotence. But God can make this air, which is here, and that air which is at Rome, to be distinct in place and in situation by destroying all the absolute accidents in them and without any quantity inhering in them; therefore, God of His absolute power can bring it to pass that those two bodies of air may be united and make one body of air, and yet that they may be distinct in place and situation without any such thing advening to them; therefore, that air will have part outside of part without a thing however added,

56 THE SACRAMENT OF THE ALTAR

and consequently will be a quantum without such a thing added; therefore, such an added thing is needlessly posited for this, that air may be a quantum.

The previous reasons can be confirmed in many other ways, which I pass by for the sake of brevity.

In the third place, it is principally argued thus according to the Master of the Sentences in Book IV., Distinction XII. Accidents of such a kind, taste, color, weight, and any other of the kind, are without a subject in the sacrament of the altar. But if quantity were another thing bearing those qualities, those qualities would not be without a subject, but would be in a subject; on the contrary the common dictum of the Doctors could in no mode be able to be verified, and very incorrectly, as it seems, the determination of the church that the accidents remain in the sacrament of the altar without a subject; for thus only one accident could remain without a subject, and all others would be in a subject; therefore, a quantity would not be such a distinct thing, et cetera. And so in carefully considering the Master and the text with the gloss on the De Consecratione and the statements of the Saints, there is not found a passage so apparent that by virtue of the sacrament of the altar it may be necessary to posit such another thing intermediate between substance and qualities, as is this against such an intermediate thing bearing qualities. No mention is made in all those places of an intermediate quantity nor is this term even once mentioned, nor does any passage speak of quantity, whether or not it be, except that many seem to posit that all the qualities in the sacrament of the altar are not in any subject; whence, the Master says thus in Book IV., Distinction XII., A:

THE SACRAMENT OF THE ALTAR 57

"Those accidents, therefore, remain," which he enumerated before; namely, taste, weight, and any other of the kind, "subsisting per se at the celebration of the mystery," et cetera. However, I do not intend to say that those who posit such a thing bearing such accidents, of which the Saints speak and which they seem to posit without any subject, may be heretical or erring in the faith or about the sacrament of the Eucharist; for they were permitted to explain such passages; nor are all who have uttered a falsehood to be considered in error. And as they were permitted to explain such passages of the Doctors approved by the church, so I shall be permitted not only to explain but even to refute the statements of the Saints who mutually condemn one another, and in no way were approved as if authorized by the church.

In the fourth place, I argue thus: no absolute accident is more simple than its primary and adequate subject; but, if a quantity were any thing other than substance and quality, it would be an accident. Therefore, I ask about its primary and adequate subject, whether it is matter or form or a composite. It is not a composite; for a subject would be more composite than its absolute accident, which seems false; nor is matter its own subject, because then some absolute accident would precede form in matter; nor is form its own primary subject, because then matter, if it were separated, could not be a quantum, which seems to be false.

Similarly, dimensions precede form without limits in matter according to the commentator; therefore, for the same reason dimensions are limited at first in matter. That reason is valid, as I think, if this opinion hold which rejects this entity distinct from matter and form, which some posit.

In the fifth place, I argue thus: according to the philosopher in the Categories, substance alone is susceptive of contraries; but quantity is not a substance according to those writers, and yet it is susceptive of contraries, which is contrary to Aristotle.

In the sixth place, it is argued thus: when a thing becomes rare from dense, I ask whether or not there is there another new quantity; but it is precisely the same quantity numerically; if it is new there, then any preceding quantity is corrupted, which seems false. If a part be new; I ask about the subject of that quantity, for it is necessary that there be a whole rarefied substance or a part of it; not the whole because then the two quantities would be at the same time, which they deny who think thus. If a part, the same argument follows, or that an accident might travel from subject into subject, as would be able to be clearly shown; but it is omitted for the sake of brevity. If it be the same quantity, then it coexists in a larger place now than before without the variation of an absolute; but this inconsistency is posited of substance; therefore, such a quantity distinct from quality and substance is needlessly posited.

Therefore, I say by virtue of those reasons and many other reasons, physical as well as theological, that quantity is not a thing really distinct from substance and quality, but any quantity is really the same as substance, and any quantity is really the same as quality; whence, quantity is not, unless 'a thing having part outside of part and having part separate from another in situation,' or 'a thing existing circumscrip-

THE SACRAMENT OF THE ALTAR 59

tively in a place,' if it be something surrounding itself. And because some substance in itself fundamentally, although causally by God or other extrinsic causes, has part outside of part; it is not necessary to posit another thing bearing one part outside of another part. But the extrinsic causes of a thing, say, efficient and final, are sufficient to produce things diverse, one in one situation and another in another, without any intermediate thing between them; therefore, the substance itself is a quantum without any other thing connected with itself or made at the same time with it.

And as I say of substance, so I say proportionately of any corporeal thing. Nor does that opinion in any way detract from the sacrament of the altar; but it avoids many difficulties respecting the sacrament of the altar, as will be obvious in replying and in objecting.

And, therefore, although some modern writers, stimulated perhaps by envy, would censure that opinion as if erroneous not by arguments but by detractions; yet the ancient Doctors, although they could not understand it, did not, however, repudiate it as heretical respecting faith or character, whose reasons I intend to cite and to explain. Whence, a certain Doctor arguing against this opinion says thus. This opinion is contrary to the philosopher, who in the Categories distinguishes quantity from substance and quality. It is also contrary to the common opinion of the Doctors. It is also contrary to experience; and when a corporeal substance is condensed without conversion of anything into itself, it is effected of a less quantity without the loss of any part. It is also contrary to reason, for in diverse subjects differing in species a

quantity the same in species seems to be able to be;
for the length, or breadth, or depth in a handful of
air is not other than that in a handful of water. That
they, however, say that the quantity of a quality really differs from the quantity of a substance and that
it itself is really the same as quality, is contrary to
authority and reason. For the philosopher in the sixth
book of the Physics says that "quality is not quantity
except through accident," which would not be true if
it were properly called quantity. It is argued through
the reasons thus: it is naturally impossible for a body,
which is a quantity, to be at the same time with another body which is a quantity; but quality is at the
same time with substance; therefore, from the previous opinion it follows that this is impossible, that two
thicknesses or even many more are naturally at the
same time; because for whatever reason whiteness
would have its proper quantity, for the same reason
taste would have its own, and coldness or frigidity
its own, and humidity and dryness, and so of others;
and so not only will the quantity of substance and the
quantity of quality be at the same time, but there would
also be at the same time the thicknesses of several
qualities; therefore, it is obvious that the opinion cited
above implies many inconsistencies. These are the
reasons of that Doctor, which are more apparent than
others. But besides these I add others; first, because
the substance of the bread is not transubstantiated
into the quantity of the body of Christ but only into
the substance of the body of Christ. But if substance
could be quantity, it would have been truly transubstantiated into quantity. It is confirmed; for the quantity of the body of Christ is not in the sacrament of

THE SACRAMENT OF THE ALTAR 61

the altar by the power of conversion but only concomitantly. But if the substance of the body of Christ were a quantity, the quantity of the body of Christ would truly be there by the power of conversion. Moreover, some argue: if substance is quantity, then since the substance of the bread may not remain in the sacrament of the altar; therefore, a quantity is not there, which is contrary to sense and contrary to the reality of the sacrament. Other reasons can be adduced; but, because the solution of these could be made clear from the explanations of those already offered, I, therefore, pass them by.

As regards the first argument of that Doctor, I say that that opinion is in no mode contrary to the philosopher either in the Categories or elsewhere. And when he says that in the Categories he distinguishes quantity from substance and quality, I reply that the philosopher does not intend to distinguish between substance, quantity and quality; as if they be absolute things really distinct from one another. But he intends to distinguish between those categories which signify things, not indeed distinct things but the same things although in diverse modes, which are not modes, unless grammatical or logical modes; and indeed although this category 'quantity' may be really distinct, if it be a thing in mind different from other categories, of which distinction a statement was made elsewhere; yet it does not signify another thing one per se, unless that thing be a substance or a quality; and so the distinction of categories, of which the philosopher speaks, obtains at the same time with this, that quantity may not be a thing other than substance and quality; as according to him 'place' and 'surface' are not really

62   THE SACRAMENT OF THE ALTAR

distinguished, and yet they are distinct species of quantity. For that there may be distinct species of quantity is obvious through the philosopher in the Categories. That these species do not imply quantities distinct from a part of a thing, is obvious; since there would then be two continuous quantities at the same time in situation and in place, neither of which would be created to inform another.

Similarly, according to the philosopher in the Categories in the chapter on 'quality'; the same is in diverse categories; therefore, categories sometimes signify the same thing; therefore, notwithstanding that quantity and substance and quality may be distinct categories, yet some of them have been able to signify the same thing, and so it is possible to agree with the philosopher that quantity is not an absolute thing other than substance and quality, as resemblance and white are in diverse categories, whether per se or through reduction; for the present I do not care, and yet they signify some thing the same.

Quite similarly I speak of 'number' which signifies no thing one per se, unless that which is under some species other than that under this common (species) 'number'; as was proved elsewhere; and yet they are different species. Similarly, 'ternary' and 'quaternary' are distinct species, and yet no thing one per se is signified through 'ternary,' but that it is or can be of the same species with another thing signified through 'quaternary,' or conversely. And, indeed, as was stated before, only a diversity of modes of signification suffices to distinguish one concept from another; not that no thing may be signified absolutely through one, but that it may be signified by another. So also it is ob-

THE SACRAMENT OF THE ALTAR 63

vious from these two 'homo' and 'homines'; for it is impossible to grant any thing signified through one that may not be signified through the rest; yet this is false, 'man is species.' So the identity of significators through some species or genera obtains with the distinction of species and of genera; and, as was frequently proved, genera or species are not, unless concepts or names.

As regards the second point; since it is said that that opinion is contrary to the common opinion of the Doctors, I reply that, if it be understood through the Doctors approved by the Roman Church, it is not true. On the contrary, this can be proved through no passage of any Doctor approved by the Roman Church. And if there be found any high-sounding passage of such a Doctor, this must be sufficiently explained. Nor is it inconsistent to explain their statements, since many statements even of the Sacred Page may also be in need of exposition; for many are not true according to a property of common speech, but are most true according to the sense which we ought to have.

Whence, such propositions which the Saviour uttered: "I am the true vine and my Father is the husbandman," "My doctrine is not mine," and many of a like kind, are not true according to the propriety of common speech; as the blessed Augustine says in a certain Homily on John: "Although in the sense in which they were spoken and in which they ought to be accepted, they may be most true." And as many passages of Sacred Scripture must be explained, so the passages of the Doctors approved by the Roman Church declaring that quantity may be a thing other than substance and quality must also be explained. But

64   THE SACRAMENT OF THE ALTAR

if through the Doctors they may understand the modern Doctors who mutually censure each other publicly and privately and even in their writings, I concede; but it is not inconsistent to contradict them; for nothing, which they say, must be accepted, except that which they can prove through clear reason or through the authority of Sacred Scripture or through a decree of the church or through the Doctors approved by the church.

And, therefore, since they can prove in none of the preceding modes that quantity is a thing other than substance and quality, although some sophistications may be able to be adduced for this; I, therefore, do not hold it as an inconsistency to refute them in this part; for by what reason they themselves mutually censure one another, and the latter reprove the former, I can refute them, when they have for their support nothing but sophisms or passages wrongly understood; nor do I think that I ought to be limited to those contrary to the dictate of reason.

On the contrary, I consider it dangerous and rash to wish to limit any one to the holding captive of his ability and to the believing of something which reason dictates to him to be false, unless it may be able to be drawn from Sacred Scripture or from a decree of the Roman Church or from the statements of the approved Doctors. Such is not this, 'quantity is an absolute thing other than substance and quality'; whence, I assert this, that no passage of any philosopher, nor any natural reason, which I have ever heard or read, moves me to believe that quantity is an absolute thing other than substance and quality more than to believe that flesh is a thing other than God and creature. Yet

THE SACRAMENT OF THE ALTAR 65

if it may be able to be proved that it may be from the mind of some Saint or Doctor approved by the church, whom it is not permitted to refute; for his sake I wish to hold in check my ability and to concede that there may be a thing other than substance and quality.

As regards the third, I say that it is not contrary to experience, but rather consonant with experience; whence, if he should not have another reason, except that experience which he adduces, I would concede that quantity is not such a thing as they themselves imagine.

Whence, when a corporeal substance is condensed, I ask whether any part or no part of a quantity is lost. If no part, and then condensation can be saved; then for the same reason, although substance may be quantity and no part of substance may be lost, condensation will have been saved. But if some part of quantity is lost, I ask about the primary and adequate subject of the quantity itself, whether it remains without any quantity, which is contrary to experience, or whether it has any quantity, and then whether new or pre-existing. It does not have a new quantity, because for the same reason another part would have a new quantity, since there may be no greater reason for one than for another; and consequently the whole substance would utterly lose the whole pre-existing quantity and would acquire a new quantity, which is contrary to experience. Nor does it have a pre-existing (quantity), since then an accident would change from subject into subject, which is not consonant with experience.

And so it is obvious that in no way is it contrary to experience to say, that quantity is not a thing other than substance and quality.

Therefore, a reply is made to that experience and by conceding that, when corporeal substance is condensed, it itself is effected of a smaller quantity without the loss of any of its part; but not without local motion of all of its parts.

Whence, through this alone, that all the parts are so moved locally that they may occupy a smaller place now than before and one part may be less separate from another now than before, the whole substance is condensed, and otherwise a substance is not to be condensed. And this is that which the philosopher says in the Categories, that "that is dense whose parts lie closer together," which is not to be understood of the parts between which there is not an intermediate; for those can not as regards themselves as wholes lie closer together; but it must be understood of the parts between which there are intermediate parts, for those parts lie closer together in a dense body than they did in the same body when it was rare. And from this itself, that all such parts lie closer together whether they may be under another thing or not; they in themselves lie closer together, and that body is more dense now than before.

Whence, I do not see that condensation and rarefication may be able conveniently to be saved, except by positing that quantity is not a thing other than substance and quality, and through that mode is easily saved. And if it be said that the whole substance remains after condensation (but the whole quantity does not remain; for, if the whole could remain, it follows that it has as much quantity as there was before); then, that preceding quantity was not itself substance. It must be said that those who perfectly understand

THE SACRAMENT OF THE ALTAR 67

logic clearly see that all such are sophistic, for such consequences inferring one of the past from two of the present are not valid; as frequently two of the past or of the future do not infer one of the present, and frequently even one of the past and one of the present do not infer one of the present. But it would take too long to tell how it must be argued from such; therefore, I pass on from this. And I say that this consequence is not valid: 'the whole substance remains' and 'so much quantity does not remain'; therefore, 'so much quantity was not in that whole substance.' And quite similarly such consequences are not valid: 'that foot of quantity does not remain' and 'this substance remains'; therefore, 'that substance will not be of the quantity of a foot'; nor does it infer more; therefore, that substance was other than a quantity of a foot. And as it is said of these, so proportionately must it be said of all of like kind, which are considered demonstrations by many.

Whence, as it does not follow: 'making happy is not.' It may be posited that 'God may make no one happy,' 'God is'; therefore, 'God was not making happy.' Similarly, it does not follow: 'the dead is not,' 'Christ is'; therefore, 'Christ is not dead.' So it does not follow: 'so much quantity is not,' 'substance is'; therefore, 'substance was not so much quantity.' And so it evidently is obvious that, although such premises may not infer that of the present, yet they do not infer that of the past. Nor does it refer quantum to a mode, whether the terms 'abstracts' or 'concretes' be accepted.

And as it is said of these, so proportionately of those of a 'possible'; for frequently two of a 'possible,' and even one of an 'actual' and another of a 'possible,' do not infer one negative of an 'actual,' although they may infer one of a 'possible'; and, therefore, such modes of arguing are not valid. This is possible, 'this likeness is not,' while this appears true, 'this whiteness is'; therefore, 'this whiteness is not this likeness'; although that follows from a 'possible'; therefore, it is possible for 'this whiteness not to be this likeness.' It does not follow: it is possible for 'this whiteness not to be this likeness'; therefore, 'this whiteness' and 'this likeness' are not the same thing. So it does not follow: 'it is possible for God not to be creating'; therefore, 'God' and 'creating' are not the same thing. But it certainly correctly follows that this is possible, 'God and creating are not the same'; and this is true.

Quite similarly is it in the proposition, that because that substance can remain, although this may not be true, 'the whole quantity is'; yet from this it does not follow that this may be true, 'this substance' and 'so much quantity' are not the same thing; but it follows that it may be possible; and this is true.

And if it be said that this is possible, 'this substance' and 'this quantity' are not the same thing, if the substance remains; by virtue of the same reason I say that this is fully possible, 'this substance' and 'this quantity' are not the same thing, so that it can be true, while this appears true, 'this substance is'; but it can not be true, while this appears true, 'this quantity is.' Whence, this will then be true by virtue of that cause of reality, 'this quantity is not,' which follows from this, 'this substance is not quantum,' which is possible.

THE SACRAMENT OF THE ALTAR   69

Another argument will be set forth later. And if it be said further that it is impossible to pass from a contradictory to a contradictory without entire newness, (if, therefore, this be at first true, 'that substance is of so much quantity' and afterwards it be false;) there is need that there be some newness or at least a destruction of something old. It must be said that it is not true; but sometimes local motion alone suffices, through which it is not necessary for something to be acquired or destroyed nor yet something old, say, a place always remaining.

On the contrary; as is shown elsewhere, a place surrounding a movable body can remain and this either in a whole or in a part. And, therefore, in the proposition regarding this, that the substance itself may be of a larger quantity or a larger quantity now than before as in rarefaction, or a smaller quantity now than before as in condensation, only local motion of all the parts of this substance suffices without entire newness of any imaginable thing whatever and without entire destruction of any thing old whatever.

As regards the fourth point; when it is said that that opinion is contrary to reason, it must be said that it is not, but is consonant with reason, as was shown before. And when it is said that in diverse substances differing in species it seems to be a quantity the same in species, it must be said that any quantity, which is not quality which is in substances diverse in species, differs in species; whence every quantity of fire, which is not a quality, differs in species from every quantity of air which is not a quality; and indeed I concede that the length of fire, and similarly the depth and the width, differ in species. And yet notwithstanding this, that the same most particular species could be predicated of them, although not 'in quid' and 'per se' in the first mode. Whence, two men and two horses differ in species, and yet 'binarius,' which is a most particular species, is applied to them. Whence, as it is not inconsistent that the same may be in diverse categories, so it is not inconsistent that the same may be in diverse species of one category, and yet they are in one most particular species of another category; and, therefore, it is not inconsistent that the same may be simply in diverse species of substance, and yet that they may be in the same most particular species of quantity. And whenever it is so, then that most particular species is not predicated of them 'in quid' and 'per se' in the first mode, and many passages concerning 'genera' as well as concerning 'species' speak of them with respect to those of which they are predicated 'in quid' and 'per se' in the first mode; yet there are many of no proper noun of any thing nor of a pronoun signifying some thing which are predicated 'in quid' and 'per se' in the first mode. Indeed, according to the intention of the philosopher relative to that which is replied in diverse modes to the question raised concerning an individual of a substance, as regards this diverse categories are accepted, as was said elsewhere; and indeed that is false which some say, that each category has a proper thing of which it is predicated 'in quid.'

As regards the fifth point; I say that quantity, which is quality, is really distinguished from quantity, which is at least some substance; say, any such, as color, heat, cold, and any other of the kind; although this may not be true of figure and of any such. And when it is

THE SACRAMENT OF THE ALTAR 71

said that quality according to the philosopher is not a quantum except through accident, I say that through all such propositions in the Categories and in the book of the Physics and elsewhere, "substance is not a quantum except through accident," and so of quality. Finite and infinite do not combine with a substance or a quality or through accident and anything else of the kind. It means nothing other than that that predicable 'quantum' is not predicated of substance and quality except through accident and not per se in the first mode. Whence, such is not per se in the first mode; neither by strictly nor freely accepting per se in the first mode: 'substance is quantum,' 'quality is quantum,' 'man is quantum,' 'man is long,' 'whiteness is wide,' and any other of the kind; since this however holds that quantity may not be a thing different from quality and substance. So 'God' and 'creating' are not distinct things, and yet this is not per se, 'creating is immortal'; as this, 'God is immortal.' Similarly, finite or infinite per se in the second or the first mode is applied to quantum and not to substance or quality. And so it appears, since those substantives and predicables, 'quantity,' 'substance,' 'quality,' are distinct; since this however holds that they do not signify distinct things, and through that mode the reply must be made to many passages.

As regards the last point of that Doctor, I say that in speaking of bodies of diverse grounds of which one was created to be in the form of another, or of which each was created to be in the form of a third, it is not inconsistent for two bodies to exist naturally in the same place; and accident and subject are so constituted; so also are constituted diverse accidents which are created to inform the same subject; so also whiteness and sweetness in milk are constituted; and, therefore, it ought to be conceded according to the virtue of common speech that several bodies can be at the same time, that is, that several things existing circumscriptively in this place, and each one of which has part outside of part, are at the same time; yet it is inconsistent that two bodies of the same ground (each of which may be completely in a genus or in some species of a substance, or that two bodies of diverse grounds, neither of which was created to be in the form of another nor both (in the form) of a third), may be at the same time; and of such bodies Aristotle speaks and other authors who say that two bodies can not be at the same time.

As regards other arguments. As regards the first; when it is said that the substance of the bread is not transubstantiated into the quantity of the body of Christ but only into the substance of the body of Christ, it must be said that according to the virtue of common speech this must be conceded, 'the substance of the bread is transubstantiated into the quantity of the body of Christ'; nor is the opposite of that found in the Bible nor in the statements of the Saints nor in the canonical law, nor in any authorized book; although it may be found in the writings of some who are censured by many Catholics and religious writers. I do not say that they censure them as heretics, but as those holding false opinions; whence, the subtle Doctor censures very much the profane and sacred writer and all, in whose writings is found the opposite of that, as regards many opinions. Many Catholic Doctors also censure the subtle Doctor in many con-

THE SACRAMENT OF THE ALTAR 73

clusions; and, indeed, although a conclusion the opposite of these may be found, it need not make much difference; for no one is bound to accept their authority, although thanks must be rendered to them, for this reason that, when they have made false statements, they have stimulated our abilities, and they have rather given to us occasions for finding the truth. I say, therefore, that this must really be conceded, 'the substance of the bread is transubstantiated into the body of Christ which is in heaven.' Similarly, this must be conceded according to the virtue of common speech, 'the substance of the bread is transubstantiated into the body of Christ which is in heaven locally.' In the same mode I say in confirmation that this must be conceded according to the virtue of common speech, 'the quantity of the body of Christ is in the sacrament of the altar by the power of conversion'; as according to the virtue of common speech this must be conceded, 'the body of Christ existing in heaven is in the sacrament of the altar by the power of conversion'; and precisely the opposite is not found in any authorized writer. But yet no matter how much each of those may be true according to the virtue of common speech and according to fact, yet according to the virtue of common speech both can be false; while this appears true, 'the substance of the body of Christ is in the sacrament of the altar by the power of conversion'; but not except in one case, say, if the substance of the body of Christ should exist nowhere circumscriptively. Whence, it does not seem to involve a contradiction, that, when the transubstantiation into the body of Christ has been accomplished and the body of Christ remains there under the species of bread, God could make the body of Christ to be nowhere locally or circumscriptively. When this has been done, the priest might be able to celebrate, and then this would be true according to the virtue of common speech, 'the substance of the body of Christ is under the species of bread by the power of transubstantiation'; and then this would be false, 'the quantity of the body of Christ is under the species of that bread,' and this by virtue of a false implication; for it would be implied that the substance of the body of Christ would be a quantum, which would not be true; for nothing is a quantum except that whose part is outside of part and whose part is separate from part. But, since the body of Christ could be nowhere locally, never could it be able in that mode to be assigned that one part could be separate from another part; but wherever it would be, one part would be in the same situation as another; and then this would be true, 'the body of Christ is nowhere circumscriptively'; and for the same reason this would be true, 'the body of Christ is nowhere a quantum'; and consequently this would be false, 'the body of Christ is a quantity'; and so by virtue of a false implication this would be false, 'the quantity of the body of Christ is in the sacrament of the altar.' And so he who would desire to excuse those who say that the quantity of the body of Christ is not in the sacrament of the altar by the power of conversion, could say that they say this, because that consequence is not valid; namely, 'the substance of the body of Christ is in the sacrament of the altar by the power of conversion'; therefore, the quantity of the body of Christ is in the sacrament of the altar by the power of conversion; for the antecedent can be true, while the con-

THE SACRAMENT OF THE ALTAR 75

sequent appears false. But this can not happen unless the substance of the body of Christ nowhere have part separate from part.

And if it be said contrary to this that, wherever the quantity of the body of Christ is by the power of conversion, there the body of Christ is a quantity or a quantum by the power of conversion. If, therefore, the quantity of the body of Christ be in the sacrament of the altar by the power of conversion, the body of Christ is a quantum or quantity in the sacrament of the altar. But every quantum is circumscriptively in a place; therefore, the body of Christ is circumscriptively in a place in the sacrament of the altar, which is heretical; for it could not then be in the whole host and in each part of the host. It must be said that that argument alone would be able to move a Catholic to hold that quantity is not a thing other than substance and quality, and would be able to be formulated thus: wherever any thing has another thing created to designate it, it is true to say that the thing there is such; as when a body has whiteness, it is true to say that the body there is white; and so is it of all. If, therefore, the quantity of the body of Christ be a thing other than the substance of the body of Christ, it is not separate from that quantity; for then those holding this opinion thus say, that the quantity of the body of Christ is there, although concomitantly; but whenever there is some quantum there, it truly has part outside of part and part separate from part; for whenever a definition corresponds to something, the defined corresponds there to the same. Therefore, since this may be a definition of quantity or of quantum, 'to have part outside of part'; if the body of Christ in the sacrament of the altar be a quantum either concomitantly or in another mode, it is necessary that the body of Christ there be 'having part outside of part, separate from part,' which is manifestly false and perilous, and it does not seem at all safe to concede that the body of Christ may be a quantum here. And indeed I say that it must be conceded according to the virtue of common speech that the body of Christ is not a quantum in the sacrament of the altar. As according to the virtue of common speech it must be conceded that the body of Christ in the sacrament does not have part outside of part, although the body of Christ may have part outside of part in heaven, and consequently may be a quantum in heaven. And if it be said that this is contradictory to a prior statement, (for it was said that this is true, 'the quantity of the body of Christ is in the sacrament of the altar'; from which it follows that the body of Christ is a quantum or a quantity in the sacrament of the altar, which was just denied;) it must be stated that this is simply true, 'the quantity of the body of Christ is in the sacrament of the altar.' But the former does not infer that; therefore, the body of Christ is a quantum in the sacrament of the altar; as this is true according to the virtue of speech, 'the body of Christ existing locally in heaven is in the sacrament of the altar'; and yet this is false, 'the body of Christ is locally existent in the sacrament of the altar.'

Similarly, this is true, 'the body of Christ existing in a place is in the sacrament of the altar'; for nothing else is designated through that except that for which it substitutes this, 'the whole body of Christ existing circumscriptively in a place,' which is not unless the body of Christ is in the sacrament of the altar,

THE SACRAMENT OF THE ALTAR 77

which is true; and yet this is false, 'the body of Christ is circumscriptively existent in a place in the sacrament of the altar.'

Similarly, this is true, 'the body of Christ having part outside of part is in the sacrament of the altar.' In the same way, notwithstanding that this may be true, 'the quantity of the body of Christ is in the sacrament of the altar'; yet this is false according to a property of common speech, 'the body of Christ is a quantum in the sacrament of the altar'; and so, although the quantity of the body of Christ be truly there, yet the body of Christ is not a quantity there; as, although the body of Christ having part separate in situation from part may be there, yet it does not there have part separate from part.

And that reply is confirmed; for, whenever some are convertibles, of whatever one term is predicated the rest is also assumed significatively; and similarly of whatever one term is predicated, the rest also. But those are convertibles: 'a continuous and permanent quantum' and 'having part separate in situation from part,' and conversely; therefore, of whatever one is said, the rest also. If therefore, this be true, 'the body of Christ is in the sacrament of the altar having part separate in situation from part,' which is manifestly false; for no part is separate in situation from another in the sacrament of the altar; therefore, this is false according to a property of common speech, 'the substance of the body of Christ is a continuous and permanent quantum in the sacrament of the altar.'

Therefore, I say that the body of Christ is not a quantum there; for it does not have there part separate

78   THE SACRAMENT OF THE ALTAR

from part; but in heaven, as elsewhere, it has part separate in situation from part, so in heaven it is a quantum. If only the quantity of the body of Christ were another thing, there would truly be a quantity there; namely, in the sacrament of the altar; and consequently the body of Christ would truly be a quantum there, and consequently would truly have there part separate from part, and consequently would not be a whole under a whole host and a whole under each part.

As to the other; when it is said that, if the substance of the body of Christ were a quantity, then the quantity could not remain in the sacrament of the altar; so the substance of the bread does not remain there.

It must be said that that argument ought not to be advanced here, unless because some maliciously provoke some frank statements contrary to the opinion; as if that opinion could posit, that every quantity would be substance; and they indeed maliciously propose this proposition, 'substance is quantity' and withdraw this, 'quality is quantity,' that they may grant through this an opportunity for the unlearned who pay no attention to the preceding opinion to understand and to posit this, 'every quantity is a substance'; and by virtue of a defect in the arguments they carefully strive to enlist some simple minded folk against the opinion.

Therefore, I say as regards the argument, that it is too stupid; for it does not follow, 'substance is quantity,' and substance ceases to be there; then some quantity does not remain there, as substance does not remain there; as it does not follow, 'substance is an entity'; therefore, no entity remains there; as a preexisting substance does not remain there.

Whence, I say that one pre-existing quantity remains in the sacrament of the altar; but quantity does not remain there, which is substance or which was substance; but one quantity remains there, which is quality; for quantity remains there, which is not a thing other than whiteness.

Similarly, a quantity remains there which is not a thing other than taste, and so of other quantities. And I say with the Doctors approved by the church, that color, taste, weight, that is, gravity, and some qualities of a like kind, remain there; none of which is a thing other than a quantity subsisting per se in situation outside of every subject by divine power; none of which is subjectively in another; but each one exists outside of a subject through the divine power, and they are preserved at the same time in the same place and situation through the divine power; and indeed there remains there one quantity having part separate from part, which never was nor ever will be substance, but is simply a thing other than substance. And these arguments concerning that matter may suffice for the present, for I shall elsewhere treat at length of it.

The introduction to the tract concerning
the body of Christ begins.

PROLOGUE

Wondrous gifts from the abundance on high, expended by Him for the redemption of the human race, place it under an infinite obligation to its glorious Redeemer; for the Only-begotten Son of God, after He
5 had assumed the substance of our frailty in order that He might redeem us from the servitude of the devil and restore us to our original liberty and also bring us at last to our heavenly inheritance, offered Himself on the altar of the cross as the price for the redemption
10 of the human race.

Moreover, that a perpetual memorial of so great a gift might remain among us and also that Christ might daily be mystically offered as a sacrifice for us who err daily, He left behind His body in the food and His
15 blood in the drink to be received by the faithful in the sacrament of the Eucharist, the unspeakable loftiness of which is deemed an improper subject for human investigation; by virtue of which there is need to speak of this sublime and most excellent sacrament with all
20 fear and modesty; for with respect to no sacrament is error more perilous, nor inquiry more laborious, nor invention more fruitful.

Accordingly, since I am about to examine carefully some views of this most worthy sacrament, I protest
25 that I will not assert anything except that which the Roman Church holds and teaches. Moreover, subjecting and exposing myself to the correction of all the skilled, orthodox Catholics who are interested, I

THE SACRAMENT OF THE ALTAR

shall explain the statements of physics which are to be inserted and whatever statements are in general to be quoted, which are not authorized by the Roman Church, with all humility and modesty, that is, not by rashly approving them but by citing them only for the sake of practice and of inquiring into the truth.

However, let all men understand that I do not undertake this present little work that I may inflict some profane novelties of speech upon the ears of the faithful, but that I may show how blamelessly and temperately I have spoken on this most worthy sacrament when I expressed my opinions.

CHAPTER I

What the Catholic Doctors discerned by the senses concerning the reality of the Eucharist

The Catholic Doctors approved by the Roman Church, who have written about the sacrament of the Eucharist, intend to assert this, that the body of Christ which was born of the Virgin Mary, suffered and was buried, which also rose from the dead and ascended into heaven and sits at the right hand of God, the Father, and in which the Son of God is about to come to judge the living and the dead, is really and truly contained under the species of bread. But, although it may really lie hidden under the species of bread, it certainly is not seen by us with the bodily eye, but with the mind the faithful believe that it is concealed under the species of bread.

And it is also held that the substance of the bread is transubstantiated, converted, or changed, so that the substance of the bread does not remain but that only the accidents existing per se remain without a subject.

And not only the body of Christ, which is one of the two parts of the human nature affected by the transubstantiation of the bread, is really contained under the species of bread; but also the whole Christ, undivided, perfect God and true man, is at the same time truly and really contained under the entire host and under each part; although by a proper assumption of 'conversion' and 'transubstantiation,' the substance of the bread may not be converted into divinity or rational soul or into some accident.

This is also my faith, since this is the Catholic faith. For whatever the Roman Church explicitly believes, this alone and nothing else either explicitly or implicitly I believe. But how much efficiency and nobility there may be in implicit faith Innocent sets forth in a gloss on the De Summa Trinitate et Fide Catholica, 'Firmiter.' "Implicit faith," he says, "prevails to such a degree, as some say, that if any one has this; namely, that he believes as the church believes; if he is impelled by natural reason falsely to think that the Father may be greater or prior to the Son or that the three persons may be three things mutually separate, he is not a heretic nor does he sin; provided he does not defend this error and believes this very statement because he believes that the church so believes, and substitutes his opinion for the faith of the church; for although he may thus wrongly think, yet that faith is not his faith; on the contrary his own faith is the faith of the church."

Therefore, if there be such great efficacy in implicit faith that it may excuse one ignorantly erring concerning those doctrines which are set forth in the canonical Scriptures, much more will it excuse the one ignorantly forming an opinion of something which is found set forth neither in the canonical Scriptures nor in the writings of the Doctors approved by the church.

CHAPTER II

That the body of Christ is really contained under the species of bread

That the body of Christ is really contained under the species of bread can not be shown through natural reason; and, therefore, it is necessary to assent through faith to a conception of this truth, concerning which we ought not to be in doubt since it may be well known to us that the same truth was revealed to the Apostles through the Only-begotten Son of God; a witness to which is the most holy Evangelist, Matthew, in Chapter XXVI. "Jesus took bread," he says, "and blessing, brake it and gave it to His disciples and said: 'Take and eat; this is my body.'" To this truth Mark also bears testimony in Chapter XIV., saying: "While they were eating, Jesus took bread and blessing, brake it and gave it to them and said: 'Take, this is my body.'" With these statements Luke agrees in Chapter XXII., saying: "When He had taken bread, He gave thanks and brake it and gave it to them, saying: 'This is my body which is given for you; this do in remembrance of me.'" In John, Chapter VI.; John, the Evangelist, also records the words of the Saviour as He points out both the reality and the benefit of that sacrament: "The bread, which I shall give to you for the life of the world, is my flesh"; and there follows: "Except ye will have eaten the flesh of the Son of Man and will have drunk his blood, ye *will* not have life in you. He who eats my flesh and drinks my blood, hath eternal life." The Apostle Paul similarly says in I.

Corinthians XI.: "The Lord Jesus," he says, "in the night in which he was betrayed, took bread, and giving thanks brake it and said: 'Take and eat; this is my body which is given for you. Do this in remembrance of me.'" Likewise, in I. Corinthians X., he says: "The bread which we break, is it not the communion of the body of the Lord?" These are the authors of the canonical scriptures, who alike affirm that the body of Christ was truly and really given to the Apostle under the species of bread and that it was also enjoined upon the same Apostles by the Saviour that they should offer the body of Christ under the species of bread in memory of the passion of the Lord.

With the previously quoted writers of the canonical Scriptures also agree the eminent Doctors, the Holy Fathers, the most illustrious expositors of the divine scriptures, and also those recognized as authorities by the Roman Church; some of whose passages preserved in the canonical law must be publicly set forth.

Whence, the blessed Augustine says as quoted in I., Question I., 'Intra ecclesiam.' "Within the Catholic Church," he says, "in the mystery of the body and the blood of the Lord, nothing greater is conferred by a good priest and nothing less by a bad priest."

Likewise, the blessed Cyprian, the bishop, as quoted in the De Consecratione, Distinction II., 'Scriptura.' He says: "As often as we offer the cup in commemoration of the Lord and His Passion, we do that which it is well known that the Lord did."

Likewise, Ambrose as quoted in the De Consecratione, Distinction II., 'Ante benedictionem.' "Before the blessing," he says, "a different species is indicated, after the blessing the body is designated. Christ is likewise in that sacrament."

Likewise, Hieronymus as quoted in the De Consecratione, Distinction II., 'Nec Moyses.' "Moses," he says, "did not give to you the true bread from heaven, but the Lord Jesus, feast and guest, the one eating and the one who is eaten."

Likewise, the blessed Gregory as quoted in I., Question I., 'Multi.' "We," he says, "desecrate the bread, that is, the body of Christ when we approach the altar unworthily."

From these and numerous other passages, it is clearly shown that the body of Christ is really contained under the species of bread; and because that was clear to all the faithful from the commencement of the Christian faith; therefore, as regards the confirmation of this, I do not wish to delay longer.

CHAPTER III

That the substance of the bread is converted into the body of Christ

Although it is expressly set forth in the canonical Scriptures that the body of Christ is to be offered to the faithful under the species of bread, yet that the substance of the bread is really converted or transubstantiated into the body of Christ is not found expressed in the canon of the Bible; but this doctrine is believed to have been divinely revealed to the Holy Fathers, or to have been proved from passages of the Bible by a diligent and skillful examination; and, therefore, I shall cite passages of the Holy Fathers to prove this truth.

Whence, Eusebius Emissenus says as quoted in the De Consecratione, Distinction II., 'Quia corpus': "The invisible Priest converts visible creatures into the substance of His body and blood by His word by a secret power." And he adds: "And so how many and how celebrated the benefits the power of the divine blessing may produce; and that it ought not to be strange or impossible to you that earthly and mortal objects are converted into the substance of Christ."

Likewise, Ambrose as quoted in the De Consecratione, Distinction II., 'Panis.' "If," he says, "there is such power in the Word of the Lord Jesus, that by a miracle He may cause that to be which was not; how much more efficacious is it that those may be which were and may be changed into another. And so that which was bread before consecration, is now the body of Christ after consecration."

Likewise, in the margin of the De Summa Trinitate et Fide Catholica, 'Firmiter,' where Innocent III. says in a general council: "There is one universal church of believers, outside of which no one at all is saved; in which Jesus Christ Himself is both priest and sacrifice, whose body and blood is truly contained in the sacrament of the altar under the species of bread and wine, since the bread has been transformed into body and the wine into blood by divine power."

Likewise, in the margin of the De Celebratione Missarum, 'Cum Marthæ.' "If, therefore, He lifted His eyes to the Father at the time when He called the soul of Lazarus back to the lifeless body, it seems to be more probable that He lifted His eyes to the Father in heaven at the time when He specially changed the bread and the wine into body and blood."

From these and very many other passages of the Saints and the Doctors, it is established that the substance of the bread is really and truly transubstantiated, converted, or changed by divine virtue into the substance of the body of Christ, yet without any increase or substantial translation of the body of Christ.

CHAPTER IV

That the substance of the bread is converted into the body of Christ, not into the divinity, or the rational soul, or the blood, or some accident of the substance

According to a proper acceptation of the term, the previously mentioned conversion or transubstantiation of the bread may not be into the soul, or the divinity, or into an accident of the substance of the body of Christ, or the blood of Christ, but only into the body of Christ. Although, by putting an improper and loose construction upon this term 'conversion' or 'transubstantiation' it might be able to be conceded that the bread is transubstantiated into the soul or an accident of the body of Christ, or the blood. For the passages of the Doctors prove conclusively that the substance of the bread is not converted into the soul or the divinity of Christ. Whence a gloss on the De Consecratione, Distinction II., above that Chapter, 'Quid est Christum manducare?' says: "The bread is converted into flesh alone and the wine into blood."

Likewise, the Master of the Sentences in Book IV., Distinction XI.: "Although," he says, "the entire Christ may be assumed under both species, yet no conversion of the bread except into flesh or of wine except into blood takes place."

From these passages it is clear that the substance of the bread, from which it is converted into flesh alone, is not transubstantiated into divinity or rational soul or blood, nor as a consequence into an accident of

90 THE SACRAMENT OF THE ALTAR

flesh or soul; but this is certainly true according to a proper use of this term 'convertitur.'

From which it must be perceived that the substance of the bread is especially converted or transubstantiated into that which is not, because it is joined to another; but, even if it were separated from others, it begins to be so by divine power under the species of the bread at the utterance of the sacramental words by the priest, with the obligatory intention, over suitable material. But of such is the flesh of Christ, and not the soul, or the blood, or some accident inhering in flesh or soul. For, if the soul were separated from the flesh, no matter how much the priest might with obligatory intention recite the sacramental words over suitable material, the soul of Christ would not begin to be there, but only the flesh.

Similarly, if the blood were separated from the flesh, the blood would not begin to be there, but only the flesh. And the judgment is the same with respect to the accidents of the flesh and the soul. And by virtue of this the Doctors say that the body of Christ is under the species of bread by virtue of the sacramental words and by the power of conversion, and by virtue of this the substance of the bread is converted into the body of Christ and not into soul or deity.

If however any one wishes to use the term 'conversion' or 'transubstantiation' more improperly, that he may say that the substance of the bread is converted into all that which at the pronouncing of the sacramental words begins now really to be under the species of bread, by so using the term it can be conceded that the substance of the bread is converted into the reasonable soul of Christ; this is to say, that at the utterance

THE SACRAMENT OF THE ALTAR 91

of the sacramental words the reasonable soul begins to be under the species of bread. If, however, the sacramental words would have been uttered with the obligatory intention during the three days of the death of Christ, the reasonable soul would not have been in the same place; and the reason for this diversity is, because the intellectual soul was then separated from the body of Christ to which it is now united.

But if they only wish to contend about a term and to say that the substance of the bread is converted into nothing, except that which will begin to be under the species of bread, even if it were separated from others, I do not wish to oppose them since the point is sufficiently obvious.

CHAPTER V

That the substance of the bread does not remain after consecration

The statement must now be considered that this conversion or transubstantiation does not happen through this alone, that the body of Christ begins to be under the species of bread though the substance itself remains; but the substance of the bread is converted into the body of Christ in such a way, that the substance of the bread does not remain by divine virtue, but the body of Christ remains only under the accidents which were in the substance of the bread before conversion; yet it is not affected by those accidents, as will be stated later.

However, it must be noted that, although it may be found expressed in the New Testament, that the body of Christ is to be received by the faithful under the species of bread in memory of the passion of the Lord and for the remission of their sins; yet it is not there clearly expressed that the substance of the bread does not remain. Whence, and in former times there have been diverse opinions concerning this, as states the Master of the Sentences in Book IV., Distinction XI., and Hostiensis at the top of the page in the margin of the De Consecratione, and the gloss on the De Consecratione, Distinction II., 'In sacramentorum,' and the gloss in the margin of the De Celebratione Missarum, 'Cum Marthæ.' Whence they say that there were three opinions about the conversion of the bread into the body of Christ. "One opinion asserts that that

THE SACRAMENT OF THE ALTAR 93

substance, which was at first bread, afterwards is the flesh and the blood of Christ. The second opinion holds that the substance of the bread and the wine ceases to be there and the accidents only remain; namely, taste, color, weight, and similar accidents; and under these accidents the body of Christ begins to be there. The third opinion holds, that the substance of the bread and the wine remains there and the body of Christ is in the same place under the same species."

The aforesaid Doctors approve the second opinion, and it seems to be the determination of the Roman Church. Whence, in the margin of the De Summa Trinitate et Fide Catholica, 'Firmiter,' Innocent says in a general council: "There is one universal church of all believers, outside of which no one at all is saved; in which He is both priest and sacrifice, whose body and blood are truly contained in the sacrament of the altar under the species of bread and wine, when the bread is transubstantiated by divine power into the body of Christ and the wine into the blood." See this passage in the preceding column; namely, in Chapter III. of this work.

But the Catholics, who agree in their approval of this second opinion, have diverse opinions concerning the mode of positing. For some posit, as Saint Thomas, in Book IV., Distinction XI., Question I., that there is a contradiction involved in the statement that the substance of the bread may remain with the body of Christ which remains sacramentally under the species of bread. And certain posit, as the subtle Doctor, in Book IV., Distinction XI., Question III., that, although the substance of the bread may not really remain with the body of Christ, yet there is no contradiction involved in the statement that through divine power the substance of the bread may be able to remain with the body of Christ; and, therefore, these concede and approve the statement that the body of Christ may be in the sacrament of the altar through a change made concerning the body of Christ. And without prejudice to any other this second opinion seems to me more probable and more in accord with theology, because it rather exalts the omnipotence of God by detracting nothing from it, nor does it plainly and expressly imply a contradiction.

However, for the present I refrain from a discussion of these opinions, since I intend, God willing, to discuss the same more fully on another occasion. However, I say that the substance of the bread does not remain, but ceases to be and the body of Christ begins to be under those species.

CHAPTER VI

That the body of Christ is not circumscribed in a place in the sacrament of the altar

Moreover, although the body of Christ may be really and truly contained under the species of bread, yet it is not circumscribed in a place in the sacrament of the altar. But the entire body of Christ is really contained under the whole host and under each part of the host, which is confirmed by the testimony of the Holy Fathers. Whence, the blessed Jerome is quoted in the De Consecratione, Distinction II., 'Singuli.' "Each individual," he says, "receives the entire Christ the Lord, and He is whole in each portion and is not lessened through each; but He offers Himself entire in each." Likewise, the blessed Hilary, the Bishop, is quoted in the De Consecratione, Distinction II., 'Ubi.' "Where," he says, "there is a part of the body, there is also the whole." From these passages it is clearly gathered that the whole Christ is in the whole host, and the whole is in a part; from which it follows that the body of Christ is not confined or circumscribed in a place.

But the faithful can be led to believe in the possibility of this in some other way. For the Christian ought to say that anything can be accomplished by the divine virtue, except that which can be clearly proved to involve a contradiction through reasoning from things known per se, which no one could doubt, and except that which can not be elicited from Sacred Scripture

96 THE SACRAMENT OF THE ALTAR

or the Doctors approved by the church. For we ought not to limit the divine power according to the mode of natural causes, since the divine power may infinitely exceed the virtue of all creatures.

Nor is experimental knowledge sufficient for saying that something can not be accomplished by divine virtue, since God might be able to change the entire order of natural causes. And it may be well known that He has done many things contrary to the common course of natural causes. For who ever experimentally knew of a virgin naturally conceiving without a husband, of two bodies existing at the same time, of the dead restored to life, of accidents existing without a subject, and of innumerable other things which, however, it is well known have been divinely wrought? Therefore, we ought not to say that some things can not be done by God, because we do not know by experience that they are done naturally. Therefore, since there is evidently no contradiction, which can be proven through self-evident propositions, involved in the statement that some substance a whole as regards itself coexists in two bodies, consequently the same substance a whole as regards itself coexists in some body and in each part of it.

I am, on the contrary, certain that it can be proved through the rules of logic, which are said to serve zealously all science and knowledge. Having conceded that the same substance a whole as regards itself may coexist in two bodies or in one body and in each part of it, every contradiction can evidently be avoided; although it may not be clearly proved from purely natural causes that the antecedent is true. For a Christian ought not to say that God might not

THE SACRAMENT OF THE ALTAR 97

through His absolute power be able to make some substance to coexist with something corporeal, so that the whole may coexist with that whole body and with each part of it; nor can the opposite be proved. For we so hold that the rationable soul is a whole in a whole body and in each part of it; and the opposite can not be proved through demonstrative reasoning.

Moreover, we similarly hold that an angel is definitively a whole in any place and in each part of it. Moreover, by virtue of the same none of the faithful ought to say that two bodies of the very same identical species, as well as those of diverse species, may not be able to exist at the same time in the same place through divine power. For the Saviour, Jesus Christ, entered thus into the midst of the disciples when the doors were closed and came forth into the world from the closed womb of a virgin and ascended into heaven with undivided celestial body. If, therefore, no contradiction appears in the statement that two bodies may exist at the same time in the same place, no contradiction appears in the statement that two parts of the same body may exist in the same place at the same time.

From which it is obvious that for a reason equal to that by which two parts of the body of Christ can exist in the same place, all the parts of the body of Christ could coexist at the same time in the same place. Moreover, from this and the former statement follows the principal intention. For if it is not impossible for God, who can do more than we can think or understand, to bring it to pass that all the parts of the body of Christ may exist in the same body, and it is not impossible for Him to place the same whole substance in a whole and to place the whole in each part, as is obvious of the rational soul and an angel.

It manifestly follows that it is not impossible for God to bring it to pass that the whole substance of the body of Christ may coexist with the whole host and with each part of it, which is the principal thesis. Nor does this obtain, that the body of Christ has organic parts really distinct, of which one is not in another, as a finger is not in a finger; of which, moreover, some are in one total part and not in another, as the eyes are not in the hand or in the foot but in the head. For local separation is not required for a distinction of organic parts, but a real distinction of material dispositions. For although the hand, if the same dispositions are retained, might be placed with the eye, so that both the hand and eye would be at the same time in the same place, yet the hand would certainly be a hand and not an eye, and a man could not see through the hand but through the eye. And so then the organs can remain distinct and created to have distinct functions, no matter how much they might not be separate locally. And, therefore, this must not be denied of the divine power. But of what kind the diversity of disposition of the organs may be, whether indeed it be substantial or accidental, does not concern the present discussion.

Similarly, also, although the organs might not be separate locally, it would not by virtue of this follow that the hand would be in the foot, or the contrary; but only that those organs would be at the same time in the same place, which is not inconsistent with the disposition of the organs, as has been shown; since with even the local inseparability of one part from another

THE SACRAMENT OF THE ALTAR 99

it obtains that one part may be in another as in its whole, after the manner in which the eye is in the head, as in a whole; and as with the local inseparability of the rational soul from man it obtains that the rational soul may be a part of man; for the rational soul is wholly in the same place in which man is, and yet it is part of man. So the eye might be able to be a part of the head and yet be in the same place with the head. And so the possibility of the existence of the body of Christ with the whole host and with each part of it is obvious.

However, I assert nothing concerning all of the previous statements, except that which is consistent with the doctrine of the Saints; but if any statement should not be in agreement with their statements, let it be said only for the training of studious minds.

CHAPTER VII

That the body of Christ in the sacrament of the altar is not seen by us with the bodily eye

Therefore, when at their words the substance of the bread only ceases to exist, this body of the Lord, which begins to exist under the species of bread by the divine power, is not perceived with the bodily eye but by faith and the understanding. This conclusion is drawn from passages of the Holy Fathers as well as from arguments.

Whence, the blessed Augustine says, as quoted in the De Consecratione, Distinction II., 'Nos autem.' "But we," he says, "in the species of bread and wine which we see, behold invisible things, that is, we do honor to flesh and blood."

Likewise, the same Augustine in the De Consecratione, Distinction II., 'Qui manducant.' "That which is seen," he says, "is the bread and the cup which also the eyes declare; but that which faith for its instruction demands, the bread is the body of Christ and the cup is the blood. These, therefore, are called sacraments, because in them one is seen and another is understood."

Likewise, Gregory in the De Consecratione, Distinction II., 'Quid sit,' says thus: "It is a great and dread mystery," the Lord says, "because one is seen and another is understood."

Likewise, Hilary as quoted in the De Consecratione, Distinction II., 'Ubi.' "A visible quantity," he says,

THE SACRAMENT OF THE ALTAR 101

"is not to be considered in this mystery, but the virtue of the sacrament is spiritual."

It is obvious from these and many other passages that the body of Christ is not seen in the sacrament of the altar, but is only understood; although the species of bread may really be seen.

Moreover, for this conclusion arguments are not wanting. For that, which is perceived with the bodily eye in some place, can certainly be known to exist in the same place without any authority. But no one without the full authority of the Saviour and of the Church would hold that the body of Christ is really contained under the species of bread; therefore, it is not seen there with the bodily eye.

Likewise, bodily vision is equal in all those equally disposed; but no unbeliever sees the body of Christ in the sacrament of the altar with the bodily eye; therefore, it remains that no believer perceives with the bodily eye that the body of Christ is there.

It is likewise manifest that no one perceives there any sensible quality by any sense whatsoever, unless a quality of the host. As is obvious, from qualities tangible and perceptible by the sense of taste and from visible qualities, the body of Christ is not, therefore, seen in the sacrament of the altar with the bodily eye.

CHAPTER VIII

That the accidents remaining after consecration are not subjectively in the body of Christ

Since little has been previously written about the existence of the body of Christ under the species of bread; it remains that some views be set forth concerning the accidents remaining after the consecration of the substance of the bread.

Let it be shown, first, that those accidents do not exist subjectively in the body of Christ; which is obvious from this, that contrary qualities in a body are not at the same time in the body of Christ. Moreover, for the same reason by which the qualities of one host might exist subjectively in the body of Christ, the qualities of another host might affect the same body of Christ. But it is obvious to sense that sometimes some qualities of diverse hosts are contrary to themselves. From which it follows that neither these qualities nor those affect the body of Christ.

Likewise, the body of Christ is not changed anew to sensible qualities, which might, however, happen if the accidents of the bread could inform the body of Christ. This is also confirmed by the passage of the Master of the Sentences in Book IV., Distinction XII. "There," he says, "is no substance except that of the body and the blood of the Lord which is not affected by those accidents. For the body of Christ does not have in itself such form, but such as will appear in the judgment."

THE SACRAMENT OF THE ALTAR 103

Moreover, those accidents do not affect the surrounding air; for no accident, neither as regards itself as a whole nor as regards any part of itself, is separate in place and situation from its primary subject. But to the sense it appears that some part of an accident of the host is separate in place and situation from the surrounding air and from each part of it; therefore, the same accident is not in the air subjectively, nor for the same reason is any of the others. Likewise, an accident never occupies a place other than the place of its subject, but it is manifest that the host and the air occupy distinct places; therefore, it is manifest that accidents are not subjectively in the air.

Moreover, those accidents are not subjectively in the substance of the bread, because that substance is not, as was shown previously. Therefore, it remains that the accidents remain without a subject; which is confirmed through the Master of the Sentences in Book IV., Distinction XII., where he says at the beginning: "But if any inquiry is made concerning the accidents which remain; namely, of the species, 'taste' and 'heaviness,' in what subject they may be found, it seems to me to cause these accidents to be without a subject rather than to be in a subject."

CHAPTER IX

That the quantity, which was before in the substance of the bread, remains

Moreover, it can be shown by many reasons that those accidents may be quanta, and that a quantity may truly remain after consecration.

First thus: according to Innocent III. in the margin of the De Celebratione Missarum, 'Cum Marthæ,' a subtle distinction must be made among three things, which are distinct in the sacrament; namely, visible form, reality of the body, and spirtual virtue. The form is that of bread and wine, the reality is that of flesh and blood, the virtue is that of unity and charity. The first is the sacrament, and not the element. The second is the sacrament and the element. The third is the element and not the sacrament.

From this it is evidently inferred that the visible form is really distinct from the body of Christ and that it is not a quantum from the quantity of the body of Christ; as it is not visible through some quality visible in the body of Christ. But it is manifest that that visible form is a quantum, since it may be long, wide, and thick; therefore, some quantity besides the quantity of the body of Christ really remains.

In the second place thus: that the quantity of the visible form is really figurated, but nothing is figurated without quantity, and does not have the figure of the body of Christ; therefore, it does not have the quantity of the body of Christ; and consequently there is there some quantity other than the quantity of the body of Christ.

In the third place thus: some quantity is seen in the sacrament of the altar with the bodily eye, but neither Christ nor any accident of Him is seen by us in the sacrament of the altar with the bodily eye; therefore, there is there a quantity remaining other than the quantity of the body of Christ.

In the fourth place thus: all that which is broken and one part of which is separate from another is a quantum. But that visible form is broken and one part of it is separate from another; but the body of Christ is not thus; therefore, there is there some other quantity besides the quantity of the body of Christ.

For the Evangelist, Matthew, is a witness that the visible form may really be broken when he says: "Jesus took bread, blessed it and also brake it." Mark offers the same testimony. "Blessing it," he says, "he brake it." Which also is obvious according to Luke and other Holy Fathers, whom it would take too long to adduce. Moreover, that the body of Christ may not be broken but may remain entire, the eminent doctor, the blessed Augustine, says, as quoted in the De Consecratione, Distinction II., 'Qui manducant.' "Christ," he says, "is eaten; though eaten, He lives; because though slain, He arose; nor, when we eat, do we make portions of Him." And he says likewise in the De Consecratione, Distinction II., 'Invitat.' "Through parts He is eaten in the sacrament," he says, "and remains an entire whole in heaven; remains an entire whole in your heart." From all these passages it is gathered that a quantity distinct from the quantity of the body of Christ remains in the sacrament of the altar.

CHAPTER X

That the sensible qualities remain

Moreover, it is not only well known that a quantity remains in the Eucharist, but it is also manifest that sensible qualities subsist in the same place after consecration. For nothing is visible without a sensible quality, but the visible form remains there, and, therefore, a sensible quality. Taste is also perceived there, and whiteness is seen, and the sense of touch also apprehends the tangible qualities. But no sense perceives any quality of the body of Christ; therefore, the sensible qualities remain, which were before in the substance of the bread and are now without a subject. As the Master says in Book IV., Distinction XI.: "The species of bread and wine is there, as taste. Whence, one is seen, another is understood." All the previous statements might be able to be confirmed by many other passages; from quoting which I refrain, for I hasten on to certain statements of physics, upon which I happened while reading the Sentences.

I have fully investigated the questions concerning the Eucharist for the sake of thoroughly examining and explaining them that I may make known to those not understanding the 'quæ' and the 'qualia' and the 'quomodo,' and that I have spoken without assertion and only by quoting for the purpose of exercising the abilities of the studious. I have undertaken the present task because of the misrepresentation of some critics.

CHAPTER XI

That every extended material substance is composed of substantial parts really distinct

However, in order that the statements, which are to be presented, may appear to rest upon a solid and immovable foundation, an exordium may then be assumed with respect to which no rational person ought to be in doubt.

Every extended material substance is composed of substantial parts separate in place or situation. For wood is not only composed of matter and form, which are essential parts and of diverse grounds; but it is also composed of integral parts, of which each is wood. But it is manifest that these parts, of which each is wood, are not in the same situation; therefore, they are separate in situation. And yet wood is truly composed of parts and is not composed of accidents; therefore, it is composed of substantial parts separate in situation.

Again, when wood is divided into two equal parts, no substance new as regards itself as a whole is generated; but there are now two substances really distinct locally; for otherwise, when wood is divided into halves, the accidents would remain without a subject in one half; from which, therefore, no substance new as regards itself as a whole is generated. It is necessary, that those two substances, each of which is a certain whole after division, were previously making one whole wood, and were not at the same time in the same place; therefore, there were before two parts of one total wood separate in situation.

Again, one half of the wood can be corrupted, the other not corrupted; but such a corruption is a substantial corruption; therefore, some substance, which was before, is now destroyed. And it is manifest that some substance, which was before, now remains; therefore, there were before two substantial parts of the same wood composing one wood.

Again, the whiteness existing in the wood is a whole in some whole and part in part; or there is, therefore, a whole in some whole substance and part in part, or there is a whole in some whole accident and part in part. If the first be granted, the thesis is maintained, that there is some substance composed of substantial parts separate in situation, as parts of whiteness are separate in situation and place. If the second is granted, it is necessary to give some primary subject to that accident, so that there may be a whole in a whole subject and a part in a part. And if, indeed, substance be such a subject, I accept the thesis; but if an accident be considered the total subject of that accident; then I inquire about the subject of that (accident) as about the former; and it is necessary to continue the procedure indefinitely, or that there may be some extended accident having some substance for a primary subject, which is a whole in a whole substance and a part in a part, which can not be, unless that substance have substantial parts separate in situation.

Again, unless wood and any material, extended substance could universally have real and substantial parts separate in situation; there could no more be such a substance really extended than there could a rational soul. For as a rational soul is a whole in a whole body and a whole in each part; so any material substance would be a whole under a whole quantity and a whole under each part; but that is absurd. It might be able to be said that there is no similarity, for the soul does not have parts; therefore, it might be able to be argued about knowledge and virtue, which have intentional parts.

Therefore, it remains that an extended material substance has substantial parts locally separate which are to such a degree distinguished from one another, that one part can be destroyed, another not destroyed, and not only this; but even if they remain, they can be mutually separated and can be certain distinct wholes; as when wood or stone is divided, those the same numerically, which were before parts, are now wholes and not parts; yet they are not now other than before.

CHAPTER XII

That an absolute thing can be prior by divine power without a posterior

To the preceding fundamental principle another must be joined; namely, that the infinite and incomprehensible power of God can make and preserve every absolute thing prior naturally, without an absolute thing really distinct as regards itself as a whole, posterior naturally. For since a thing prior naturally to another may depend less upon and require a thing posterior less than an effect its essential cause, and since we manifestly hold that sometimes the divine power produces, maintains and preserves its effect without a natural cause, we ought not to doubt but that God can produce and preserve a thing prior naturally without a thing posterior.

Again, a thing posterior can not be a cause of a thing prior. Therefore, if a thing prior can not be without a thing posterior, this must not be posited, unless because a thing posterior is a natural effect naturally following a thing prior; but it is manifest that divine virtue sometimes has suspended the action of a created cause, and preserved a cause without an effect. For who, except God, prevented the fire of the glowing furnace from consuming the servants of God who were cast into the midst, and yet the flame of fire slew the Chaldean attendants. Countless other instances are found in Sacred Scripture and in the saying of the Holy Fathers and the acts of the Martyrs.

From all these it is evidently obvious that natural

THE SACRAMENT OF THE ALTAR 111

causes are prevented through the virtue of God from producing their own effects; therefore, no contradiction is involved in the statement that a thing prior naturally is produced and preserved without a posterior.

Again, an accident depends more upon its subject than any thing prior by nature upon a posterior. But so great is the divine power that notwithstanding the dependence of an accident upon its subject, the accident will be able to exist and to be preserved through divine power without any subject; therefore, notwithstanding by whatever natural sequence of a thing posterior from a prior, the thing prior could be preserved by divine virtue without a posterior.

Therefore, it must not be denied that by divine power God might be able to preserve and make any absolute thing prior naturally without a thing posterior. For so great is the divine power that concerning His creatures He could do whatever would please Him. Accordingly, if He make a cause of a natural object, He is not necessitated to make the effect.

CHAPTER XIII

That the omnipotence of God can make a substance without any absolute accident formally inhering in it

If the Creator of all, according to the good pleasure of His will, can make, preserve and maintain a thing prior without a posterior, there ought to be no doubt but that the same power may be able to produce and preserve any substance whatever without any absolute accident formally inhering in it. For if the virtue of God preserves and maintains an accident without a subject, will He not have so much power that He may preserve and maintain a substance without any accident? For since a substance may be more perfect and more actual, approaching also more nearly to divine subsistence than an accident may be, it may also depend less upon an accident than an accident upon a substance. But according to reason it may be characteristic of a substance for it to exist per se, but an accident naturally depends upon another. It also depends more upon a substance than conversely. No believer, who believes and holds that the accidents are in the sacrament of the altar without a subject, ought to doubt that a substance could by the same virtue subsist without an accident.

Again, no contradiction appears in the statement that an absolute thing may exist without all that which is neither a part of it nor an essential cause of it. But no accident is a cause nor a part of the substance in which it inheres; therefore, no contradiction is in-

THE SACRAMENT OF THE ALTAR 113

volved in the statement that a substance can subsist per se without an accident.

Again, it is necessary that everything, which is not God, if it really have being, be really produced by God; therefore, if a substance is produced, an accident could not be, unless God of his own free will had given being to it. But the divine power is subject to no creature; therefore, there is no contradiction in the statement that, if a substance is created, an accident may not acquire being, if it should be pleasing to God.

Again, if for the being of a substance the being of an accident may necessarily follow, this can not happen except by virtue of one of three reasons: either because an accident is part of a substance and a whole can not be without its parts; or because a substance is the effect of an accident and an effect presupposes its cause; or because a substance is the natural cause of an accident; and, if a cause is posited, the effect follows in order. But that an accident may not be part of a substance is as manifest to the Saints as to the philosophers. Since it may be known to all that a substance may be composed of substances and not of accidents; therefore, no accident could be a part of any substance.

Nor does it suffice to say, that a substance is an effect or a cause of an accident; since it was shown before that the omnipotent God, to whom all creatures yield perfect obedience, can suspend the action of a natural cause and preserve an effect without a secondary cause.

From the previous statements, it is especially gathered, that it will not be denied that the omnipotent God, to whom every word is not impossible, will be able to preserve a substance without an accident inhering in it; as it is not impossible for Him to preserve a thing prior without a posterior, which can be confirmed thus far by another reason. For the omnipotence of God has no less efficacy over all the individuals of some species than created virtue may have over a single individual of the same species.

Therefore, if created virtue can make this substance without this accident, if some individual of that species of accident was designated, could not the infinite power of God make this substance without any individual of any species of accident? And for the same reason, if imperfect created virtue has so much efficacy that it could preserve some substance without any individual of some species of accident, will not infinite virtue have so much efficacy that it may conserve the same substance without any individual of the whole genus of that accident?

Therefore, since the sun could preserve wood without any tangible quality, could not God preserve wood without any color? And if a natural cause; namely, fire, can preserve water without the cold, will not the immeasurableness of divine power have strength enough to preserve water without any tangible quality? From this it seems probable that since inferior causes, impotent except with the assistance of divine power, can preserve and produce a substance without this and that accident, it will not be impossible for God to maintain a substance without any accident. And if it should please God, He could bestow being upon any substance whatever without any accident; for God has made many things wonderful and contrary to the common course of nature.

CHAPTER XIV

That a substance, which is extended, can be preserved locally unmoved, although all of its absolute accidents may be destroyed through divine power

But it is not only not incompatible with the divine power to produce and preserve a thing prior without a posterior, and consequently it will be able to sustain a substance without an accident; but it is also not incompatible with the omnipotence of God to produce and preserve a substance existing under an absolute accident inhering in it without a local change of substance and to destroy that accident and to preserve the substance. For what believer may dare to say, if God wills to separate or destroy an absolute accident inhering in a subject without the destruction of the substance, that He is compelled to transfer the substance or some part of it from place to place?

For if natural causes expel many absolute accidents and introduce them into that space though not locally changed, could not God without the moving of the substance locally preserve it, and also destroy an absolute accident inhering in it; even, if He should be willing, without the introduction of any other?

Again, God can destroy a thing posterior and separate a thing prior from its nature, so that He may permit it to excite the proper motion. Therefore, God can destroy every accident of that wood and separate the substance of the wood from its nature, that He may excite the proper motion. When this has been done,

either this substance of the wood will be locally moved, and this is the intention; namely, that every absolute accident inhering in a substance can be destroyed without transference of the substance or any part of it from
5 place to place; or this substance will be moved locally, which can not be granted.

From which, this substance is separated from its own nature. At one time, because it could tranfer itself in respect to no difference of place; not down-
10 wards, since it may not have the principle of penetrating the earth, as neither when it had its own accidents; nor can it move itself upwards, as neither before; and by virtue of the same neither forwards nor backwards; nor will it be moved by some natural external agent,
15 as is obvious by induction. At another time, because, either the whole substance will change the whole place, which can not be granted, or because the parts of the substance, which were before separated, come together, as it were, into one point, which can not be granted;
20 since there may not be there such a principle of being moved. And, if there were, there could not be a stronger reason why they should meet at one point more than at another; nor could there be any reason why an intermediate part should be moved to one inter-
25 mediate point more than to another point near the end.

Again, if while preserving the whole substance of that wood, God should both destroy all the absolute accidents of one part and preserve the absolute accidents of the other part, which is not impossible with
30 God, as neither is it impossible for Him to destroy a half of the whiteness of one white body and preserve the other half of the whiteness; and at the same time while doing this separate the whole substance of wood

THE SACRAMENT OF THE ALTAR 117

from its nature, where would that half of that substance go? Could that part of the substance, all of whose accidents were destroyed by a proper virtue, enter into another part of a substance or separate itself totally from that part? It is not possible to concede that any such result might be able to be done by created power. Therefore, that part of the substance separated from its nature will remain locally unmoved; although God through His omnipotence may remove all absolute accidents inhering in it by destroying or even separating them. Therefore, God can preserve a substance locally unmoved and destroy every absolute accident inhering in it.

Again, every material substance is naturally in a place either circumscriptively or definitively, especially if there be a place surrounding it. Therefore, substance existing by natural accidents is in a place and is present in a place; and as it is prior naturally to the accidents themselves, so it is naturally present in the place itself before its accidents may be present in the same place. Therefore, no contradiction is involved in the statement that God may preserve a substance present in a place without local translation of any part of a substance without the presence of accidents at that place. It is, therefore, established that He, who spake and all things were made, can by the same virtue preserve a substance immovable locally and destroy or separate the absolute accidents inhering in it.

CHAPTER XV

That a material substance through its intrinsic parts is present in the place in which it is circumscribed

In connection with that which has been shown before concerning the distinction of substantial parts separate in situation and composing an extended material substance, it must now be shown that an extended material substance through itself and its parts, which are substances, is present in the place in which it is circumscribed, so that through itself as a whole it is in a whole place and through a part in a part of a place; for indeed everything, which is present in a place either through itself or through something else, to which it is present, is present in that place. Therefore, since a material substance may be present in a place circumscribing itself, it is necessary that it be present in that place either through itself or through something else, to which it is present; therefore, it is present in that place. For I do not now speak of that through which as if through an efficient cause something is present in a place; as a worm produced by the sun is present in a place through the sun as if through an efficient cause; for the sun, as is obvious, makes the worm to be, so it makes it to be present in a place; but I speak of that through which something not separate from a place is present in a place.

If it be conceded that material substance through itself and through its substantial parts is present in a place, that is accomplished which is intended. But if

THE SACRAMENT OF THE ALTAR 119

it be said that that material substance, which is extended, is present in a place through something else which is neither substance nor part of it, to which the substance itself is present, say, through some accident inhering in a substance which is present in a place and with which the substance itself is present; from this I deduce the thesis. For when any two things locally inseparable are present, whatever is present locally with one of them, through the same is present with the other of them. Therefore, if an accident of a substance and of a place be present locally, through that same through which the substance itself is present with the accident itself, through the same it will be present in the place itself. But a substance through itself and through its parts is present with that accident; therefore, it is present in its place through its same parts.

Again, the substance itself is present with that accident through that which is present in that which is its own place, so that the whole substance is present with that whole accident and part with part, as the whole substance is informed by the whole accident and part of the substance is informed by part of that accident; for otherwise either the substance or the accident would not be extended or be a quantum. Therefore, either the substance is in the manner already stated present with that accident or through some accident intermediate with which the substance itself is present, and which is present with that accident.

The second proposition can not be conceded; for concerning that intermediate with which the substance is present, I raise the question, as before, concerning the prior accident and the process will be endless, or it will be established that substance itself through itself is present with that accident. And so it is necessary to concede that such a substance, which is extended through itself, is present with that accident 'quantum,' so that the whole, locally inseparable, is present in a whole and a part in a part.

Since this is conceded, I proceed further thus: every substance (which through itself and through its parts intrinsic in it is present in some quantum having part outside of part so that the whole substance is present with that whole having part outside of part so that the whole substance is present with that, and its own part is present with a part of that whole, through itself formally and through parts intrinsic in it,) has part outside of part and part distant from part, and every such is through itself circumscribed in a place surrounding it. For nothing more is required for this, that something may be circumscribed in a place through itself, except that it may have being through itself formally, although it may have causally by another 'part separate from part and part distant from part'; therefore, a substance is circumscribed in a place by itself and by parts intrinsic to it.

From this it follows that a substance through itself and through parts intrinsic to itself is present in a place. That the accidents are present in a place would not be in opposition to these statements; for, when more are not separate locally, they themselves are present in the same place. Therefore, since a substance is not separate locally from its accidents, notwithstanding that the substance may be present in a place, the accidents themselves were able to be present in the same place.

CHAPTER XVI

In which certain arguments are advanced
to prove that the quantity remaining in
the sacrament of the altar is not really
distinct from the qualities remaining

In the former statements, certain immovable fundaments, as it were, have been examined and in consequence of those statements some reasons must be adduced by virtue of which it might appear to anyone that the quantity remaining in the sacrament of the altar is not an absolute thing really distinct from the qualities remaining with the substance of the body of Christ, and that before the consecration there preceded some quantity, which was not an absolute thing really distinct from the substance of the bread, which does not remain after the consecration by virtue of this, that the substance of the bread ceases to be.

However, I repeat through the testimony advanced in the beginning of this little work that, although I shall say nothing assertatively except that which the Roman Church teaches, I am prepared in all things to hold in check my inclination by virtue of the authority of the same church and also to believe with the heart and to confess with the lips the universal truths which the Roman Church expounds or will expound; but others to be cited only, under whatever form of words I shall have expressed them, I shall publicly set forth for the purpose of exercise and of supplying material for thought.

But before I shall approve the principal thesis, some

fundaments must be premised; namely, that every thing one per se, whether substantial or accidental, having part separate from part or part outside of part, is a quantum; for every such thing is really extended. But no thing can really be extended unless it be a quantum. Therefore, whether every quantum be per se one having part outside of part or part separate from part or not, makes no difference at all; yet this seems to be understood by all, that everything per se one having part outside of part or part separate from part is truly and really a quantum and is extended.

From which it further follows that, since it may be possible for something to be a quantum without a quantity, (and every quantum is either subjectively in a quantity as if in its subject or is a subject of a quantity or is a thing not distinct from quantity; for it can not be understood in several modes that something is a quantum,) it is necessary for that quantum, which is neither subjectively in a quantity nor is a subject of a quantity, to be a thing not really distinct from quantity.

From these statements it can be gathered that everything, which is circumscribed in a place, is a quantum; for everything, which is circumscriptively in a place, is a whole in a whole place and a part in a part; for this is to be circumscribed in a place. For by virtue of this, that an angel is not a whole in a whole place and part of an angel in a part of a place; by virtue of this an angel is not in a place circumscriptively. Therefore, that, which is in a place circumscriptively, is a whole in a whole and a part in a part. But every such has part separate from part, as parts of a place are separate in situation. But that which has part sep-

THE SACRAMENT OF THE ALTAR 123

arate from part is a quantum; therefore, everything per se one existing in a place circumscriptively is a quantum; and by virtue of the same it is obvious that every quantum having part separate from part is circumscriptively in a place; especially if there be some place surrounding it. For every such is in a place so that a whole is in a whole place and a part in a part, and consequently is circumscriptively in the place.

CHAPTER XVII

That any quantity is not an absolute thing really distinct from substance and that any quantity is not an absolute thing really distinct from quality

Since those propositions have been advanced, some conclusions must now be proved; one of which is, as it were, common and general; namely, that any quantity is not an absolute thing really distinct from substance, or that any quantity is not an absolute thing really distinct from quality. And that I may not appear to depend upon a proper sense and to deviate from the patristic definitions, as a fundament I make use of a passage of the most Holy Father, the illustrious Doctor, John of Damascus, who asserts that the same thing is of the genus 'substance' and of the genus 'quantity'; which can not be true if every quantity were a thing really distinct from substance. Whence, says the aforesaid doctor, the venerable Father, John of Damascus: "Therefore, we say," he says, "since it is possible for the same thing to be classified as number, according to one intention under one category and according to another intention under another category. Indeed, obvious facts, which were previously mentioned, are classified under 'quantum,' as however mutually having condition or mutually classed under those which are in relation to another; for great and small are named in relation to another. For great is called great in relation to small, and double in relation to half, and similarly the rest. But a body, according to that which is natural, is classified under 'substance,; but according to that which is mathematical, that is, measured, under 'quantum.' "

Notice how plainly that Saint asserts that the same thing is contained under diverse categories because of a distinction of intentions. He also asserts that the same thing, as body, may be of the genus 'substance' and of the genus 'quantity.' For the same body, because it is a certain natural thing composed of matter and form, is of the genus 'substance.' Moreover, the same thing, because it has part separate from part, by virtue of which it can be measured, is of the genus 'quantity'; which could not be true if every quantity were a thing really distinct from substance. And as the same thing, since it is a certain natural thing composed of matter and form, is of the genus 'substance'; and, since it has part outside of part, is of the genus 'quantity'; so the same whiteness, since it is a certain natural thing created to qualify a subject, is of the genus 'quality'; and, since the same whiteness is a certain thing having part outside of part and part separate from part by situation, it is of the genus 'quantity.'

And so it is established that in saying that any quantity is not a thing really distinct from substance and that any quantity is not a thing really distinct from quality, I do not deviate from the patristic definitions. Whence, I have never read that any Saint or the Prince of philosophers, Aristotle, has made a distinction between 'quantum' and 'quantity'; on the contrary, he indifferently uses 'quantum' and 'quantity' as the same. And I say this, that according to Aristotle it would be the same to say, 'quantum is substance' or 'quality and quantity is substance or quality.' And, indeed, that which is commonly said, that Aristotle says in the first book of the Posteriores, that this negative is immediate, 'no substance is quantity,' is false; for he does not even remotely make any mention there of substance or quantity or of other categories.

CHAPTER XVIII

That all the qualities in the sacrament of the altar are not one subject of one quantity

Since the former conclusion has been shown, as if uniform, some special conclusions must now be proved; one of which is, that all the qualities remaining in the sacrament of the altar are not one subject of one quantity by virtue of which all those qualities may be called quanta. Just as a man is called white because he is the subject of whiteness, or fire is called hot because it is the subject of heat; for no accident one numerically can be one per se in a primary as if in an immediate subject in something which is one only through aggregation, so that that whole accident may be in any one of them and may not be one part of an accident in one of them and another part in another; which I say in order to refute one sophistical cavil; for some say that sometimes it happens that, when some wood is placed in water so that one part may be in the air and the other in the air or outside of the water, the part existing in the water is converted into stone and the other part remains wood as before. When this has been accomplished, they say that any quantity existing in a whole is one numerically and yet the subject is not one per se, since one part may be stone and the other wood. And so any accident one numerically could be in one subject which is one only through aggregation. But this sophistical cavil, whether it contain the truth or not, is excluded through this which

128 THE SACRAMENT OF THE ALTAR

is accepted, that an accident one numerically can not be in something one through aggregation, so however that one part of that accident may not be in one of them and another in another. For in the instance advanced one part of that quantity is placed subjectively in one of those aggregations and another part in another. Therefore, it is obvious that an instance can not be found contrary to the proposition asserting that no accident one numerically can be in something one through aggregation only, and yet that one part may not be in one of them and another in another. But it is manifest that these qualities remaining in the sacrament of the altar, if they be one, are not one except through aggregation. And it is manifest that one part of that quantity is not subjectively in one of those qualities and another in another. Therefore, it follows that all those qualities are not the subject of a quantity one numerically by virtue of which they are called quanta.

Again, no accident one numerically can be successively in diverse primary subjects through the action of a natural cause. But I consider a primary subject not that which is a subject of some accident through a part, as a man is called the subject of whiteness, because a hand or foot is the subject of whiteness. But I consider that a primary subject which is the subject of some accident, and no part of it is the primary and adequate subject of it. And if a primary subject is thus accepted, it is manifest that no accident one numerically can be naturally in diverse primary subjects.

If this is conceded, one part of those qualities may be removed, as it is obvious to sense that it can be done. Then I ask whether or not the same quantity

THE SACRAMENT OF THE ALTAR 129

remains, which was before. If so, then it follows that a quantity the same numerically is at first subjectively in this whole aggregation of prior qualities and afterwards is not in that, since it does not remain, and yet is in something; therefore, it is in another, and consequently is in several successively.

If a quantity the same numerically does not remain; therefore, when whiteness has been destroyed, any one of the other qualities might change its quantity, which seems absurd.

Furthermore, if this quantity is one in that aggregation, either it is a whole in a whole and a whole part in any part of them or a whole in a whole and one part in one of them and another part in another of them. The first can not be conceded; for then an accident the same numerically would be at the same time in several subjects, which is false. Nor can the second be conceded; for no part of that quantity can be accepted which may have more regard for one quality than for another, since those qualities may in no mode be separate locally.

From the previous statements it is gathered that, since an accident may be counted according to the enumeration of subjects, the qualities can not be distinct unless the quantities were distinct, if any one of them be the subject of a quantity.

CHAPTER XIX

That not any quality may be the immediate subject of a quantity

Moreover, it is not only impossible that those qualities may be one subject of one quantity; but it is also impossible to say that any quality is the subject of some quantity, so that a distinct quality is the subject of a
5 distinct quantity; for such a plurality of quantities distinct from qualities is altogether superfluous and is granted without necessity.

Again, for the same reason before transubstantiation the substance of the bread was a distinct subject
10 of a quantity distinct from all those quantities whose subjects after transubstantiation are qualities, which is incompatible; for it would then follow that a substance would be a quantum with distinct quantities; for there would be a quantum with one quantity of
15 which there would be an immediate subject and there would be a quantum with other quantities, of which there would be a mediate subject, because with those mediating qualities of which there is a subject.

Again, all, whom I have seen who posit that quan-
20 tity would be a thing other than substance and quality, hold to the incongruity that two dimensions may be at the same time. But if a substance be the subject of one quantity and a quality be the subject of another quantity, it is necessary to posit that not only
25 two dimensions may be at the same time, but even that more than two may be at the same time; from which

THE SACRAMENT OF THE ALTAR 131

it follows that those, who talk in this fashion, do not speak consistently.

Therefore, although according to some it is not inconsistent to posit that distinct quanta are at the same time, which are of a different ground or of the same ground, making however one; nevertheless it seems impossible naturally or through created power that diverse quantities of the same species, most especially those not making a quantity one numerically, are at the same time.

But if each quality could be the subject of a distinct quantity, those quantities could not make a quantity one numerically nor could they be distinguished in species; therefore, they can not be at the same time in the same place; and so it is manifest that each quality is not the subject of a distinct quantity.

CHAPTER XX

That the quantity remaining is not subjectively in one quality and not in another

Moreover, that one quantity only, which may be subjectively in only one quality and not in another, may not remain so that the remaining qualities may not be subjects of that quantity, follows from this; that, if only one quality could be the subject of that quantity, the remaining qualities could not be quantities and could not be subjectively in a quantity, nor could a quantity be subjectively in them. But it was stated before that that, which is neither a thing really distinct from a quantity nor is subjectively in a quantity nor is the subject of a quantity, is not a quantum; and so the remaining qualities distinct from that quality, which might be the subject of that quantity, could not be quanta, which is well known to be false.

Besides, since it may be manifest that all the qualities remaining in the sacrament of the altar are broken and divided and, when the host is divided, all similar qualities remain with each part of the host, it can not be said that one quality is the immediate subject of a quantity, but each other quality is the mediate subject of a quantity; and, therefore, each is a quantum, because in qualities there is subjectively a quantity mediately or immediately.

This, I say, can not hold; since, if only one quality could be the subject of a quantity, one would be mediate and another immediate. This would not be able to be true, unless because a quality, which is the im-

THE SACRAMENT OF THE ALTAR 133

mediate subject of a quantity, could be subjectively in that quality which is the mediate subject of a quantity. But this is clearly found to be false, for one corporeal quality is not a subject of another corporeal quality; for color is not a subject of taste, nor contrariwise. Nor is heat the subject of odor or color; for then heat would truly and really be white or black, which is absurd. From this, therefore, it follows, among other statements, that no concrete of any quality is predicated of an abstract of another. For it is manifest that one quality is not the subject of another quality.

This conclusion also obtains by another reason; for the destruction of an accident follows either mediately or immediately upon the destruction of a subject. If, therefore, one quality could be the subject of another quality, it would be necessary that, when a quality is destroyed, which is immediately in the substance as in a subject, all other qualities would be destroyed. And so, if a tangible quality could be an immediate subject of another sensible by another sense and that of another, and so by continuing in logical order, it would be necessary that, when the color of any body changed, the other qualities would be removed.

Therefore, from all the previous statements, it can evidently be understood that a quantity is not any accident existing subjectively in a quality, as in a subject.

CHAPTER XXI

In which it is proved by the testimony of the Catholic doctors that qualities are not subjectively in a quantity other than a substance

After the previous statements it remains to show that the qualities remaining in the sacrament of the altar after consecration are not subjectively in a quantity, as if in a subject sustaining them. And, indeed, this conclusion is to be confirmed by the testimony of the venerable Doctors. Whence, the illustrious Doctor, the Master of the Sentences, says in Book IV., Distinction XII., in the beginning of the Chapter, 'Damnamus.' Whose doctrine a general council, in the margin of the De Summa Trinitate et Fide Catholica, 'Damnamus,' also approved. "If a question is raised," he says, "concerning the accidents which remain; namely, concerning the species, taste and heaviness, in what subject they may be found; it seems clear to me that they exist without a subject rather than that they are in a subject."

From which it is obvious that it is in accordance with the intention of that Doctor, that such qualities, taste, heaviness, and similar qualities, remaining in the sacrament of the altar, are not subjectively in something and consequently are not in a quantity as if in a subject; because then they would not be without a subject but in a subject. Nor is it sufficient to say that he does not intend that those qualities are outside of the whole subject; but that they may not be in some

THE SACRAMENT OF THE ALTAR 135

substance as if in a subject; whence, assigning a reason why those qualities are without a fundament, he adds, that there is no substance there, except that of the body and blood of the Lord, which is not affected by those accidents.

This response, I say, does not suffice because it never follows, that any accident is without a subject as long as it subsists in its primary and immediate subject. But if the qualities remaining after consecration could be in a quantity as in a subject, a quantity would be the immediate subject of them and consequently, as long as they would subsist in a quantity, they would not be without a subject.

Again, any accident can never be said to be existing per se, so long as it subsists in its immediate subject. But according to the same Doctor the qualities remaining in the sacrament of the altar are subsisting per se; for when he speaks of the qualities of which he spoke before, that they are without a subject, he says: "Those accidents, by which the body of Christ having its form and nature is concealed, remain subsisting per se at the celebration of the mystery, for the tasting and assent of faith." Therefore, it is apparent that it is in accordance with the intention of that Doctor that taste and weight and the like, the qualities remaining in the sacrament of the altar, are subsisting per se and without any subject. From which it follows that they do not exist in a quantity, as in a subject.

Whence, the aforesaid Doctor adds in the same place: "Do not be surprised or scoff," he says, "if the accidents there may appear to be broken, since they may be there without a subject." From this it is more wonderful that the accidents exist without a subject than that they may be broken.

Again, there is no stronger reason that one quality may be in a quantity as in a subject, than for another quality; but any quality remaining in the sacrament of the altar is not in a quantity but in a subject. Therefore, there is nothing there in a quantity, as if in a subject. But it is obvious that some quality may remain after the consecration which may not be in a quantity as if in a subject. For heaviness is a quality; for according to it something is called 'quale'; and yet the heaviness remaining in the sacrament of the altar is not in a quantity as in a subject; for, if heaviness were in something as in a subject, that subject would truly and really be heavy, as the whole subject, in which there is whiteness, is white; and the whole subject, in which there is heat, is warm. But nothing remaining in the sacrament of the altar after consecration is heavy by that heaviness which remains in the same sacrament; which a certain gloss on the De Consecratione, Distinction II., above that chapter, 'Si per negligentiam,' clearly asserts. Whence, objecting to this that he said that accidents fall to the earth, he says thus: "But it is likewise objected, since the accidents alone remain there, and accidents do not have weight, for body alone has weight; how, therefore, are accidents said to fall, since they may not have weight." And solving this objection he says: "Say that heaviness still remains with other accidents and yet nothing heavy is there." From this gloss it is obvious in part that, although heaviness may remain with the other accidents after consecration, yet it is not in some subject which may be able to be called

THE SACRAMENT OF THE ALTAR 137

heavy from that heaviness. And for the same reason there is not something white there, but whiteness only is there, and there is nothing white there as heaviness is there, and nothing is heavy there.

And in the same manner, although taste may be there, yet there is not there a subject sustaining taste deriving its name from taste. From which it plainly follows that quantity is not a subject informed by those qualities nor deriving its name from them. For if it were under those qualities, it would truly be heavy, warm or cold, white, sweet or bitter, which is plainly contrary to the aforesaid gloss.

Another point can also be drawn from the preceding gloss; namely, that in the sacrament of the altar there is not some body having weight. From this it follows that there is not there a quantity having weight, since every permanent and continuous quantity may be a line or a surface or a body. Therefore, if a quantity having weight were there, then it would be necessary that there should be there either a line having weight, or a surface having weight, or a body having weight. But it cannot be said that a line or a surface has weight, and not a body; for the previously mentioned gloss says that body alone has weight. From this it follows that, if there were there some quantity having weight, there would be there a body having weight, which is denied; therefore, there is there no quantity having weight. From this it is, furthermore, proper to infer that no quantity there is the subject of that heaviness, and by virtue of that it is necessary to say that no quantity there is the subject of those qualities; but all those qualities there are subsisting per se by divine virtue.

138 THE SACRAMENT OF THE ALTAR

Again, the Holy Mother Church when celebrating the sacrament of the body of Christ reads thus: "The accidents exist without a subject in the same that faith may have a place, while the invisible concealed by another species is visibly received, and the senses, which judge of accidents known to them, are rendered immune from deception."

From the preceding authorities and very many others it clearly obtains that not only one accident may exist without a subject in the sacrament of the altar, but that accidents exist without a subject, say, all the qualities of which the senses judge; which would be true if all the qualities were in a quantity as in a subject.

Whence, since this may be the opinion of many revered Doctors; namely, the Master of the Sentences, Hostiensis, Gaufridus, and of many other glossators upon the decrees and decretals, it seems consistent with the Catholic faith to say that all the qualities remaining in the sacrament of the altar after consecration may not be in something, neither in a quantity nor in anything as in a subject. And it appears that this may be the opinion of the Doctors; for Hostiensis at the top of the title of the De Celebratione Missarum, and Gaufridus in the same title, and the gloss in the margin of the De Celebratione Missarum, 'Cum Marthæ,' and the gloss on the De Consecratione, Distinction II., Chapter, 'In sacramentorum', and the Master of the Sentences in Book IX., Distinction XI., cite three opinions concerning the conversion of the bread into the body of Christ. "One," as they say, "asserts that that substance, which was bread at first, is afterwards the flesh and the blood of Christ. The second opinion holds that the substance of the bread and of

THE SACRAMENT OF THE ALTAR 139

the wine may cease to be there and the accidents only remain; namely, taste, color, weight, and similar accidents; and by those accidents the body of Christ begins to be there. The third opinion holds that the substance of the bread and of the wine remains there and that the body of Christ is in the same place and under the same species." The second opinion is approved by all the previous authorities.

From all these it is obvious that the ancient and authorized Doctors have posited that only the qualities remain per se without a subject; and, indeed, they have not posited that qualities were subjectively in something.

These, and many, who posit that the qualities remaining in the sacrament of the altar are in a quantity as if in a subject, adduce many passages of the authorized Doctors to prove that accidents; namely, qualities, are without a subject; but they can not, indeed, adduce one passage of any authorized Doctor to prove that the qualities in the sacrament of the altar are in a quantity as in a subject.

Whence, although I have diligently read the entire tract of the Master of the Sentences concerning the Eucharist and the entire tract, which is found in the canonical law concerning the same matter, along with the glosses, and other Doctors, as Hostiensis, Innocent and others, yet I have not found that they mention quantity even by denying it, except in three places; namely, once in the De Consecratione, Distinction II., 'Quia corpus'; where, when speaking to the man receiving the body of Christ, he says thus: "Continuing in thy visible stature thou hast invisibly become greater than thyself without increase of quantity, although you yourself would also be the same."

Again, the gloss over that chapter of the De Consecratione, Distinction II., 'Dupliciter': "It can be understood, either, according to that form and quantity which he had on the cross or according to the quantity of the glorified body which seems spiritual; for it is subject to no sense."

Again, before, in Chapter 'Ubi,' Hilary says: "A visible quantity is not to be considered in this mystery; but the spiritual virtue of the sacrament"; where the gloss says: "The quantity must not be so estimated that the body of Christ may be less under a smaller quantity and greater in a larger quantity; for, wherever there is a part whether of species or of body, that is, the foot or the hand, the whole body is."

I do not remember that I have read in very many places that the Saints or the authorized Doctors, who discussed the sacrament of the Eucharist, touch upon any thing about quantity.

But it is mainfest that from the preceding places that it can neither directly nor indirectly be gathered that qualities may be in a quantity as if in a subject. But they expressly say of qualities that they remain and that they themselves are broken and are used up.

Whence, the gloss above that Chapter of the De Consecratione, Distinction II., 'Ego Berengarius,' says: "I not only confess that weight and the other qualities of the sacrament are perceived by the bodily senses; but I confess that under those broken species and very much wasted parts the whole and unbroken body of Christ is, that the whole is eaten, and that the whole is consumed." Notice that he calls the species, qualities, which species, he says, are broken and worn. Therefore, needlessly would there be posited any quantity, which would be the subject of them.

CHAPTER XXII

That a quantity really distinct from a substance may not be a subject of qualities in the sacrament of the altar, is also confirmed through the statements of the philosophers

That a quantity really distinct from a substance may not be a subject of qualities could be confirmed not only by the testimony of the Holy Fathers but also of the philosophers. Therefore, let it suffice to adduce Aristotle, the Prince of philosophers. However, he says in the Categories that substance alone is susceptive of contraries through a change of itself; and he says that this is properly characteristic of substance. But if there could be between substance and qualities one intermediate quantity differing and sustaining sensual and corporeal qualities, it is manifest that that quantity would be susceptive of contraries through a proper change of itself. For that would at one time be sweet, at another time would be bitter, when it would support whiteness, when it would support blackness, when it would be warm, and when it would be cold; and so a thing other than a substance would be susceptive of contraries through a change of itself.

Again, according to the same philosopher alteration as regards a sensible quality is distinguished from condensation and rarefaction to such a degree that, when any body is rarefied or condensed, it is not necessary that it lose all its qualities. Therefore, a white body may become rarefied; and, when this has been done, it can not be granted that it may lose the prior whiteness and may have a new whiteness; for there is here nothing efficient enough that would be able to induce whiteness into this body. But this can not obtain if quantity be a thing intermediate between substance and qualities; for, if it be an intermediate thing, it is necessary that a rarefied substance have a new quantity, as will be said and shown later. But since the newness of its accident may follow in consequence of the newness of the subject, it is necessary that whiteness should be new and for the same reason each quality existing subjectively in that quantity would be new.

CHAPTER XXIII

That the quantity remaining in the sacrament of the altar is not an absolute thing really distinct from the qualities remaining in the same sacrament

From the preceding statements, it evidently follows that the quantity remaining in the sacrament of the altar is not an absolute thing really distinct from the qualities remaining in the same sacrament. For nothing is a quantum unless it be a subject of a quantity, either existing in a quantity as in a subject or a thing not really distinct from a quantity. And it has been shown that the quality remaining is not a subject of a quantity and is not subjectively in a quantity. And it is manifest that the qualities after consecration are quanta, since they may be long, wide and thick. Therefore it remains that those qualities may be quanta, and not through quantity which may be an absolute thing really distinct from those qualities.

Again, everything having part separate from part is a quantum. But it is evident that the heaviness remaining in the sacrament of the altar has part separate from part; and it was shown before that that heaviness is not subjectively in a quantity nor is it the subject of a quantity; therefore, it is a quantum and not through a quantity, which is an absolute thing other than that heaviness. And for the same reason any other quality will be a quantum and not through a quantity really distinct from it.

CHAPTER XXIV

That before consecration there was one quantity, which was not an absolute thing really distinct from the substance of the bread

Since it has been seen that the quantity remaining in the sacrament of the altar is not an absolute thing really distinct from the qualities remaining in the same place, it now remains to adduce some convincing arguments by virtue of which anyone might be able to see that before consecration there preceded one quantity which was not an absolute thing really distinct from the substance of the bread, which does not remain after consecration, as the substance of the bread does not remain.

And this could, indeed, be regarded as settled from the statements in the first and the last Chapters. For if a quality could be a quantum without a quantity really distinct, this could not be except by virtue of this, that a quality has parts really distinct and created to be separate in situation. But the distinction of parts of a material substance is as great as is the distinction of parts of a quality; so also the parts of a substance are created to be separate in situation, as the parts of a quality. On the contrary, by nature and by created virtue, as the parts of a quality can not be without a substance, so they can not be separate without separation of substantial parts. If, therefore, qualities be quanta without a quantity really distinct from qualities, it is necessary to say that a substance alone could

THE SACRAMENT OF THE ALTAR 145

be a quantum without an added quantity really distinct, and that that substance of the bread was a quantum not through a quantity, which was a thing other than a substance and consequently was the same. And, indeed, as the substance of the bread does not remain, so that quantity does not remain. Again, the substance of the bread was not a quantum from a quantity, which was really the same as a quality, and any quantity really distinct from a quality does not remain after consecration, as was proved.

Therefore, it is necessary to say that some accident is corrupted when the body of Christ is consecrated, which seems to refute the statements of the Holy Fathers, or it is necessary to say that the substance of the bread was a quantum from a quantity, which is not a thing really distinct from the substance of the bread and consequently does not remain, as the substance of the bread does not remain.

CHAPTER XXV

That a substance can be a quantum without any absolute thing really distinct added to it

However, that the principal thesis may appear more obvious, I desire now to prove, besides those former statements, that a substance can be a quantum without any absolute thing really distinct added to it. For it was shown before that the divine power can make and preserve a whole substance without a whole absolute accident inhering in it. It was also proved that, if it should have pleased the divine will, it is possible to preserve in the future any substance now extended and present under its accidents and to separate or destroy or annihilate all the accidents; and the divine power is not compelled by virtue of this to transfer a substance from place to place or to change it locally.

From which I deduce such a proposition: that the divine power can preserve however freely or contingently, this substance, which is now a quantum, unmoved locally as regards itself as a whole and each substantial part of it, and it may destroy a whole quantity really distinct from this substance and inhering in the substance. On the contrary also, and without reason, it seems to curtail the divine power to say that, if God wills to preserve in being a substance prior naturally with every accident inhering in it and to destroy an absolute accident inhering in it, it is necessary for God necessarily to change the substance locally and to transfer it from one place to another.

THE SACRAMENT OF THE ALTAR 147

Since we may also frequently see that a natural agent destroys any accident of the same subject without the destruction and local change of a subject; it must not, therefore, be said that it may be impossible for the divine power, to which all things are completely subjected, to destroy a whole quantity which is an absolute accident inhering in this wood, without the destruction of that wood and without local change of the same. When this has been done, it is necessary to say that this substance is a quantum, since it may have part outside of part, as before; for unless the parts of that substance could be separate, as before, there could not be a whole substance in a whole place and part in part, as before, before the destruction of the accident; and consequently this substance would be moved locally, which is contrary to the thesis.

This substance is, therefore, a quantum and it is posited that no accident, which is an absolute accident, inheres in it; for according to the thesis every such is destroyed through the divine power; therefore, this substance is a quantum without a quantity, which may be an absolute accident inhering in it.

However, if that event is posited, it can not as yet be concluded that this substance may remain a quantum; for it is manifest from this statement, this whole substance is preserved in being through divine power, that no part of it is corrupted or destroyed; therefore, the same substantial parts remain which were before.

I ask concerning those parts; whether they are separate locally in situation; (if this is conceded, the thesis is maintained, since it may have been proved before that every thing per se one having parts separate in place and situation is a quantum;) or

whether these parts are not separate in place and situation, which can not be granted; for it would follow from this that they would be changed locally. For if they are not now separate locally and were formerly
separate locally and one is not converted into another, since both may truly remain, it is necessary that one of them be changed locally.

Again, I take one part of that substance, say, A, and I ask, whether A coexists with that part of the place with which it previously coexisted, or does not coexist with that part of the place. If A does coexist with that part of the place; for the same reason another part of that substance coexists with another part of the place with which it coexisted before. From which it follows that the whole substance coexists with the whole place and part with a whole part; and consequently, this whole substance has parts separate from parts in situation; as parts of a place, with which they coexist, are separate in situation. But if A does not exist with that part of a place with which it coexisted before; therefore, that part is changed locally; for everything, which is present in a thing at first and remaining afterwards is not present in that place, is necessarily transferred from place to place; since it may not be outside a place and so a part would change the place, which is contrary to the thesis.

Nor is it sufficient to say that this substance is not in a place unless through a quantity which is an accident of that substance; and, indeed, when a quantity is destroyed, that substance is neither in a place nor is it changed locally; for that is not stated catholicly. For according to the Holy Fathers and the authorized Doctors, and it is satisfactory according to the inten-

THE SACRAMENT OF THE ALTAR 149

tion of the canonical scriptures, an angel is in a place and is transferred from one place to another, in as much as it may not be a quantum but indivisible lacking all the parts created to be separate locally.

Therefore, it would be much more suitable for a substance having parts created to be separate locally to be in a place and to be changed locally, although it may not have a quantity which may be an absolute accident really distinct from it and inhering in it. On the contrary, no matter how much a substance may be separate from every accident, thus far it will be in a place unless it were placed outside of the world. And not only the whole substance will be in a place, but indeed each part of it will be in a place. And then I ask about this part A; whether it is in the place in which it was before, and is held intent, or is in another place and consequently is changed locally, which is contrary to the thesis.

Nor is it sufficient to say that this substance is not in a place circumscriptively but definitively; for to say this is to concede the thesis. For if the prior case is posited; from this very statement that this substance is in a place definitively, it will be in a place circumscriptively. The reason for this is; because if that substance is in some place definitively; from this it follows that A, which is part of that substance, may be in a place definitively. Then I ask, whether or not A is in that part of a place definitively. If it be granted that it is, for the same reason another part will be in another part definitively; from which it follows that these parts are separate locally and in situation. But every whole having parts separate locally is in a place circumscriptively. Therefore, this whole substance is thus in a place circumscriptively. But if it be granted that A is not definitively in a place or in that part of a place in which it was before, either this is because it is elsewhere definitively and consequently is changed locally, or because it is not anywhere, which can not be conceded, since even an angel must be placed somewhere; however, if this is granted, it follows that it is changed locally, from which it is not definitively nor circumscriptively in the place in which it was before; and yet in the nature of things it reàlly remains.

So, therefore, since the divine power may be able to preserve a substance in the same place and destroy every accident inhering in it, which is an absolute accident, there is no contradiction involved in the statement that a substance may be a quantum without a quantity, though an accident inhere in it.

CHAPTER XXVI

In which other reasons are adduced to prove the same conclusion, which was stated before; namely, that a substance can be a quantum without a distinct quantity added to it

Besides the former reason, it can be concluded from other reasons, that substance can be a quantum without a distinct quantity added to it; for it requires no less virtue to preserve two substances created to make and constitute one substance without all the absolute accidents inhering in it, when they do not make or constitute one whole substance, than when they constitute one whole substance; as when two bodies of water are taken, say, A and B, it requires no less virtue to preserve A and B in distinct places without all the absolute accidents inhering in them, when they do not make one total body of water than when they make parts of one water. But the omnipotence of God can separate A and B from all their accidents and preserve A and B in distinct places; as A here, and B at Rome, if it pleases Him. For, if the omnipotence of God could separate the one water at Rome from its every accident, and another here existing from its every accident, it is not necessary that God should transfer that water, which is at Rome, even here, or this water even to Rome; nor would it be necessary that He should transfer them to some intermediate place; but He might be able to preserve that there and this here. Therefore, with equal facility, if it should please Him, if A and B should be joined together and constitute one water, the omnipotence of God might be able to preserve A and B in distinct parts of a place, although He could separate A and B from all their absolute accidents. If this is posited, that total substance would have parts separate in situation, and A and B would be their own parts which were separate in situation; and consequently that total substance would be a quantum and yet without a quantity really distinct from the substance itself.

The argument is confirmed; for there appears to be no contradiction to the statement that God might be able through His infinite power to preserve that substance and destroy the accidents, as He voluntarily and freely created the whole water of the ocean under its accidents. But, if this is posited, God would never be necessitated to transfer the part of the ocean, which is in the West, even to the other part, which is in the East, or the opposite; or to transfer both parts to some intermediate place. For it does not appear to be in accord with theological statement that God would be necessitated to this; therefore, God might be able in the nature of things to preserve the whole water of the ocean and destroy every absolute accident inhering in it and yet preserve other waters, which are in the East and the West, where they were before. If this is done, that whole water would have parts separate without water added to it, and consequently would be a quantum without a quantity added.

Again, when subject and accident have parts corresponding to themselves so that the distinct parts of the substance correspond to the distinct parts of the accident, it requires no less power to preserve the parts

THE SACRAMENT OF THE ALTAR 153

of an accident by destroying the subject without local change of the accident or some part of it, than to preserve the parts of the substance without local change by destroying an absolute accident. But a material substance and an accident are at the same time, so that the distinct parts of an accident correspond to the distinct parts of a substance. For one part of an accident is in another part of a substance; so that distinct parts of an accident are in distinct parts of a substance, as is obvious through this which was proved before; namely, that material substance has substantial parts separate in situation.

For God can preserve an absolute accident in the same place and situation by destroying the substance, as is obvious in the sacrament of the altar; therefore, there is no contradiction involved in the statement that God preserves a substance in the same place by destroying whatever absolute accident inheres in it. If this is done, that substance will be circumscriptively in a place, as before, and consequently will be a quantum without a quantity added to it.

Nor is it necessary maliciously to misrepresent by saying that it is contrary to the faith to say that the substance of the bread is corrupted in the sacrament of the altar; for this is not my statement but it is the statement of the Catholic doctors. Whence, the gloss says on the De Consecratione, Distinction II., 'Quia corpus.' The gloss above the word 'convertuntur' says: "It well states: they are converted or transubstantiated, or pass over" (supply: earthly and mortal things into the substance of Christ); "but they do not become or begin to be; for nothing becomes or begins to be the body of Christ; yet it can be conceded that

154 THE SACRAMENT OF THE ALTAR

the body of Christ becomes and is formed from the bread, as a crystal becomes from water, yet it is not a crystal. But it is safer not to concede this; and wherever the bread is found, the body of Christ either becomes or is produced from the bread. It is thus understood: it becomes, that is, it passes over into the body of Christ, as later this, 'Panis': the body of Christ either becomes from the bread, that is, it is under the species of bread, or it lies concealed or begins to be or to lie concealed, where it was not before consecration; for if the bread should become the body of Christ, there would be added to it on each single day something which was not before, and thus it would be constantly augmented." And the gloss adds: "Do not understand, therefore, that any augmentation may be assumed from such conversion, nor in the same mode in which food is converted into flesh; but there is corruption there, that is, the substance of the bread and of the wine ceases to be there, yet there is no generation."

Again, the gloss on the De Consecratione, Distinction II., 'Ante benedictionem': "Although the words may be uttered successively, yet the consecration does not become successively; but the bread is corrupted in one instant; namely, in the last instant of the utterance of the words; and, although the bread becomes the body of Christ, yet the corruption of it is instantaneous."

Again, the gloss in the same distinction of the Chapter, 'Panis est,' says that "the substance of the bread ceases to be in the subvening consecration," et cetera, in the same place. Therefore, it is not contrary to the Catholic faith to say that the substance of the bread

THE SACRAMENT OF THE ALTAR 155

is corrupted or destroyed in the sacrament of the altar. Therefore, since God may preserve an accident in the same place by destroying a substance, it is not impossible for Him to preserve a substance in the same place by corrupting an accident, and thus a substance will be a quantum without such an accident.

Again, if God could destroy a half of any absolute accident informing one half of that wood and could preserve the other half of the accident informing the other half of that substance, these two parts of the substance would be separate and yet one of these would be lacking every accident informing it. From this it follows that a part of a substance can be separate from a part of a substance without an accident informing it, and consequently a substance could be a quantum without a quantity added to it.

Again, it involves no greater contradiction (to say) that a substance having parts really distinct created to be separate locally may be without a whole accident added to it in a whole divisible place, so that the whole may be in a whole place and a part in a part, than that some substance lacking every such part may be in some divisible place so that a whole may be in a whole place and a whole in each part. But an angel, lacking every integral part without every absolute accident added to it, can be a whole in any divisible place and a whole in each part; therefore, it is not a contradiction that some substance having parts created to be separate locally may be a whole in a whole divisible place and a part in a part without some quantity added to it. From this it follows that it will be circumscriptively in a place without a quantity added to it. This reason is confirmed.

It involves no more of a contradiction that a corporeal substance is in a place in a mode consistent with itself without any thing added to it than that an incorporeal substance is in a place in a mode consistent with itself without an entire thing added. But the proper mode of being in a place consistent with a corporeal substance is to be in a place circumscriptively, as the proper mode of being in a place consistent with an incorporeal substance is to be in a place definitively; but an incorporeal substance can be in a place definitively without any absolute thing added to it. Therefore, it involves no contradiction that a corporeal substance is in a place circumscriptively without an entire absolute thing added to it; and so there is a quantum without an entire absolute thing added to it. Therefore, as it appears, it involves no contradiction that any substance may be a quantum without every absolute accident added to it.

CHAPTER XXVII

That the same conclusion, which was stated before, seems to follow from the statements of adversaries

Aside from the former reasons, some can be adduced based partly on the statements of other Catholic doctors who, however, deny the previous conclusion. For it appears that that proposition follows from the statements of some adversaries, 'every absolute thing existing under any absolute accident through information so that a whole subject may be under a whole accident and a part under a part,' can through divine power coexist with the same without information and this inherence, as is obvious. For according to many who say that substance can not be a quantum without an accident inhering in it, the extrinsic respect advening to it can be taken from the extremes remaining. And according to the same the respect of inherence of an accident to a subject is an extrinsic advening respect; therefore, it does not involve a contradiction that a substance and that thing, which they call quantity, remain without respect of such inherence. But if this is posited, the whole substance coexists with that whole quantity which is an accident; therefore, as this quantity has part separate from part so that substance will have part separate from part, and so that substance is a quantum without a quantity informing it. Nor can they say that, when a respect of inherence of a quantity to a substance is removed, the substance will not be present in the quantity so that the whole may

158 THE SACRAMENT OF THE ALTAR

be present in the whole quantity and a part in a part.

They can not, I say, thus evade the issue. For according to the same the respect of presentiality of a substance to a quantity is prior to the respect of inherence of a quantity to a substance, and similarly the respect of presentiality of part of a substance to part of a quantity is prior to a respect of inherence of part of a quantity to a part of a substance. This can be proved through this, that it is impossible that there may be a respect of inherence of a quantity to a substance without the respect of presentiality of a quantity to a substance, and consequently without the respect of presentiality of a substance to a quantity; for these mutual presentialities are by nature at the same time according to their principles. But the respect of presentiality can be without the respect of inherence; for a substance is present or can be in many which do not inform it nor inhere in it. But according to these writers a prior can be through divine power without a posterior; therefore, it involves no contradiction that there may be preserved a respect of presentiality of a whole substance to that whole quantity which is considered an accident inhering in it, and a respect of presentiality of a part of a substance to that part of a quantity without a respect of inherence of a quantity to a substance and without a respect of inherence of a part of a quantity to a part of a substance.

If this is posited, a whole substance is present in a whole quantity and a part of a substance is present in a part of a quantity without a respect of inherence; and consequently without this, that a substance may be informed by a quantity. And so this substance will

THE SACRAMENT OF THE ALTAR 159

have a part distinct from a part without a quantity informing it, and consequently there will be a quantum without a quantity informing it; for no thing per se one has part outside of part and part separate from part unless it be a quantum.

Again, the respect of presentiality of a substance in relation to 'ubi,' according to those writers, does not depend upon the respect of inherence of a quantity to its subject; for, if the respect of inherence of a quantity to this substance is destroyed, still this substance could be present in a place, and for the same reason the respect of presentiality of a part of a substance to a part of a place does not depend on the respect of inherence of a part of a quantity to a part of a substance. And yet according to those writers, everything, which does not depend upon another, can be preserved through divine power without it.

Therefore, the respect of presentiality of a whole substance to a whole place and of a part of a substance to a part of the place could be preserved without the respect of inherence of a quantity to a substance. When this is done, a substance will be present in the whole place and part in a part; and consequently will be circumscriptively in a place, and yet will not be informed by some quantity which may be an absolute thing really distinct from a substance; and so a substance will be a quantum without such a quantity.

CHAPTER XXVIII

That a substance may be a quantum through its substantial parts without every quantity which is called a thing really distinct from substance and quality

After this it remains to show that not only a substance can be a quantum without a quantity added to it, but also that a substance is a quantum through its substantial parts without every quantity which may be another absolute thing really distinct from a substance and a quality.

In the first place it is settled thus: that, which can be accomplished through fewer, is needlessly accomplished through more; for this is a principle which ought not to be denied, that no plurality ought to be posited, unless it can be demonstrated through reason or through experience or through the authority of that one who can not be deceived or err. But from this a substance can be a quantum and similarly a quality can be a quantum without such a quantity distinct from a substance and a quality. It can be demonstrated neither through reason nor through experience, that there may be another such quantity. Neither is this found expressed by any author who can not err; for it is not found to have been revealed by God. Therefore, it is not necessary to posit such a quantity; and so it would be posited needlessly; for all, which can be saved through such a thing, can be saved without it through this, that a substance has substantial parts really distinct created to be separate locally, which

THE SACRAMENT OF THE ALTAR 161

parts of the substance as well as of the qualities, as they are brought into being, so they become separate by virtue of an efficient and a final cause. For by the same virtue by which different parts of a substance and of qualities proceed from non-being to being, they also take on being in distinct places. And, indeed, as nothing is necessarily required aside from an efficient, formal, final, and material cause; nor is it previously demanded for this, that a substance and parts of a substance may be brought from non-being to being; so nothing aside from the previous causes is necessarily acquired for this, that one part of a substance be outside of another part or separate from another part. For it appears wonderful that one accident later than a substance and the parts of it might be able to make one part of a substance to be outside another part, and yet the essential causes of a thing would not be able to make this without such an accident; for such an accident is not required for a separation of some things, since two substances may be able to be separate, even if they were separated from all the accidents. And such an accident is not required for this, that some parts which may contribute some whole, since there may appear to be no reason why parts naturally prior to every accident can not constitute a whole, the parts of which were created to be without such an accident.

From all these statements it is gathered that a quantity of the genus 'accident' is neither required for the local separation of those which are created to constitute one substance; nor required for the constitution of the whole, since it may be later than the whole, and so separate parts can constitute another substance without such an accident. From this it is obvious that all things, which can be saved by the assumption of such a quantity, can be equally well saved without it. For it will be so saved that the parts of the substance and the qualities informing the substance are separate locally, and that the substance as well as the qualities are quanta; for they have part outside of part without such a quantity through this, that essential causes produce a substantial thing and a quality and produce parts of a substance and of qualities in distinct places, as if there be posited such a quantity following a substance already produced. For who could prevent God from producing one substance or quality without every accident distinct from substance and quality; and who could prevent God from placing one part of that substance and quality outside of another without the dissolution of that substance and quality without another absolute thing really distinct, if He be able to do this with such a distinct mediating thing? For this seems to limit too much the divine power to say that, although one thing having parts really distinct was produced by God, God could not be able to make them separate locally, except by giving to them a new thing or unless He break asunder or destroy the unity of them.

Again, that a substance may be a quantum through its substantial parts intrinsic in it, I show thus. That, which is circumscriptively in a place through its intrinsic parts, is a quantum through its intrinsic parts; for it was shown before that every thing, which is circumscriptively in a place, is a quantum. But every material substance is circumscriptively in a place through its substantial parts; for, as was shown be-

THE SACRAMENT OF THE ALTAR 163

fore, every material substance, which is extended, is present in a place through its essential parts, so that a whole substance is present in a whole place, and a part of a substance is present in a part of a place. But any such is in a place circumscriptively, and so every such substance is a quantum through its parts intrinsic in it.

Nor is it sufficient to say that a substance does not have parts except through quantity which is a thing distinct from substance; for a substance does not depend on any accident of its own, and consequently the parts of a substance do not depend upon the parts of an accident. Therefore, if quantity may be an accident of substance, the parts of a substance do not depend either upon a quantity or upon parts of a quantity; and so substance does not have parts through quantity. Which conclusion is confirmed, for a thing has 'being' and 'being distinct' through the same; therefore, through that through which there are parts of a substance, through that those parts are also distinguished. But the parts of a substance are not through quantity; therefore, they are not distinguished through quantity; therefore, substance does not have parts through quantity, which is a thing other than substance.

Again, if quantity be a thing other than substance, then it does not make a part of a substance to be separate from a part of a substance, unless it be an efficient or final cause. But the causality of an efficient or final making parts to be separate does not prevent that thing from being a quantum through its parts intrinsic to it; for then, since God as an efficient and final cause may make the parts of any quantity at all to be separate, no quantity could be 'quantum' or 'having part outside of part' through its parts.

From this it is obvious that no matter to what extent one other quantity might be added to that substance, which has part outside of part, that substance would still be a quantum through a thing itself and its intrinsic parts; as parts of a substance are locally separate from themselves and through nothing else except through their intrinsic causes, say, efficient and final.

Nor is it sufficient to say that quantity, which is an accident, is a formal cause by which a substance is a quantum, as whiteness is a formal cause why something is white. This does not obtain; for it was shown before that every thing one numerically having part separate locally or in situation from part is a quantum. Therefore this, through which a thing is neither one numerically nor through which parts of a thing are separate in situation, is not a formal cause why that thing is a quantum. But a quantity, which is an accident, is not that formally through which a substance is one numerically; for through the same a substance is and is one numerically. But no accident is a formal cause why its subject is or will not be; therefore, the formal cause why its subject is one. Nor, indeed, is quantity a formal cause through which the parts of substance are separate locally, as something is white through whiteness; for then as it is impossible that some may be white without whiteness, whether they be separate from one another and be certain wholes existing per se or may be parts constituting some whole, so it would be impossible that those things, which are merely separate in situation through quantity, which is an accident, as a body is white through

THE SACRAMENT OF THE ALTAR 165

whiteness, could be separate in situation or in place without such a quantity; even if they were mutually separate and were whole quanta not making one whole, which is false.

For the omnipotence of God may be able at first to divide a piece of wood into two parts and place one of them at Rome and the other here, and afterwards separate them from all their absolute accidents. When this has been done, they would be separate locally and yet would not have such a quantity; for they are separate from that per casum. From which it is obvious that parts of a substance are not separate through such a quantity, as a body is white through whiteness.

CHAPTER XXIX

The same conclusion, which was stated before, is proved through arguments taken from the statements of Catholic doctors

In addition to the preceding reasons, some others must be added, based partly on the statements of other Catholic doctors, who, however, posit such a quantity intermediate between substance and quality. For a certain Doctor, whom I think reputable, says it; for I have no desire to detract anything from the omnipotence of God since He may be able to do more than we are able to think or understand, unless I may see that an evident contradiction follows. For that Doctor, namely, Scotus, says in Book IV. of the Sentences, Distinction X., Question IV., that the infinite power of God might be able to preserve sacramentally the body of Christ under the species of bread without this, that it could have being locally and circumscriptively in heaven or elsewhere. Therefore, let it be posited that the body of Christ may be sacramentally under the species and that it may cease to be in heaven locally and that it may begin to be nowhere locally and circumscriptively. When this has been done, I ask, whether this quantity, which was before distinct from substance and quality, remains or does not remain but is corrupted. It can not be said that that quantity is destroyed; for according to those writers in the same place an absolute is not altered by virtue of a variation of respective, and consequently an absolute thing is

THE SACRAMENT OF THE ALTAR 167

not destroyed by virtue of a variation of respective. But according to the same writers 'ubi' is not in heaven except as a respect. Therefore, it is not necessary to posit that some absolute thing may really be destroyed by virtue of this, that the body of Christ ceases to be in heaven locally. Therefore, every absolute thing, which was before, remains, and so that quantity remains; since, therefore, according to them that substance is a quantum through that quantity, as a body is white through whiteness.

As it is impossible and involves a contradiction, that any body may be informed by the whiteness inhering in it and yet that it may not be white; so it is impossible that that substance may be informed by that quantity inhering in it, unless it be a quantum. Therefore, it would be necessary to say this, that that body of Christ would truly and really be a quantum by that quantity, if the prior case is posited.

But that this ought not to be conceded, I am convinced, first, thus: that, which does not have part separate from part, is not a quantum. But, if the prior case is posited, the substance of the body of Christ does not have part separate from part; for, if so, then that body would coexist with the species of bread. It follows that distinct parts of a body coexists with distinct parts of that species.

It is the proof of consequence; for, if parts of the body of Christ are separate locally, I take those two parts, say, A and B. Then I ask concerning A, whether it coexists with the whole host and with each part, or whether it coexists with any one part and not another. If you say that it coexists with the whole host and with each part; for the same reason B coexists with the whole host and with each part; and through position the body of Christ is not elsewhere than under the species of bread. Therefore, with whatever one part coexists, with the same another part also coexists, and consequently they are not distinct locally. But if you say that A coexists with one part of the host and not with another, B would then also coexist with a second part and not with the former, and so distinct parts of the body of Christ would coexist with distinct parts of the species of bread, which is false; since from that it would follow that not the whole body of Christ would be in each part of the host; on the contrary the whole body of Christ would be in no part of the host. It would also follow that the body of Christ would be in a place circumscriptively, all of which are false. Therefore, it remains that, if that case is posited, the body of Christ would nowhere have part separate from part in situation, nor would it have part outside of part, and consequently could not be a quantum, which is the thesis.

But they suggest one response to that and similar arguments, when they say that position, which is a difference of quantity, necessarily is in a quantum or is in a quantum continuous and permanent; and it is necessary for that to be saved in a thesis, namely, which speaks of the order of the parts in a whole.

For it is not well understood that something is a measurable quantum, but that it may be to designate in a whole the order of this part in relation to another according to the intervening quantity. But position, which is posited by certain persons, adds another category. For, if the order of the parts in a whole is presupposed, it further posits an order of parts in re-

THE SACRAMENT OF THE ALTAR 169

lation to place or to parts of a place or locality. This is certain, that parts are coextended with parts, as a whole is said at first to be commensurate with the whole place, in which it has its 'ubi,' so that 'position' as a category presupposes 'position' as a difference of quantity and specifies 'ubi.' And it is possible for God to separate this position from a quantity remaining in the first position not only through the negation of 'ubi,' as He would be able to make some body outside of the universe, and then it could not have this second position; for it would not have some thing continuous with whose parts the parts contained would be commensurate. But even if a terminus is posited to that which is present, a commensuration or coextension might be able to be made with another body of Christ. It would be possible for God to save a quantum and the coexistence of it in relation to another quantum; and yet without this coexistence of the parts of one in relation to the parts of another which this second position says.

These points have been subtly stated, yet no lover of truth ought to be offended if they are assailed for the cause of seeking the truth and of training. For, if they are true, it is profitable to hear objections in order that they may be explained that the truth may thus be more clearly known. If they are false, it is expedient that they be refuted. But, that this response may not be sufficient, it can in the first place be proved thus: if position, which is a difference of quantity, indicates the order of parts in a whole and is sufficient for this, that something may be a quantum; I ask, of what kind is this order of parts in the whole; whether it is an order of parts situated so that one part is lower

170 THE SACRAMENT OF THE ALTAR

and another higher, one part before and another behind, one towards the East, another towards the West; or is it an order of perfection, for surely one part may be more perfect and another more imperfect; or is it an order of whole and of part, as the eye is part of the head; or is it an order of causality, and one part is the cause of another; or is it an order of origin or of nature; for surely one part prior by nature is produced and is in the nature of things prior to another. For in another mode, as it appears, it can be understood that there may be an order of parts in a whole; if however an order of parts in a whole which is occasioned through position, which is a difference of quantity.

Let it be the first order; namely, situal. It is manifest that that order can not be without local separation of parts, and so there never is any quantum unless the parts be separate in situation. Since, therefore, if the first case is posited, the parts of the body of Christ may not be separate in situation; the body of Christ will not be a quantum if that is conceded. But the order of parts in a whole, which is position which is a difference of quantity, can not be understood by other modes; for any such order could be so suitable to the substance of the body of Christ, if the whole substance of the body of Christ were separate from an entire quantity, which it is possible for God to do according to those writers, as when it is joined with a quantity. For if the whole substance of the body of Christ is preserved without this, that it be a quantum; so there would be one part of a substance more perfect than another, as it now is; for one part is not now any more a part of another, nor is one part any more

THE SACRAMENT OF THE ALTAR 171

the cause of another when more prior by nature than another would then be; and so it is obvious that no order of parts in a whole can be suitable to the parts of a substance when it is joined with a quantity without its being able to be suitable to them when it is not conjoined with a quantity aside from that order which is situal; and so a situal order of parts alone suffices for this, that something may be a quantum. But such an order of parts requires local separation of parts, and consequently nothing is a quantum continuous and permanent, unless it have parts separate in situation.

Again, every situate quantum is long; but no 'long' is without local or situal separation of parts. If, therefore, the body of Christ be a quantum when the prior case is posited, it is necessary that it be long; and consequently one part will be separate from another and one will be outside of another, and it is not true if the first case is held.

Again, every quantum is extended, but nothing is extended, unless one part be separate from another and be outside of another; for the presence of a thing in some quantum is not sufficient for extension, for then the rational soul would be a quantum since it may coexist and be present in the entire body and in each part of it. And so it is well known that, if the body of Christ were a quantum in the sacrament of the altar, if the first case is held, it would have part outside of part, since it would truly be extended and so would have position which indicates the order of parts in a place.

Again, every finite quantum continuous and permanent has form; but an order of parts in a place is required for form, if it be present in a place; nor does any other order of parts in a whole suffice for form, which is obvious from this; for it is possible for form to be changed if a local change alone of parts is made. For if all the parts of the human body were changed locally so that the hand, or so that the stomach could be placed above the head or the feet above the stomach or any such local change of parts could be made, it is manifest that the form would be changed; and yet it could not be unless another order of parts in a place or some diverse situal position is required. And so it is manifestly obvious that a situal order of parts is required for form. Whence, if parts may not be separate locally, it is manifest that form is not there. For if God could through His own omnipotence create anew the substance of wood with all its absolute accidents under the species of bread without this, that it would be elsewhere locally, which is possible for God according to those writers; I ask of what form would that wood be. For no reason can be assigned why it may be square more than triangular or round, and a foot of quantity can not be posited any more than two feet, since it may be able to be rarefied and condensed, and sometimes be of a greater quantity and sometimes of a less quantity. Nor could it be able to be posited that that wood would be rare or dense, since it would not be able to be said that the parts would lie near or not near; although however according to the opinion of the wise, that may be rare whose parts lie remote.

Again, a homogeneous body is truly a quantum and consequently truly has position which is a difference of quantity. But it is manifest that there is no order of homogeneous parts except situal. For, if a situal

THE SACRAMENT OF THE ALTAR 173

order of such parts is circumscribed, no part could be prior to another nor one part after another, since they may be entirely of the same ground; therefore, a situal position is not other than that, which is the order of parts in a place or which is a situal order of parts, and is required for this, that something may really be a quantum. Whence, he, who says that for this, that something may be a quantum, a certain order of parts in a whole is sufficient, which is not a situal order of parts. It is necessary, to indicate of what sort that order of parts may be; and it appears that no order could be assigned but that according to those they can be among the substantial parts, after such a quantity is circumscribed.

From the previous statements it is gathered that, if the body of Christ were precisely under the species of bread sacramentally and nowhere else locally and circumscriptively, it would not be a quantum by any quantity distinct from substance and quality. If however everything one numerically, having parts really distinct, created to be separate locally and created to be produced by a natural agent in distinct places, be called a quantum; it can be conceded that, the body of Christ would be a quantum if that case is posited.

Again, I intend to show through the principles of those previously mentioned, that material substance is quantum through its substantial parts. For according to those writers as a whole substance is prior to a whole quantity, so the parts of a substance are prior to the parts of a quantity; therefore, the parts of a substance are before the parts of a quantity. Then I ask; whether they are in that prior in the same place or in distinct places. They are not in the same place, for they are not more in one place than in another; therefore, in that prior they are in distinct places; but a substance having parts existing in distinct places will be circumscribed in a place; therefore, a substance in that prior is circumscribed in a place, and consequently is a quantum in that prior and so a substance is a quantum through itself and through its intrinsic parts.

Again, everything, which is circumscribed in a place through itself and through its intrinsic substantial parts, through that same is a quantum. But a material substance is circumscribed in a place through itself and through its intrinsic parts, which is obvious from the principles of those writers; for according to them there is not a passive circumscription of location except a certain respect. But according to those holding such an opinion, a respect is altered according to a variation of a fundament which is a terminus. Therefore, since substance and quantity may really be distinguished, 'a passive circumscription, by which substance is circumscribed,' and 'a passive circumscription by which a quantity is circumscribed,' will be distinct; and so a substance is in a place by one passive circumscription, and quantity by another; and consequently substance is fundamentally circumscribed in a place by itself and its substantial parts and is formally circumscribed in a place by a proper circumscription. But, when all the others are circumscribed, these two are sufficient for this, that something may be quantum; therefore, substance is a quantum without an absolute quantity really distinct.

Again, there is one local distance of one part of a substance from one part of a substance and there is another distance of one part of a quantity from an-

THE SACRAMENT OF THE ALTAR 175

other part of a quantity; for from this fundament and terminus are distinct fundaments of one respect and of another respect according to them. It is necessary that respects be distinguished, therefore, these distances are distinguished. But the local distance of parts constituting any whole can not be without a quantity; therefore, since the parts of a substance may be separate locally before the parts of a quantity, as they are before; the substance will be a quantum before that other quantity may be posited in being.

And so from the arguments advanced and from others which I omit by virtue of brevity, it would seem to anyone that there is not a quantity except the extraposition of parts or the local or situal distance of parts making one whole for which extraposition, whether local or situal distance of parts, parts are not required, except those which are separate, and essential intrinsic causes, if they have intrinsic causes, and extrinsic causes; say, efficient and final; and so consequently the parts of a substance making one can be separate in situation and one can be outside of another by virtue of its natural causes.

But quantity, which is an absolute thing other than substance, is neither an intrinsic nor an extrinsic cause of those parts; by virtue of which such a quantity is not required for that extraposition or situal distance of parts.

Whence, from the principles of many writers it can be argued thus: respect, fundament, and terminus suffice for real existence, and extrinsic causes; but according to these situal distance of parts or extraposition of parts of a substance beyond the parts themselves does not add a respect, which it does not have, in place of fundament and terminus, except those parts of the substance. Therefore, when the parts themselves of substance and the extrinsic causes which make them to be separate are assumed, that respect will be sufficiently posited. Therefore, if there is required for that distance of parts of a substance another quantity, which may be a thing other than a substance, that quantity either will be a fundament or a terminus of that respect; which can not be granted, as has been shown before, or it is the extrinsic cause of that respect, and consequently without it that respect can be posited. Since whatever God can do by a mediating and extrinsic secondary cause, God can accomplish immediately per se; therefore, without any such distinct quantity that extraposition or situal distance of substantial parts can be posited. But when the extraposition or local or situal separation of parts is posited, it is considered quantity; for it is considered some whole having part outside of part; therefore, without such a quantity there might be able to be a quantity; and so a quantity other than a substance and a quality seems to be entirely superfluous.

And many of the preceding arguments, through which it was proved that substance can be a quantum without a quantity other than substance, can be employed to prove that quantity can be a quantum without another quantity; the discussion of which I pass over for the sake of brevity.

Yet from the previous arguments it can be deduced that there is no necessity for positing a quantity other than substance and quality; because for this, that substance as well as quality may be a quantum, it suffices that substance and qualities be produced by virtue of essential causes, and that parts of these are produced in distinct places by virtue of the same causes without the production of any other, or that one part may take on being outside of another. For another thing does not seem to be required for this, that one part of a substance or of a quality may take on being outside of another, unless it be an intrinsic or extrinsic cause of it. But such a quantity can not be posited as an intrinsic or extrinsic cause of substance or of quality; and so for this, that one part may be brought into being outside of another, such a quantity is not required; therefore, it is needlessly posited.

CHAPTER XXX

Concerning objections contrary to the previous statements

For a fuller explanation of the preceding statement some objections must be raised. For from various sources diverse reasons theological as well as philosophical, of which I shall cite a few, are adduced to prove that every quantity may be a thing other than substance; for, if they could be solved, the remaining reasons would easily be refuted. But it is argued thus: if any quantity could not be an absolute thing other than a substance, then as the substance of the bread is converted into the body of Christ, so similarly some quantity is converted into the body of Christ.

Again, as the bread is converted into the body of Christ, so the substance of the bread will be converted into the body of Christ and consequently the quantity of the body of Christ will begin to be under the species of bread by virtue of the sacrament; from which it follows that the body of Christ would be a quantum both locally and circumscriptively in the sacrament of the altar by virtue of conversion; which is false.

Again, if any quantity were not a thing distinct from substance, a quantity would not remain in the sacrament of the altar, as the substance of the bread does not remain there, which is false.

Again, no accident is really the same as a substance; but every quantity is an accident, which is proved to be in accordance with the intention of the Saints and the philosophers by their testimony. For the blessed

THE SACRAMENT OF THE ALTAR 179

Augustine says in the De Trinitate, Book V., Chapter V.: "In created and also in changeable things it remains that that, which is not said according to substance, may be said according to accident; for all are accidental to those, which can be either lost or diminished, both magnitudes and qualities; and that which follows in relation to anything, as friendships, relationships, services, likenesses, equalities, and if anything else of the kind; both situations and conditions, both place and times."

Again, the same writer in the same book in Chapter X.: "In things," he says, "which are great by participation of magnitude, to which it is one thing to be, another to be great; as a great house, a great mountain, a great mind; in these things, therefore, magnitude is one thing, that which is great from the same magnitude is another; and certainly this, which is a great house, is not magnitude."

Again, Aristotle posits nine categories as accidents, among which he enumerates quantity. From all of these statements it follows that magnitude is an accident and consequently it is a thing distinct from substance.

Again, this, which is contrary to the common opinion of the Doctors, is not, therefore, to be received as if a Catholic opinion. It is also contrary to experience; for, since a corporeal substance may be divided without the conversion of anything into that, it is effected of a less quantity without the loss of any of its part; which could not be, if quantity were not another thing really distinct from substance.

Again, in diverse substances differing in species there is a quantity the same in species; for there is not a longitude or a latitude other than species in a handful of air and of fire; which would not be true if longitude were not really distinct from substance. It is also thus shown that no quantity may really be the same as quality; for according to the philosopher, quality is not a quantum except through accident; but if quality were really the same as quantity, then it would be a quantum per se without addition.

Again, it is naturally impossible for one body, which is a quantity, to be at the same time with another body which is quantity; for dimensions mutually expel one another. But quality is at the same time with a substance. Therefore, if some quantity were really not distinct from quality and some quantity were really distinct from substance, two quantities would naturally be at the same time, and so two solidities or depths, and two longitudes and two latitudes would be at the same time; indeed many more than two; since for whatever reason whiteness would have its proper quantity, for the same reason taste would have its own, and heat its own, and humidity its own, and dryness its own; and thus of others. And so as many bodies would be long, wide, and thick as there are qualities at the same time, and so in the sacrament of the altar there would be many bodies at the same time. If this is conceded, it is possible to inquire how those qualities remaining in the sacrament of the altar remain at the same time, whenever they are moved. From this none of them is in another as if in a subject, nor are all in any one subject, if quantity may not be the only one and the subject of them; so then it is obvious that by virtue of the preceding and other arguments, it is necessary to posit a quantity differing from substance and quality.

CHAPTER XXXI

In which replies are posited to the previous objections

But it now remains to show that all these reasons do not sufficiently agree that there may be some quantity really distinct from substance and quality.

For when it is first deduced to this inconsistency, that some quantity is converted into the body of Christ, it can first be said that the opposite of that is not found in sacred scripture; for I have never read either in the Sacred Scriptures or in the canonical law or in any authorized work that quantity is not converted into the body of Christ. For they make no mention at all whether a quantity may be converted into the body of Christ or may not be converted, as they make no mention whether a quantum may be converted into the body of Christ; although some, whom one is permitted to contradict because they mutually condemn one another, may assert that a quantity is not converted into the body of Christ.

In the second place, although it might be found that a quantity is not converted into the body of Christ, it would not be necessary to concede that quantity is a thing other than quality and substance; for the mode of signification might be able to preclude such a predication, 'a quantity is converted into the body of Christ,' as according to many writers. Although 'humanity' may not be a thing really distinct from 'man'; yet this could be conceded, 'man is white,' and this may be denied, 'humanity is white'; not be-

182 THE SACRAMENT OF THE ALTAR

cause 'humanity' may be some thing really distinct from 'man,' but because this name 'humanity' and this name 'man' have another mode of signification; namely, grammatical or logical. For it ought to be shown elsewhere how possible it may be that predication may be false, without a distinction of the things introduced by virtue of diverse modes of signifying 'gramaticales' or 'logicales.'

In the third place, it might be able to be said that no matter how much this will be conceded, that 'a quantity is converted into the body of Christ'; yet this happens, that this may be true, 'a quantity is converted into the body of Christ'; while this appears true, 'the substance of the bread is converted into the body of Christ.' And frequently those may be denied by writers, which are through accident; although according to the virtue of signification they may not be under obligation to deny them. Wherefore, no matter how much some quantity may not be a thing really distinct from the substance of the bread, yet these two stand at the same time: 'the substance of the bread is converted into the body of Christ,' and 'no quantity is converted into the body of Christ.' Just as according to many writers and appointed Catholic doctors 'fundament' and 'relation' are not distinct things and consequently 'whiteness' and 'likeness' are not things really distinct; yet these two stand at the same time: 'whiteness is,' and 'likeness is not.' But, notwithstanding that some quantity may not be a thing really distinct from substance, how can this be true, 'the substance of the bread is converted into the body of Christ,' while this appears false, 'quantity is converted into the body of Christ,' can be explained thus. Although some quan-

THE SACRAMENT OF THE ALTAR 183

tity may not be a thing other than substance, yet this name 'quantity' connotes that one part is outside of another or that one part is separate from another part. But this name 'substance' does not connote that one part is separate in situation from another part; and by virtue of which I do not see that it involves a contradiction that this may be true, 'the substance of the bread is converted into the body of Christ,' while this appears false, 'the substance of the bread having part outside of part or separate from part is converted into the body of Christ.' On the contrary, it can be false, while another appears true; for it can implicate a fallacy; namely, 'one part of the bread is separate in situation from another part.'

Whence, if God, who can make all things, should make some substance of bread to be somewhere precisely in that mode, in which the body of Christ is under the species of bread, so that that substance of that bread would be nowhere locally or circumscriptively; then this would be true, 'this thing is substance,' and this false, 'this thing is a substance having part separate from part.' And so, if God could then convert that substance into the body of Christ, which I do not think a Christian ought to say could not be done by God, this would be true, 'the substance of the bread is converted into the body of Christ,' and this is false by virtue of a false implication, 'the substance of the bread having part separate from part in situation was converted into the body of Christ'; and consequently the opposite of it is true, 'the substance of the bread having part separate from part was not converted into the body of Christ.' From which this follows, 'a quantity is not converted into the body of Christ.' Therefore, it is obvious that, although this may in a mode be true, 'the substance of the bread' is in a mode 'the substance of the bread having part separate from a part'; yet this could be true, 'the substance of the bread is converted into the body of Christ,' while this appears false, 'the substance of the bread having part separate from part is converted into the body of Christ'; and consequently while this appears true, 'the substance of the bread having part separate from part is not converted into the body of Christ,' which negative could be true, while the first also appears true by virtue of this cause of reality; namely, 'the substance of the bread does not have part separate from part'; and so it can easily be said that although this may in a mode be true, 'some quantity is not a thing distinct from the substance of the bread'; yet this could be true, 'the substance of the bread is converted into the body of Christ,' while this appears true, 'a quantity is not converted into the body of Christ.' And the whole cause is; because, although this may be in a way true, 'the substance is really the same as some quantity'; yet this could be true, 'the substance of the bread is really not the same thing as a quantity'; as, although this may in a mode be true, 'the substance of the bread is a substance having part separate from part'; yet this could be true, 'the substance of the bread is not a substance having part separate from part'; for it follows from this possible, 'the substance of the bread does not have part separate from part,' even while this appears true, 'the substance of the bread is.'

Therefore, it is obvious from the premises that this name 'quantity' connotes something, or permits one to understand that which is not denoted or permitted to

THE SACRAMENT OF THE ALTAR 185

be perceived through this name 'substance'; for this name 'quantity' permits one to understand that that, of which it is predicated, may be 'having part separate from part'; but this name 'substance' does not connote either in a proposition or outside a proposition that that, of which it is verified, may be 'having part separate from part.' And, indeed, no matter how much this may in a mode be true, 'substance is quantity'; yet it might be able to be false, even though a substance remains; as this is in a mode true, 'the substance of the bread is a substance having part separate from part'; and yet, though a substance remains, this could be false. Just as some say that this name 'likeness' connotes that two qualities of the same ground exist at the same time in the nature of things; but this name 'whiteness' does not connote that two qualities exist at the same time in the nature of things, and yet many Catholics say that 'whiteness' and some 'likeness' are one thing and are not things really distinct; although this may be able to be true, 'whiteness is,' while this appears false, 'likeness is.' And, indeed, although they might concede that this could be true, 'whiteness' and 'likeness,' are said to be two whitenesses existing in the nature of things; yet this might be able to be false, while whiteness remains, 'whiteness (is whiteness,' 'white) is likeness'; for it would imply a fallacy, namely, 'two whitenesses are really outside of the mind.'

Therefore, it is obvious from the previous statements that, although some quantity may not be a thing really distinct from the substance of the bread; yet this could be true, 'the substance of the bread is converted into the body of Christ,' though this appears

186 THE SACRAMENT OF THE ALTAR

false, 'a quantity is converted into the body of Christ'; and this by virtue of a diverse mode of signifying or of consignifying of those two names 'substance' and 'quantity.'

Through this it is obvious that, although it may not be found expressed in the canon of the Bible, nor in the canonical law, nor in the writings of the Saints approved by the Roman Church, that the substance of the bread is not converted into the quantity of the body of Christ; for they do not make mention of this; yet in virtue of the diverse mode of signifying or consignifying of these names 'substance' and 'quantity,' this might be able to be verified, 'the substance of the bread is converted into the substance of the body of Christ'; although this would be false, 'the substance of the bread is converted into the quantity of the body of Christ,' as by virtue of the diverse mode of signifying these names 'substance' and 'quantity,' this would be able to be false, 'substance is quantity,' although substance and some quantity would not be things really distinct.

And that this may not even be contrary to the faith of the church is obvious in a similar case; for many Catholic doctors say that 'relation' is not a thing really distinct from its 'fundament.' For I do not think that anyone of sane mind, unless he, who alone would wish to be called a rabbi, wishes to say that all, who hold that relation is not a thing distinct from its fundament, are heretics. It is, therefore, not heretical to say that relation is a thing distinct from its fundament. It is, therefore, never heretical to say that the substance of the bread is converted into a relation, even to say that this is true, 'the substance of the bread is con-

THE SACRAMENT OF THE ALTAR 187

verted into the body of Christ,' and this is false, 'the
substance of the bread is not converted into a relation';
notwithstanding that some relation, say, relation of
dependence itself upon God is not a thing other than
the body of Christ.

And so it is manifestly obvious that the whole truth
concerning the sacrament of the Eucharist can so
easily be saved; although it may be conceded that some
quantity is not a thing really distinct from substance,
as I concede that some relation is not really distinct
from substance, which many Catholics concede. For
it is no more to be found in sacred scripture that a
quantity is not converted into the body of Christ or
that a substance is not converted into the quantity of
the body of Christ, than that a relation is not converted into the body of Christ or that the substance
of the bread is not converted into a relation. And, indeed, as it can be posited according to the Catholic
faith that some relation is not a thing really distinct
from the substance of the bread, and some relation is
not a thing really distinct from the substance of the
body of Christ; and then it is necessary to concede
that some relation or some respect is converted into
the body of Christ, and the substance of the bread is
converted into relation as 'next,' or it is necessary to
assign some mode of signifying or of consignifying
the diversity of those names 'substance' and 'relation'
by virtue of which some thing can truly be attributed
to one and truly denied of another; and similarly one
of them can truly be attributed to one, and the other
truly denied of the same. So a Catholic can posit that
some quantity is not a thing really distinct from substance; and then either it is necessary to concede as

if not opposed to the faith, that 'a quantity is converted into the body of Christ' and 'the substance of the bread is converted into the quantity of the body of Christ,' or to assign some diverse mode of signifying those names, 'substance' and 'quantity'; by virtue of which one can be conceded, another can not be conceded; no matter how much some quantity may not be a thing other than a substance, which it is easy to do, as was shown elsewhere.

Nor is this more difficult to do than to show how some quantity may not be a thing distinct from substance; and yet that this may be false, 'quantity is substance'; but because this pertains more to logic than to theology, I, therefore, pass on.

With reference to that which is introduced under the last head in the second argument, it must be said that this does not follow; namely, that, if some quantity of the body of Christ could begin to be in the sacrament of the altar by virtue of the sacrament, then by virtue of the sacrament the body of Christ could be a quantum both locally and circumscriptively in a place in the sacrament of the altar. For as it is not established according to some writers that 'the quantity of the body of Christ' or 'the body of Christ existing in a place locally is in the sacrament of the altar'; therefore, the body of Christ there is a quantum and is locally in a place. So it does not follow that 'the quantity of the body of Christ begins to be in the sacrament of the altar by virtue of the sacrament'; therefore, by virtue of the sacrament it begins to be there locally. Whence, whether this be conceded or not, 'the quantity of the body of Christ begins to be under the species of bread by the power of conversion'; yet

THE SACRAMENT OF THE ALTAR 189

this I simply deny, 'the body of Christ is a quantum under the species of bread by the power of conversion.' And, indeed, I make this assertion, that the body of Christ is a quantity or a quantum neither by the power of conversion nor by the power of the sacrament; as notwithstanding that this may be true, 'the body of Christ having part separate from part,' say, in heaven, is there under the species of bread by the power of conversion; yet this is simply false, 'the body of Christ by the power of conversion has part separate from part under the species of bread.' Whence, he who would desire to concede that this would need to be conceded by virtue of language, 'some quantity is substance,' could easily reply to all the arguments about this matter by conceding or denying the propositions and by positing the consequences in place of this name 'quantitas,' this whole, 'a thing having part separate from part'; since they would then have to say that these two, 'quantity continuous and permanent' and 'a thing having part separate from part,' would be convertibles; in fact, one would be a definition expressing something of another name, if there could be some name convertible with this, 'quantity continuous and permanent.' And, therefore, in replying to whatever proposition or consequence in which this name 'quantity' would be posited, it would be necessary to posit in place of this name this whole 'a thing having part separate from part'; and it could be easily seen, if the proposition or consequence were to be conceded or denied; and then this proposition would necessarily be conceded, 'a quantity is converted into the body of Christ,' as this, 'a thing having part separate from part is converted into the body of Christ.' Similarly, this would necessarily be conceded, 'the substance of the bread is converted into a quantity,' as this must be conceded, 'the substance of the bread is converted into a thing having part separate from part'; although this thing may not have part separate from part in the species of bread; for it is not there locally and circumscriptively in a place, but is elsewhere.

And I certainly confess that I have never read either in the canonical law or in the original sources of the Saints or in decrees of any High Pontiff or in any general council or in any authorized writing, such a proposition, 'quantity is not converted into the body of Christ,' 'the substance of the bread is not converted into quantity,' or any similar proposition; although I seem to posit an opinion contrary to many modern Doctors who mutually condemn one another, and, indeed, their writings are not authoritative; on the contrary, many opinions of some have even been condemned in the established universities; for they have presumed to approve such propositions. However, this is in every mode false, 'the bread is converted into the body of Christ, which is a quantity under the species of bread.'

And if you say; if they concede such propositions, they have not done this unless influenced by sacred scripture or at least by some authentic scripture; I reply that they have said many things for which they did not have either sacred scripture or any authentic scripture. I ask from what authentic scripture have they the statement that the accidents in the sacrament of the altar do not subsist per se without a subject, and that all qualities are in a subject. I ask from what authentic scripture have they the statement that in the

THE SACRAMENT OF THE ALTAR 191

sacrament of the altar there is some subject of ponderosity, which is ponderous. Also from what scripture have they the statement that God can not make several angels in the same species, that God can not make a man or an ass without an absolute accident inhering in it, that a quality can not be without a subject, that there are not many substantial forms in man, that the will can will nothing contrary to the judgment of reason; and many such statements, which disagree with authentic statements and reason.

Whence, I ask, are the modern writers inspired, or what authentic scripture do they have per se for positing that there is some thing of which God can not be the cause, that there is some thing which God can not destroy through His omnipotence, that a dead man is a man, and innumerable statements which are manifestly not in accord with the authentic scriptures.

So then it is easy to see that it is not contrary to the Christian faith to posit that some quantity is not a thing really distinct from substance by virtue of this, that a quantity is then converted into the body of Christ, and the substance of the bread is converted into a quantity; so however that it may be converted into a substance which may be a quantity there.

Nor does it contradict the statement which is afterward adduced, that a quantity would not then remain in the sacrament of the altar; for, although some quantity may pass over, say, that quantity which was not a thing distinct from the substance of the bread; yet one other remains, namely, that which is not really distinct from quality.

Nor does it seem more in conflict with the statements of the Holy Fathers that one quantity, which is not a thing other than a substance, may pass over; and another, which is not a thing other than a quality, may remain, than that one relation or respect, which is not really a thing other than a substance, may pass over; and another relation or another respect, which is not really a thing other than a substance, may pass over; and another thing or another respect, which is not really a thing other than a quality, may remain. But in what way two quantities can be at the same time will be shown later.

CHAPTER XXXII

In which it is shown that both propositions stand at the same time; some quantity is not another thing really distinct from substance, and quantity is an accident

It now remains to show that any quantity is not another thing really distinct from substance; notwithstanding that it may be conceded by the philosophers as well as by the Saints that quantity is an accident and that quantity is some category other than substance.

But that I may rest upon a solid foundation, I shall begin from one distinction of this name 'accident' which can be deduced from the words of the venerable Father Anselm. According to this source this name 'accident' can be taken in a three-fold sense; namely, strictly, liberally, and very liberally.

By taking this term 'accident' in the strict sense, accident signifies thus a thing distinct from substance and inhering in that thing, namely, substance, and without which that substance can exist at least through divine power, so that there is no contradiction involved in the statement that that substance exists and is not informed by that accident really distinct.

And then an accident is called a thing really advenient to another thing and receding from it, or able to recede without the destruction of that substantial thing, not making one per se with that to which it really advenes; which I add by virtue of matter and

194 THE SACRAMENT OF THE ALTAR

substantial form. But such an accident can in no mode accede to a subject or recede from a subject without an entire change of that subject. For it is unthinkable that some subject may now be informed by one
5 thing really distinct from it and afterwards may not be informed by that same thing, or conversely; and yet that it may in no mode be changed. For every thing really advening to another thing or receding from it really makes some change about that thing.

10 But 'accident,' when used in the liberal acceptation of the term, is called everything predicable of something contingently, which can be successively affirmed and denied of that by virtue of a real transmutation of that and not so much by virtue of a real transmu-
15 tation of another; although it is not always necessary that it be successively verified and denied of that by virtue of a transmutation of that; but it can be successively affirmed and denied by virtue of the transmutation of another. And so likeness is called an
20 accident of Sortes; not that likeness may be a certain thing really distinct from Sortes and from a quality of Sortes, really informing Sortes or a quality of Sortes; but because these can be successively verified, 'Sortes is similar,' 'Sortes is not similar' by virtue of
25 the transmutation of Sortes. For if Plato be white, and Sortes black, and afterwards Sortes may become white and may be transmuted from blackness to whiteness by virtue of this alone, that Sortes is transmuted from blackness to whiteness, and Plato may not be
30 transmuted; this proposition is true, 'Sortes is not similar to Plato'; and afterwards this, 'Sortes is similar to Plato'; and so then likeness thus advenes to Sortes by virtue of the transmutation of Sortes, although it

THE SACRAMENT OF THE ALTAR 195

may be able to happen to him without a transmutation of Sortes by virtue of a transmutation of Plato. For from this very fact, that Plato could become black, and could be transmuted from whiteness to blackness, while Sortes remains black and not changed; this proposition would be true, 'Sortes is not similar to Plato,' and afterwards this, 'Sortes is similar to Plato.' And so it is obvious that this relation 'likeness' can advene to or recede from Sortes through a change of Sortes and without a change of him. This is said, 'Sortes can be similar at first and afterwards is not similar'; and conversely, both with a change of Sortes and without a change of Sortes. And that is called 'accident' when using the term in a liberal sense.

In a very free use of the term, 'accident' is called all that which can be suitable to something at one time and at another time can not be suitable to it, or might be able to be suitable to it and not suitable by virtue of a proper change as well as an inadequate change, or might not be able to be successively suitable to it and not be suitable through a proper change but specially through an inadequate change.

And in thus accepting the term it is not inconsistent to concede that some accident is suitable to God, for such an accident occasions no change either actual or possible in God.

'Accident' taken in the first way is most properly an accident; 'accident' taken in the second way is less properly an accident; but the third way is not properly an accident. And lest some one may believe that this distinction procedes from my head, let him read the venerable Anselm in his Monologium in Chapter XXV., where he says: "Of all things, surely, which are called accidents, some are understood to be able to be present or absent not except with some variation of the participant, as all colors; others are known not to effect any change at all about that of which they are said, either by acceding or receding, as certain relations. For it is, indeed, well known that I am neither older nor younger nor equal nor like the man who will be born after the present year; but I shall undoubtedly, be able to have and to lose all these relations to him, when he will have been born, without any change of myself, in proportion as he shall grow, or will be changed through diverse qualities.

And so it becomes plain, that of those, which are called accidents, certain to a certain degree bring commutability, but certain by no means impare immutability. Therefore, as the Supreme Nature in its own simplicity has never attributed a place to accidents effecting a change; so it sometimes does not disdain to say something about those accidents which by no means resist the supreme immutability; and yet there is nothing accidental about its essence, whence variableness itself can be conceived.

Whence, this can also be drawn, that it is susceptible of no accident. Surely, according to this mode those accidents, which by acceding or receding make some change, by this very effect are considered truly to happen to the thing which they change; so those, which are deficient by a similar effect, are discovered to be improperly called accidents."

From these words the previous distinction can be deduced. For when he says that there are some accidents, which make some change by acceding or receding, which are not conceived to be able to be present

THE SACRAMENT OF THE ALTAR 197

and absent except with some variation of the participant, as all colors, it shows that some accidents, which produce some change, are things really distinct from their subjects and inhere in the same. For color is a certain quality really distinct from substance, and inherent in it. But through this, which he says, there are some which either by acceding or receding are known to effect no change at all about that of which they are said, as certain relations. It evidently shows that there is an accident which is not a thing really distinct from a subject outside advening to that subject and really receding from that. For it is impossible that some thing may really and truly inhere and inform some thing really distinct and afterwards may not inform it unless that thing be commuted. The same writer also gives assent to this through this which he says, that there are some accidents which do not at all impair immobility.

From this it is obvious that not every accident is really retained in its subject, for Anselm says that the Supreme Nature "sometimes does not disdain to say something about those accidents which by no means resist the highest immutability; and yet nothing is accidental about its essence, whence variation itself can be conceived." For nothing is accidental to that Supreme Nature through real inherence and real information; and yet Anselm does not deny but concedes that some accident is suitable to it.

From which, according to the statement of Anselm, it is obvious that not every accident is really sustained in a subject; whence, this can also be concluded, that surely Supreme Nature is susceptible of no accident; for although some accident may be suitable to God, yet He really sustains none in Himself; and as it is of an accident, which is suitable to God, which is not really sustained in God, so an accident, which makes no change about that of which it is said, is not really sustained in that subject.

For if it could really be retained in a subject, as if a distinct thing in a distinct thing, the subject would necessarily be changed; for it would truly and really have in itself some thing inhering in itself, to which it was potentially prior, for it can not be without any change. For every thing which has at first one thing and afterwards another, either at first is deprived of some thing and afterwards may really be informed by it, or on the contrary it necessarily passes rapidly from one thing to another and consequently is changed; for according to Saint Gregory "to change is to go from one to another"; and according to the philosopher, "to change is to have yourself now otherwise than before."

Therefore, it is obvious that an accident, which advenes to that, of which it is said, without any change, is not really sustained in a subject; for then the divine nature would be susceptible of some accident. And, indeed, when Anselm says that "some accidents make no change at all by acceding or receding," he does not understand that such accidents may really accede as distinct things to a subject in informing it and may recede through the destruction or separation of one thing from another; for when, although Sortes appears black, Plato becomes white from black, no thing is separated from Sortes; but then that likeness is said to recede, by which Sortes was similar to Plato; for Sortes ceases to be similar to Plato. Whence, for

THE SACRAMENT OF THE ALTAR 199

likeness to accede to Sortes and to recede, is nothing other than that Sortes sometimes begins to be similar and sometimes ceases to be similar; and yet by virtue of this it is not necessary that Sortes receive some thing into himself or cease to have some thing in himself; as God, without the assumption of any thing into Himself and without the loss of anything existing in God, sometimes begins to be the justifier of the sinner and sometimes ceases to be the justifier of the sinner.

And so it is thus clearly established that it is according to the intention of Anselm to posit some accident which is a thing really distinct from the subject, really retained in that subject; as color is really retained in a body as a distinct thing in a distinct thing. But any accident is not a thing really sustained in a subject but is, indeed, called an accident; for it is contingently predicated of that, even if the constancy of the subject is posited. And that any of them can accede and recede through a change of that of which it is said, and even through an inadequate change, as is manifestly obvious; for that is obvious of relative accidents through an inadequate change, which Anselm says can advene to itself either through this, that another might increase or will be changed through diverse qualities. But that any may be able to advene to myself through a proper change of myself is also manifest, as was declared of likeness advening to Sortes. But that some accident may not be able to advene to that, of which it is said, except through an inadequate change is obvious through this which posits, that some accident can advene to God, even though God can in no mode be considered mutable.

And so it is obvious that this term 'accident' can be accepted in a three-fold sense; although that, which can not be suitable to anything except through an inadequate change, may improperly be called an accident to it, as Anselm says.

CHAPTER XXXIII

It declares how quantity is an accident, and how it obtains with this, that some quantity is not a thing distinct from substance

Besides the proposed distinction, it must be declared how quantity is an accident. When this has been shown, it will be obvious how these obtain at the same time, 'some quantity is not a thing really distinct from substance,' and 'quantity is an accident.' Whence, it must be known that, as, for instance, not every relation is an accident in the first mode; for not every relation is a thing really distinct from substance inhering in it, as many ancient Catholic doctors say and some modern Catholics agree with them.

And, indeed, not every relation is an accident in the first mode of accepting the term 'accident,' nor even is every relation an accident in the second mode of accepting 'accident'; for some relatives are suitable to God according to circumstances; sometimes suitable and sometimes not suitable; but this is not possible through a change of God, but precisely through a change of a creature; and yet it is conceded that relation is an accident and that it is one category of accident.

So it can be said of quantity, that not every quantity is a thing really distinct from substance and yet that a quantity is an accident. For which it must be understood that not every quantity is a thing really distinct from a substance inhering in it; as neither is

202 THE SACRAMENT OF THE ALTAR

every thing having part outside of part in situation or having part separate from part a thing really distinct from a substance.

And, indeed, as 'to have part separate from part' is not called an accident in the first mode; so not every quantity is called an accident in the first mode; but 'to have part separate from part' is called an accident in the second mode. For, if something substantially the same can at first 'have part separate from part' and afterwards can not 'have part separate from part' through a proper change (as some Catholics say. And it has already been mentioned before, that the body of Christ has in a mode 'part separate from part'; for), it is locally and circumscriptively in heaven; and the same body though not destroyed can cease to be locally and circumscriptively and can begin to be sacramentally under the species of bread; and so then it does not have part separate from part, yet the substance itself of the body of Christ is not destroyed. And so, when the same substance has at one time 'part separate from part' through a change of itself, at another time does not have 'part separate from part,' it is an accident; and yet it is not a thing always distinct and inhering in substance as if a thing really distinct from a substance; so also quantity is an accident not in the first mode, but in the second mode. For, although some quality may not now be a thing really distinct from substance; on the contrary some substance is really the same as substance, the substance itself however remaining.

This can manifestly be true, 'no quantity is really the same as substance'; for when it is assumed that God can thus bring it to pass, that it may not have part

THE SACRAMENT OF THE ALTAR 203

separate from part in situation, as in a mode the body of Christ is under the species of bread; then this is true, 'no substance is a quantity'; and some quantity is then not really the same as substance. So then this is true, 'no substance having part separate from part' is really the same as that substance, for it has that cause of reality. This substance is not 'having part separate from part' in situation; and so a substance 'having part separate from part' in situation can be called accident, if the term 'accident' is accepted in the second mode; for sometimes this is true, 'this substance is substance having part separate from part,' and sometimes it is not true without the corruption of that substance; although for this, that those contradictories may be successively verified, there is required a local change of that substance. So these obtain at the same time, 'any quantity is not a thing other than a substance,' and 'quantity is an accident.' For so many state, that any relation is not a thing other than a substance, and yet that relation is an accident.

And this, for these contradictories can be successively verified by virtue of a change of that substance: 'this substance is really the same as quantity,' 'this substance is not really the same as quantity.' But for the verification of such contradictories nothing is required except a local change of that substance and no other. And, therefore, it is necessary that every quantity be some absolute thing really distinct from substance; and certainly for all such, unless it should displease those loathing logic, it might be able to be briefly and easily stated that this is true, 'quantity is not a thing really distinct from substance,' if quantity be substituted significatively or personally; but this is true, 'quantity is an accident,' if quantity be substituted simply, and even if it be substituted personally; for an indefinite is verifiable for one singular. For thus John of Damascus posits in his Logic in Chapter XXXIII., that "number is an accident" and yet he posits that "number itself is things enumerated." Whence, he says under 'discretion': "Number is reduced to a quantum and language is reduced into number, but we call these 'enumerated.'" From which it is gathered that number, since it may be a quantity, is called an accident; and yet number is itself a thing enumerated. So we also say that white is an accident and yet something white is man. Thus we also say that man and white differ and yet we say that man is white. Whence, through this mode it can easily and evidently be shown that, although these two may be conceded; 'some quantity is not a thing really distinct from substance,' and 'some quantity is an accident'; it is not necessary to concede that the same thing may be substance and accident. Whence all arguments, which can be offered against these, are sophistical; nor do they not have any other way of being solved except through the fallacy of equivocation; for they do not have another defect.

CHAPTER XXXIV

In what way it must be replied to the passages of Augustine, introduced before in Chapter XXX, in the fourth and the fifth arguments

Having seen how these obtain at the same time: 'some quantity is not a thing really distinct from substance,' and 'quantity is an accident'; it remains to show that the opinion of Augustine does not contradict the previous statements; for Augustine does not intend that magnitudes are accidents really distinct from substances and inhering in them. For it seems wonderful that one accident might be able to make one part to be separate from another and yet God might not be able to do this, unless He would join one other thing to the parts of a substance. For when two distinct things are brought into being, who could prevent God from making one to be outside another, although He could join no other thing to them? And so that whole thing composed of them might be able to be great, although no other thing would be produced in it. For the blessed Augustine posits that magnitude is an accident; for a substance itself can be larger or smaller through a proper change of substance, according to that which can have parts more or less separate, which can touch without every thing inhering de novo in the substance itself. For when a substance having parts separate in act and in situation is produced, those parts can be still more separate without any added thing inherent in them, and then that substance is con-

sidered larger; because for a substance to be larger is
nothing other than to have parts more separate in situation. Moreover, those parts can be less distant by
virtue of an active cause, and then the substance is
also smaller, because for a substance to be smaller is
nothing other than to have parts less separate; and
that this is not surprising, can be shown through a contrary opinion. For if quantity be an absolute thing
really distinct from substance and quality, air may be
rarefied; if this is done, either the total preceding
quantity is corrupted or the total preceding quantity is
not corrupted.

It is not possible to grant; first, for in any rarefaction infinite absolute things distinct as regards themselves as wholes, not making one numerically, would
then be destroyed. For since there may be an infinite
substance in each continuous time, such infinite quantities would be destroyed in that time in which something without interruption becomes rarefied; because,
from this, that rarefaction is continuous in each instant, there would be quantity distinct according to
itself as a whole and distinct from a prior and posterior quantity. But it is obvious that they do not make
one numerically; for one does not remain with another.

Nor is it sufficient to say that those quantities have
not been actually, but potentially only. For every
accident really distinct and denominating its subject,
which is not part of another, is actually; but these
continuous quantities now corrupted were of this kind;
therefore, it follows that things infinite actually, distinct according to themselves as a whole, not making
one, would now be corrupted, which seems sufficiently
absurd.

THE SACRAMENT OF THE ALTAR   207

Nor can an agent even be granted that could destroy one quantity and generate another; for which reason God would not even be able to preserve one of those quantities while another is advening. Therefore, it does not appear reasonable to say, that a whole preceding quantity is corrupted and a whole new quantity is generated when air or another body becomes rarefied; for then it would follow that all the qualities would be corrupted no matter how much some body would become rarefied; for if quantity, which is posited as a subject of qualities, is corrupted and an accident itself is destroyed by the destruction of the immediate subject of some accident, it is necessary that all the immediate qualities inhering in that quantity be destroyed. But if you wish to say that not the whole preceding quantity is corrupted but something remains, now then that specially remains without any new part, or there is some new part which was not before. But that there may not be another new part of quantity which was not before, can not be said; since that part would not be retained in any subject, and it is manifest that it is not retained unless in some part of air or of fire; therefore, either it is then at the same time with that quantity which preceded in the same part, or that quantity recedes and no longer informs that part which it informed before; and yet it itself is not corrupted.

Since there may be no greater reason that one part of a preceding quantity is corrupted than another, it follows that that part of the quantity either remains without a subject or withdraws from that subject, in which it was before, to another; each one of these is unreasonable. Therefore, it remains that in rarefaction there is not some new part of a quantity but precisely that which was before; and yet notwithstanding this that a quantity the same numerically is at first smaller and afterwards larger; for parts of the same quantity were at first less separate in situation when the air was dense; but afterwards are more separate in situation when the air is rare. And so it is established that a thing numerically the same having parts distinct without any absolute new thing advening to it can be larger sometimes and sometimes smaller. And if this be possible of any quantity, there seems to be nothing inconsistent in conceding this of substance; for substance itself having parts sometimes becomes larger, sometimes becomes smaller, without any absolute thing advening to it.

But now Augustine calls everything 'accident' which can or can not be affirmed as true of a thing by virtue of a change in the object, and which can be affirmed as true of a thing according to the various modes. Whence, because the same substance can be larger and can be smaller, and can be great, which before was not great, and conversely; and this by virtue of a change of that substance. By virtue of this Augustine says that magnitudes are accidents in the second mode, not in the first; for the same proper substance through a proper change can be larger sometimes and sometimes can be smaller without any absolute thing really distinct added to it. Magnitude is not such an accident which may be an absolute thing really distinct from a substance inhering in it.

But, perhaps, you may say: how can a substance be changed unless some new thing be added to it? I say that this is the difference between substantial

THE SACRAMENT OF THE ALTAR 209

change, and change which is properly alteration, and local change; that through the first two some thing inhering in the changed advenes. But through a local change it is not necessary that a thing inhering in the changed may advene to the changed; but it suffices for it that a thing acquire for itself a place which it did not have before. Whence, from the very statement that a thing is in a place quiescent in which it was not before, but was in another without any other thing intermediate between the place and the thing placed; and there is that thing which is changed. And if you ask: what is it for a thing to be located in a place? It can easily be said that for a thing to be located in a place is for no corporeal thing to be intermediate between a thing placed and a place, so that, when the things themselves have not been changed locally from one place to another, there can not be local motion.

Therefore it is obvious from the previous statements how it can be safely held that magnitude is an accident according to the intention of the blessed Augustine, although magnitude may not be another thing really distinct from substance inhering in it. For as Augustine posits that accidents are in relation to "something," as "relationships, services, likenesses, equalities and anything else of the kind"; yet according to many Catholics relations of this kind are not certain things really distinct from absolutes. For as the venerable Anselm posits that many relations are accidents which however can advene to something without any change, and consequently are not distinct things inhering in it; thus also the same Anselm posits that some accident is suitable to God, and yet no thing really distinct from

God is retained in Him through real inherence or information.

Whence, in short, I have never read in any sacred writer, that he posits that quantity is an accident and is distinguished from substance any more than that he posits that 'ad aliquid' and 'relations' are accidents and distinct from substance. And, therefore, as according to many Catholics it is not inconsistent with the statements of the Saints to say that 'relation' is not a thing other than its fundament, so it is not inconsistent with the Catholic faith to say that some quantity is not another absolute thing really distinct from substance; and at the same time with this I say, that some quantity is another absolute thing really distinct from substance; for some quantity is really the same as quality which is really distinguished from substance.

Through the previous statements another opinion of the same blessed Augustine can be posited; for he does not intend to say that every magnitude may be a certain absolute thing inhering in substance and really distinct from it; but he intends to say that one thing is magnitude, another is that which is great by means of it in proportion to so much, for the thing itself can remain, although it may not be great; which can occur in a two-fold manner.

Whence, it may occur in one mode through condensation; for if a large thing be condensed, so that it become an object of small quantity, through this alone that the parts of the substance, which were locally much separated, become less separate in situation without any new thing having been generated and any old thing having been destroyed; then the thing is not great and yet the thing itself remains. And so it is

THE SACRAMENT OF THE ALTAR 211

one thing for a thing to be, and another for a thing to be great; for a thing can be although it may not be great.

This can happen in another way through the omnipotence of God, if He should bring it to pass; as many say, that it is impossible for God to bring it to pass, that a thing formerly great might afterwards come to be somewhere in that mode in which the body of Christ is under the species of bread; and yet would be nowhere locally or circumscriptively; for then, because the thing might not have parts separate in situation, it would not be great; and so it can be a thing, although it may not be great. And Saint Augustine intends this alone, and thus it is obvious that there is no statement of the blessed Augustine contrary to the previous statements.

In another way it can be declared that the blessed Augustine does not contradict the previous statements, for the blessed Augustine speaks of magnitude, which is a relation; for, as for instance, great is relative, a magnitude is relation. But now according to many Catholics it is not contrary to the statements of the Saints, that relation is not another thing really distinct from an absolute; therefore, it is not contrary to the Catholic faith to say that magnitude, of which Augustine speaks, is not a thing other than substance; yet with this it is established that the blessed Augustine says the truth when he says that magnitude is an accident, since it is accidentally predicated of a natural thing; therefore, the blessed Augustine can thus be explained.

In still another way it can be explained that through magnitude, by which created things are great, he does not understand one absolute accident inhering in created things; but through that magnitude he understands an efficient cause making these to be great, of which there is no doubt that there may be a thing other than created things, which are great by the participation of that magnitude, not indeed through information but through real dependence upon it; and that he may hold this opinion, his last words declare, which he adds there in the De Trinitate, V., Chapter X. Whence, he says that "that is true magnitude, by which not only great is a house which is great, and by which, whatever mountain is great, is great; but also by which great is whatever else is called great; as that magnitude may be one thing, another those which are called great from that magnitude; which magnitude certainly is primarily great and in a much more excellent way than those which are great by partaking of it. But since God is not great by this magnitude which is not Himself, so that God may be, as it were, a partaker of it, God is however great; otherwise that will be magnitude greater than God, but there is not anything greater than God; therefore, He is great by this magnitude by which He Himself is the same magnitude."

From these words it can be gathered that the blessed Augustine speaks of magnitude by which created things are causally great; for however he speaks of magnitude "by which great is whatever else is called great," whether it be a corporeal thing, or it be a spiritual thing. Whence, he speaks of the magnitude, as he premised before, by which a home is great, by which a mountain is great, by which a mind is great,

THE SACRAMENT OF THE ALTAR 213

which is a spiritual thing, although home and mountain may be corporeal things.

But it is manifest that there is no magnitude inhering in a substance as if in a subject, by which every other is great, which is called great, whether it be corporeal or it be spiritual. Therefore, he does not speak of magnitude which inheres in substance; but of magnitude which is the cause of all great things and by which "great is whatever is called great." For without it no thing great is by far great. However, because the blessed Augustine speaks of magnitude, which is "primarily great and in a much more excellent way than" another, magnitude of such a kind is not any accident inhering in a substance; for as nothing can be before substance, so nothing can naturally be great before substance. Then because he speaks of magnitude which is greater than that which is great when magnitude is not that which is great, it is established that no accident inhering in a substance can be more than the substance of which it is an accident.

Therefore, it is obvious that the blessed Augustine speaks of the magnitude which is the cause why other created things are great. Whence, the blessed Augustine wishes to show in the same place that God is neither causally nor in any mode great by some magnitude which is not God Himself. But creatures are great by some magnitude which makes them to be great; which magnitude is, however, not itself a created object, but "is primarily great and in a much more excellent way than those which are great by participation of that magnitude."

Whence, this term 'participation' is often accepted equivocally in various places by the philosophers as well as by the Saints; yet for the sake of brevity I pass by the discussion of that mode.

And so it is well known that the blessed Augustine can be explained in two modes; and all the passages of the Saints can be explained by the second of those modes, which passages appear to call out loudly, that quantity or magnitude is another thing really distinct from substance and quality; and the expositions can be proved through the processes of the same Saints in other places; yet for the present I refrain from discussing them. Nor is there any inconsistency in explaining the statements of the Saints, since all the writers later than they make this statement, although some may not have the intention of the Saints, and various writers may think differently of the intention of them, although neither may be considered heretical.

CHAPTER XXXV

How quantity is a category distinct from quality and substance; notwithstanding that no quantity may be distinct from part of a thing, from substance and quality. In which there is a reply to the sixth argument, showing that categories are signs predicable of things

This must also be considered: how quantity is a category distinct from quality and substance, notwithstanding that no quantity may be a thing really distinct from part of a thing, from substance and quality, which can be declared in a similar way according to the statements of many Catholic doctors; for, as has often been said, relation is a category distinct from other categories, and yet according to many of them relation is not another thing distinct from absolute things; therefore, quantity could be a distinct category, although no quantity may be another thing really distinct from quality and substance.

Again, it is not more inconsistent for categories to be distinguished, although distinct things may not correspond to them, than for species to be distinguished, which do not have distinct things content under themselves; but it sometimes happens that species are diverse, although the same thing may be arranged under those species. Which is proved by the testimony of John of Damascus, for he says: "Place is a surface of air"; from which it is obvious that the same thing is a place and a surface; (yet, notwithstanding this, the same Doctor posits with others that place and surface are distinct species of quantity), and also a continuous quantity and a discrete quantity are distinct species; yet no thing corresponds to a continuous quantity that may not correspond to the other; for nothing is continuous that may not constitute number with another, according to the intention of the present Doctor.

Again, the same thing is also placed in diverse categories according to the same Saint, as was asserted before; therefore, there is no inconsistency that quantity may be a category distinct from quality and substance, and yet that every quantity may be an absolute thing really not distinct from substance and quality. Whence, it must be known that there are no categories except certain predicables and signs of things, by virtue of which John of Damascus fittingly says: "It is necessary to know that there are in all ten categories; that is, very general genera under which every word simply stated belongs." Whence, the same Saint wishes, that every word, which can be called the extreme of a proposition or can be that through which an answer may be conveniently made to any question raised through any interrogation whatever, is placed under some category, and is placed under diverse categories through which an answer is made to such distinct questions raised through diverse interrogatives.

Whence, all words, through which an answer is conveniently made to the question raised concerning some substance per 'ubi,' are placed in the same genus, 'ubi'; and all words, through which an answer is conveniently made to the question raised per 'quando,' are arranged under the genus, 'quando'; and all words, through which an answer is made to the question raised per 'quale,' are in the category 'qualitas'; and all words through which an answer is made to the question raised per 'quantum' or per 'quot' or any such interrogative which is posited by the grammarians as an interrogative of quantity, are placed in the genus 'quantity as.'

And thus it is of other words placed in diverse categories, unless, per chance, such interrogatives may fail us, because we have a great dearth of terms. But not only nouns are placed in diverse categories, but even verbs and other parts of speech, and sometimes words composed of diverse parts of speech, as frequently words composed of diverse prepositions and their cases; by virtue of which the celebrated Doctor afterwards stated in his Logic in Chapter XXXII.: "That every word, namely, simple, belongs under those categories." He further explains, saying: "They are indeed these: 'substance' as stone; 'quantity' as two or three; 'relation' as father and son; 'quality' as white and black; 'place' as in Tyre in Damascus, but this is a manifestation of place; 'time' as yesterday, tomorrow, but this is a manifestation of time; 'possession' as to put on a garment; 'situation' as to sit or to stand; 'action' as to burn; 'passion' as to be burned." From this it is gathered that adverbs as 'yesterday,' 'tomorrow'; verbs as 'to burn,' 'to be burned'; composites of prepositions and their cases as 'in Tyre,' 'in Damascus,' are contained under one of those categories. And indeed there are no categories except certain predicables and signs of things and simple terms; from which are made combinations true and false; but simple terms of this kind can be distinct to such a degree that the predication of one of another is impossible; although no thing one through one is signified, but that the same thing may be signified by the rest; as no substantial or accidental thing is signified through this name 'angelus' but that it may be signified through this name 'angeli,' and conversely. Yet this is impossible, 'angelus is angeli,' and conversely; and indeed it is not inconsistent to posit that distinct predicables imply the same thing; notwithstanding, therefore, that substance, quality, and quantity may be distinct categories; yet every quantity could be a thing not really distinct from substance and quality. But it must be observed that such categories are not only signs fixed arbitrarily, of whatever kind the words are; but are also concepts or intentions of the mind which are signs naturally signifying things; and indeed as words can be distinguished, notwithstanding the identity of the things signified, so concepts or intentions of the mind can be distinguished, although they do not signify distinct things. And thus these names 'substance,' 'quality,' and 'quantity' may be distinct, although the things signified may not be distinct. Nor are names synonyms by virtue of this; for this name 'quantity' connotes or enables one to understand something; namely, part of a thing separate in situation from a part, which is connoted or is able to be understood neither through this name 'substance' nor through this name 'quality'; by virtue of which this could be true, 'substance as well as quality is'; notwithstanding that this may be false, 'quantity is.'

CHAPTER XXXVI

That the previous opinion ought not to be rejected as heretical, contrary to certain writers who condemn that opinion as heretical; and through this the seventh reason, adduced before in Chapter XXX, is explained

After the previous statements it remains to see and to show that it is not necessary to reject this opinion as heretical, although many modern Doctors writing of that may condemn and oppose it. First, because no doctor of much reputation condemns this opinion as heretical, although he may deny it as he may deny other opinions of theology and of philosophy, which he does not understand to be true. On the contrary, a certain Doctor intimates that that opinion is probable; namely, Scotus, in Book IV., Distinction XII., Question II., and he presents a mode of explaining many arguments which might be offered against it, as will appear later. Moreover, the same Doctor cites it, and disapproves of it, as of other opinions of Catholic theologians, which he believes are false.

Again, although he might oppose this opinion as heretical, as none of them does, it would not necessarily be settled by their judgment, since it may belong to the Roman Church alone to determine a question of faith, as Pope Innocent says in Causa XXIV., Quæstione I., Capitulo XII., 'Quotiens.' "As often," he says, "as a ground of faith is under discussion, I think that all our brothers and our fellow bishops ought to report only to Peter, that is, to the authority of his name and position, just as now your love prompted, that it may be able to be of profit to all the churches throughout the whole world." In the same place a gloss objecting states the opposite of this. The opposite of this seems to be in the margin of the De Hereticis, 'Ad abolendum': "For there it is intimated that those must be shunned as heretics, whom the bishops have declared are to be shunned." Whence, Pope Lucian says in the same place: "All who, concerning the sacrament of the body and the blood of our Lord Jesus Christ or concerning baptism or concerning the remission of sins through obligatory confession or concerning matrimony or the rest of the ecclesiastical sacraments, have not feared to teach or to think otherwise than the Sacrosanct Roman Church prescribes and observes, and in general whomsoever the same Roman Church, either each bishop individually throughout his diocese with a council of clergy, or the clerical bishops in a vacant See with a council of neighboring bishops, if it will have been necessary, have declared heretics, we condemn with a bond of perpetual anathema."

From these words it might be gathered that it pertains to the bishops and to the clergy in a vacant See to determine a question of faith. But the gloss previously cited replies to that when it states: "That that must be understood, when they decide any such question, which is certain to be heresy; but this when there is doubt." The argument for this is in the margin of the De Hereticis, 'Cum Christus,' in the gloss.

From which it can be concluded that with respect to heretics asserting something which is manifestly a heresy, the bishops can examine and condemn as heretics those who have confessed or have been convicted, who are then to be excommunicated by the authority of the Pope. But it is not allowed them to determine a question raised about some article concerning which there are opinions among the Catholic sages; where the gloss before says: "It is one thing to decide a question raised concerning the faith, which is the privilege of no one other than the Roman See, as is here said; it is another thing to discuss it without a defense, which the Patriarchs and Primates can do." And thus they reply to that decree of Pope Clement, who seems to intimate that it belongs to the bishops to decide a question of faith, in Distinction LXXX., 'In illis,' where he says as follows: "But in those states in which formerly their chief priests and also the chief doctors of the law were among the heathen, the blessed Peter advised that the primates of the bishops and also the patriarchs be appointed, who should consider the causes of the other bishops and the more important matters of the faith." According to this authority anyone might believe that it belongs to the bishops to decide a question of faith; which is not true. Whence, the gloss in the same place replies: "In faith, that is, faithfully," and that "a question of faith" must be referred to the Apostolic See, as Causa XVI., Question I., 'Frater noster' proves that; and for that reason it says: "But explain this, 'in faith, that is, faithfully'"; either they can discuss the causes of faith, but they can not proceed to a decision, or they can distinguish who are those who doubt; for if they are laymen, it appears that the bishops can decide according to the gloss in the margin of the De Hereticis, 'Ad abolendum'; and if the clergy, the Pope; in the margin of the same title, 'Cum Christus,' this gloss.

It is, therefore, obvious that, when there may be a controversy among theologians concerning some article as to whether it may agree or disagree with the Christian faith, it must be referred to the Supreme Pontiff. For when the office of inquisition of heretical perversity may be at any time entrusted to the unlearned or inferior teachers, it seems absurd that it belongs to such an inquisition to decide by proper authority any difficult and profound question concerning any articles whatever pertaining to theology, and to condemn as a heretic any one great and famous in theology and worthy because of his understanding of life as well as the office of a doctor of science, and approved by an established university, if he should contradict its opinion. Therefore, it appears that it must be referred to the Roman Pontiff, when a question is discussed concerning something which is not expressed in the canonical scriptures and is not determined through the Roman Church, which we also see is done in modern times.

Therefore, it must not stand upon the judgment of any modern writers who condemn the previous opinion, especially since many Catholic doctors, praiseworthy because of knowledge and of life, have held this opinion; and, as I have understood through a relation worthy of faith, a certain great Doctor, the Archbishop of Lyons, canonized by the Roman Church, held this opinion and left it in his writings; whose book containing the aforesaid opinion I have

THE SACRAMENT OF THE ALTAR 223

not, however, seen; but I hope to receive it in a brief time.

It is also much more permissible to deny the statements of those who mutually condemn one another and of whom some hold a doctrine suspected and condemned by the established universities than the statements of the Holy Fathers before they be approved by the Apostolic See, which however is permitted, than the statements of the Holy Fathers after they may be approved by the Apostolic See. How one may be obligated to hold with devout faith, Innocent says in the margin of the De Constitutionibus on that Chapter, 'Ne innitaris.' "Observe," he says, "that it is permitted to stand upon the statements of the Holy Fathers or of others acknowledged by the Church."

And he, who says that which they themselves say, can not be determinately contradicted, unless they have retracted the same, as Augustine has retracted many of his statements, or unless they be corrected by the Church. If indeed they among themselves have diverse opinions, as concerning the assumption of the body of the blessed Virgin Mary or concerning the condemnation of Salome, it is permitted to anyone to say what he pleases; if indeed no diversity is found among the Saints, it is necessary to observe even to the smallest iota that which they say, after their little works are authorized by the Holy Church. But formerly, before they were authorized, it was permitted to hold these opinions or not. Therefore, any one can not be contradicted, although he may deny the Doctors not authorized by the Roman Church. Whence, the presumption of some modern writers must be depreciated, who puffing themselves above themselves, desiring that they alone be called rabbi, inspired by envy, condemning every opinion dissenting from their teachings. Since they do not know how through reason to refute it as dangerous and heretical, they are incessantly rending it to pieces by their dog-like barkings, not considering that the most Holy Father and the illustrious Doctor, the blessed Augustine, wished thus to be devoted neither to his own writings nor to those of other bishops, but that some things in their writings might be able to be censured by a just judgment and with no rashness. Whence, Saint Augustine says as cited in Distinction IX., 'Noli.': "Do not," he says, "servilely regard my writings as though canonical scriptures."

Again, the same writer in the first book of the De Trinitate in the second Chapter: "I shall not be ashamed to ask," he says, "if in any place I am undecided; nor shall I be ashamed to learn, if in any place I am in error."

Again, in the same book in Chapter III.: "Indeed he, who," he says, "on reading these statements says: I understand whatever may be said, but it has not been truly said, asserts, as it pleases, his own opinion, and refutes mine, if he can. But if he would do this with charity and truth and would take care to make it known to me also, if I am still alive, I shall then have received the most abundant fruit of this my task. But if it would not be possible for me to know; willingly and gladly would I be that he should be responsible for informing them, as he will be able. I, however, meditate on the law of the Lord, if not day and night, at least during those moments of time I can," et cetera.

Again, the same author says, as cited in a letter to

THE SACRAMENT OF THE ALTAR 225

Vincent in the De Constitutionibus, Distinction IX., 'Negare': "I can not deny," he says, "nor ought I, as in the larger works themselves, so there are many statements in so many of my smaller works which can be censured with judgment and with no rashness." Again, the same author in Distinction IX., Chapter 'Ego solus': "I read others," he says, "so that no matter with how much sanctity or with whatever doctrine they may prevail, I may not indeed think a thing true because they themselves think so; but because they have been able to convince me through other authors or through the canonical or through probable reasons, that they do not swerve from the truth."

Again, the same author says of individual baptism, as cited in Distinction IX., 'Quis': "Who may not know," he says, "through the letters of the bishops which either were written after the canon was confirmed or will be written, and through, perhaps, the wiser language of any one more experienced in this thing, and through the weightier authority and more acute sagacity and through councils of some of the bishops, that it is permitted to censure anyone who, among them, perchance, is diverted from the truth."

Again, the same author in a letter to Vincent says, as cited in Distinction IX., 'Noli frater': "The writings of the Holy Bishops," he says, "are not thus read, as if testimony may be so cited from them, that it may not be permitted to think the opposite, where, perchance, they may thus have been understood other than the truth demands. We are indeed in this number, that we may not disdain even to take to ourselves the saying of the Apostle. And if you are wise in any other matter, this also God will reveal to you."

Again, in a letter to Fortunatus the same Augustine says, as cited in Distinction IX., 'Neque quorumlibet': "We ought," he says, "not to regard the discussions of each and every one, even though Catholics and noteworthy men, as we ought to hold the canonical scriptures, that it may not be allowed to us with the proper regard which is due those men, to reject and also to condemn anything in their writings, if we, perchance, might discover that they should think otherwise than the truth has it, as understood either by others or by us with divine help. Such as I am with respect to the writings of others, such I wish the judges of my own writings to be."

According to these authorities and very many others it evidently can be gathered that it is permitted to censure and also to condemn the writings of any one before they may be authorized by the Roman Church. And indeed although many may hold the opposite of the opinion proposed, it is not necessary to condemn this opinion, especially since it may thus concur with the statements of Saints and Doctors accepted by the Church. Yet I confess this, that if it could be able to be shown that it may be from the mind of any Doctor accepted by the Apostolic See, that quantity is another absolute thing really distinct from substance and quality, I am prepared to defend and to hold this, although I am unwilling by virtue of the dictum of any one of the plebs, to hold in check my intellect and to affirm something contrary to a dictate of reason, unless the Roman Church may teach that this view must be held; for the authority of the Roman Church is greater than the whole capacity of human genius.

CHAPTER XXXVII

That the previous opinion is not contrary to experience, and the eighth reason, cited before in Chapter XXX, is explained

From the previous arguments it can easily be seen that it is not contrary to experience to posit that quantity is not a thing other than substance and quality; for, when substance is divided without the loss of a part, it is not more necessary for quantity than for substance to be destroyed. For quantity, as substance, can be thus divided without the loss of part; for whenever wood is divided, it is not necessary for any absolute thing to be destroyed.

It is also possible that a substance, which at first is of a greater quantity, may become that of a smaller without the corruption of any absolute thing; which is obvious in the condensation of a thing. For when anything is condensed, it is inconsistent to posit that the whole preceding quantity may be corrupted; therefore, it is necessary that some preceding quantity may remain, or therefore, the whole remains without the newness of any part; and then a thing becomes a smaller quantity without the corruption of any absolute thing, and consequently by virtue of this it is not necessary for quantity to be distinguished from substance; or the preceding quantity remains so, however, that some part of the preceding quantity may be corrupted, which can not stand. Because if any part of a preceding quantity be corrupted, I take that part of a substance which was at first the primary subject of that quantity or of that part of the quantity; and I ask whether it now remains without quantity, which can not be granted; for then a substance or part of a substance, which was before a quantum, would naturally not become a quantum, if it itself remains, which is false and impossible; or it is the subject of some part of a quantity, and then even of a new part, which can not be granted; for there is no greater reason that one part of a condensed may take on a new quantity than another; and so it is necessary that either a whole substance according to any part of itself or according to nature take on a new quantity, or is the subject of some pre-existing thing, which can not obtain; for then some part of a quantity would pass from subject into subject, which is impossible through nature, although God could be able to do this; but God administers things that He may allow them to control their own proper movements.

Therefore, according to all the previous statements it remains that, when some thing is condensed and becomes a smaller quantity, no absolute thing is lost or corrupted; but the same thing, which was at first a greater quantity, is afterwards a smaller quantity without the entire corruption of an absolute thing through this, that parts of the same thing were before more separate in situation than now. And so it is evidently obvious that by virtue of such an experience it is not necessary to posit that quantity is an absolute thing other than quality and substance.

On the contrary, by virtue of experience it is necessary to posit that quantity is not another absolute thing bearing qualities and really distinct from substance, of whose substance some part or the whole

THE SACRAMENT OF THE ALTAR 229

may be destroyed, when some substance may be a quantity smaller than before. For it is obvious through experience that sometimes some thing becomes a less quantity, although no part of whiteness or of taste or of another like quality may be lost. If this is admitted, I ask whether or not each preceding part remains now as before. If you say that each part of the preceding quantity remains, it is necessary to concede that, when a thing becomes a smaller quantity, no part of the quantity is lost, which is the proposition.

But if you say that some part of the preceding quantity is lost or corrupted, and it is manifest that there is no greater reason that one part is corrupted than another; therefore, the whole is corrupted, which is inconsistent.

Similarly I ask whether the entire preceding quantity be corrupted or only a part. Since, at the destruction of a primary and immediate subject, there may follow a destruction of an accident existing in that, it follows that either the whole whiteness or a part of it is corrupted whenever any thing is condensed. And similarly it is necessary to concede this of taste and of any sensible quality, which is contrary to experience; and so it is contrary to experience to say that whenever any substance is condensed or becomes a smaller quantity, some absolute thing bearing qualities may be destroyed. And, indeed, it is in harmony with experience that, when any substance becomes a smaller quantity through condensation or through another mode without the loss of any part of a substance, no absolute thing bearing qualities is corrupted, neither as regards itself as a whole nor as regards its parts; as it is in agreement with experience that then many qualities neither as regards themselves as wholes nor as regards their parts are destroyed or lost. And indeed that substance does not become a smaller quantity through the destruction of any absolute accident, but through this, that parts of that substance are now less separate in situation than before; and in the same mode the parts of extended qualities in this substance are now less separate than before without the destruction or loss of any absolute accident at all.

And if you ask in what way substance is now a quantity smaller than before, if it has lost no thing, it must be said that this is by virtue of an active cause which, as it can move some thing locally, so it possible for parts reciprocally to approach which were before more separate. And, therefore, for this thing to be a smaller quantity now than before, is not other than for the parts of that thing to be less separate locally or in situation now than before.

Nor is any thing required for these except parts, which are separate, and an agent effectively causing them to be separate, together with a final cause. On the contrary, it appears wonderful that a single cheap created thing might be able to distend those parts of a substance; and yet the omnipotence of God might not be able to make the very same parts of a species to be separate, unless He should join one such thing distinct from them.

CHAPTER XXXVIII

How all lengths are of the same species,
and how some differ in species; and the
ninth reason, adduced in Chapter XXX,
is explained

After these statements it must be seen how all lengths are of the same species; and how some differ in species. Whence, it must be noticed that, as it was proved through John of Damascus, the same thing can be in diverse categories according to one or another intention. And consequently two things of the same category can be in diverse categories; for according to the aforesaid Doctor the same thing is in the genus 'substance' according to one intention, and is in the category 'quantity' according to another intention; and consequently when two such things are accepted, each of which is classified in the category 'substance' and in the category 'quantity' according to one or another intention; those things are of the same category, because each is in the category 'substance,' and yet they are in diverse categories according to the illustrious Doctor and Saint; so it is possible that some things may be contained under one species and under different species, by virtue of which those things, each of which is 'length,' can be contained under this species of quantity 'length'; and yet they could have been contained under different species of substance.

Nor is this a greater inconsistency than to concede that the same things, which are in one category, are at the same time contained with this under diverse categories. Therefore, it must be conceded that length of air and length of water are of the same species in the category 'quantity'; and yet they are of diverse species in the genus 'substance'; as many Catholics have posited, that diverse relations of the same species in the genus 'relation' are things really not distinct from the fundaments distinct in a species.

Whence, whiteness, heat, sweetness, blackness, and such qualities are distinguished in species; and yet all similitudes, which are not things outside the mind really distinct from those qualities, are contained under one species in the genus 'relation.' So it can be of lengths which are not things other than substance and quality; and yet they are contained under one species in the genus 'quantity.' However, it must be perceived that such distinct species not subordinately placed are never predicated of any thing or of a pronoun indicating that thing extra in quid et per se in the first mode. And through this many passages of the philosophers can be explained, which seem to be contrary to the previous statements, just as is shown elsewhere.

CHAPTER XXXIX

Concerning a diverse mode of predicating quantity according to diverse categories, explaining the tenth reason posited before in Chapter XXX

After these there must be a discussion of a diverse mode of predicating quantity according to diverse categories. Whence, this must be understood, although 'per se' be taken in diverse modes in different places by the philosophers. Whence Aristotle in one place holds that only the necessary are 'per se,' and in another place holds that wood is white 'per se,' although it may however be contingently white; yet one mode of acceptation suffices for the thesis. 'Per se' is taken in one way when the predicate does not connote or signify something, but that something similar may be connoted or may be allowed to be understood through a subject. And indeed when a subject is purely absolute and connotes nothing and does not enable one to understand something, and the predicate is connotative and enables one to understand something else, then such a proposition is not said to be 'per se.' And in thus accepting 'per se' always for this, that the proposition may be 'per se,' it is required that the proposition can not be false with the constancy of the subject; that is, if 'to be' is called 'to exist' in relation to a subject significatively assumed, as it is possible that this may be true, 'Sortes is,' though this appears false, 'Sortes is a man.' And, therefore, this consequence is good: 'Sortes is,' therefore, 'Sortes is a man.'

234 THE SACRAMENT OF THE ALTAR

And similarly it follows: 'man is,' therefore, 'man is an animal.'

And in accepting 'per se' thus, this is not 'per se,' 'quality is a quantum'; nor is that 'per se' 'substance is a quantum,' but that, 'quantity is a quantum' is 'per se.' And the reason for this is according to the philosopher; for this name 'quantum' connotes that part of a thing is outside of part. But nothing such connotes or enables one to understand this name 'quality,' nor this name 'substance'; but this name 'quantity' thus enables one to understand that part is separate from part, as this name 'quantum.' And by virtue of this, this is 'per se,' 'quantity is a quantum,' and no such is 'per se,' 'substance is a quantum,' 'quality is a quantum,' 'whiteness is a quantum,' 'man is a quantum.'

On the contrary, it is possible that this may be true, 'quality is,' while this appears false, 'quality is a quantum.' Similarly it is possible, that this may be true, 'man is,' while this appears false, 'man is a quantum.' For if the omnipotence of God could preserve the substance of man present in the same mode in the species of bread in which He may preserve the body of Christ present in the subject of the bread, and yet that substance would be nowhere locally and circumscriptively and at the same time with this could destroy every absolute accident existing in man; then this would be true, 'man is,' and this would be false, 'man is a quantum.' And in the same mode the omnipotence of God would preserve any substance and any quantity, no matter how much any such might be false: this, 'substance is a quantum'; this, 'quality is a quantum.' And to that extent do the philosophers and the Saints say

THE SACRAMENT OF THE ALTAR 235

that 'substance is a quantum through accident'; and similarly, 'quality is a quantum through accident'; but this is 'per se,' 'quantity is a quantum'; and likewise this, 'length is a quantum'; and so of others. For it is impossible that this be true, 'length is,' while this appears false, 'length is a quantum'; and similarly of others. For it is impossible that this may be true, 'length is,' while this appears false, 'length is a quantum'; and similarly of others. It is impossible that this may be true, 'quantity is,' while this appears false, 'quantity is a quantum.' But it does not follow from this, therefore, that quantity is an absolute thing other than substance and quality; but it is shown that this is possible, 'quantity is not the same absolute thing as substance and quality,' which I concede to be possible. And supposing that substance as well as quality be in the nature of things; as no matter how much this may be in a way true, 'a thing having part separate from part is as much substance as quality'; yet this is possible, 'no thing having part separate from part is substance or quality.' And if it be said that these are really distinct, one of which can be without the other; but it is possible that substance may be, though quantity does not exist; there substance and quality are really distinct.

I say that there is a fallacy of a figure of speech in any such mode of arguing; for this reason, that the purely absolute is changed into the connotative; as this, 'those are really distinct, one of which can be, while the other does not exist.' 'Man' can be, though 'musician' does not exist; therefore, 'man' and 'musician' are really distinct. And similarly this, 'those are really distinct one of which can be without another.'

But 'God' can be, though 'making happy' does not exist. Because these obtain at the same time; for 'God is,' and yet 'making happy is not'; therefore, 'God' and 'making happy' are really distinct. But in what mode there is a fallacy of a figure of speech in such a mode of arguing pertains to logic; and I have spoken elsewhere of this; therefore, I now pass on for the sake of brevity.

CHAPTER XL

In what manner diverse quantities can be subjectively in a substance, since two bodies may not be able to be naturally at the same time; and the last reason is explained

Moreover, in what manner diverse quantities can be subjectively in a substance, since two natural bodies can not be at the same time, must now be considered. Whence, it must be observed that body is accepted in a two-fold sense. In one way as an individual existing per se in the genus 'substance,' which was not created to be part of another existing per se in a genus; or more universally for all that which can exist naturally per se without this, that it may be part of another or depending on another, which however is composed of parts created to be separate in situation; and it is impossible through nature for two such bodies to be together. But all authors, who posit that two bodies can not be at the same time, speak of such a body; and the previously mentioned gloss speaks of such a body when it says in speaking naturally that body only has weight; but such a body is not primary matter nor substantial form nor any quality.

But in another sense body is taken for all that which is long, wide, and thick through parts intrinsic to it; and thus body is rarely or never accepted. If it be, however, thus accepted, it is not impossible for two such bodies, of which one was created to be the form of the other, to be at the same time; nor is it impossible for many others, which have been created to inform one subject, to be at the same time. And indeed it is not impossible for more such lengths and more solidities to be at the same time; for it is however impossible through nature for more solidities, which can naturally exist, to be at the same time, although they may not be parts of something nor in others as in subjects. Solidities of such a kind are not qualities; for no quality can exist per se by created virtue although it can by divine virtue. If you say that two bodies can not be at the same time, this is by virtue of the repugnance of those dimensions; therefore, no dimensions can be at the same time.

It must be said that not any dimensions resist being at the same time; but only the dimensions which can naturally subsist per se. And such alone can not naturally exist at the same time; but they mutually expel each other from a place, if they be left to themselves, although some dimensions can be at the same time through divine power. But it is not impossible for the remaining dimensions, which were created to inform another and one of which can inform another, to be at the same time.

Nor have I ever read the opposite in sacred scripture. And if you ask in what manner these dimensions more than others resist that they may not be at the same time through nature, it suffices for me at present to reply; because there is no such distinction of thing, which is plain to me, partly through reason, partly through experience. For it is easily established through reason that substance and quality created to inform it do not have any intermediate and distinct thing bearing quality.

THE SACRAMENT OF THE ALTAR 239

From which it is obvious that for this, that substance as well as quality may be extended, it suffices that it have distinct parts really distant created to be separate in situation with an active cause which can effectively produce those parts in distinct places, and thus cause them to be separate locally and preserve the same in the same condition. From this it is necessary to confirm, that the parts of the substance are naturally produced in distinct places by an agent before they may be informed under some absolute accident. It is also obvious through experience, that substance and quality are at the same time in situation; and it is similarly established through experience that, when one body exists per se naturally and enters into some place, some body very similar to it withdraws.

And if you say that it is obvious through similar experience that a body subsisting per se in the accidents in the sacrament of the altar withdraws, it can be said that this is either because a preexisting quality was not created to inform a subject in which it never was produced, or because that body has very similar qualities, or because this is by the will of God, willing that something contrary to the common course of nature may evidently appear to the sense; and this that we may be entitled to merit; for faith does not have merit for him for whom human reason provides experiment.

Whence, many Catholics posit there that many things are done by God alone, that the merit of faith may not be made of no avail, as reduction of substance, creation of a new quantity, and any other of the kind. And concerning this, see Scotus in Book IV., Distinction XII., Questions IV. and VI. And indeed it can be said with equal facility of all these that God has ordained that all things apparent to the sense, which are done about the host when not consecrated, may also be done about the host when consecrated. And indeed those, which can not be done by created virtue, He has arranged to do immediately through Himself.

From the previous statements it can be concluded how those accidents remain at the same time, although they may not be in some one subjectively nor one be the subject of another; for whether this may be able or not to be done by created virtue, there ought not to be doubt but that it can be done by divine virtue.

And in the same way whether that heaviness remaining in the sacrament of the altar can or can not move with itself other qualities with which it is joined, by created virtue, there is no doubt but that this may be able to be done by divine virtue. And, therefore, as certain say that, when the host is moved, the body of Christ is moved at the same time by God alone, so that created virtue can not move the body of Christ, no matter how much the host may be moved. So it can easily be said that, when heaviness is moved, other qualities are moved either by created virtue or by divine virtue. Thus also we can save all transmutations, which we see are made about the qualities remaining in the sacrament of the altar, that those, which can not be made by created virtue, can be done by the virtue of God, as many writers posit about many things.

And so all, which are apparent to the sense, can be equally saved by positing with the approved ancient Doctors, that taste, weight, color, and the other qualities of this kind, in the sacrament of the altar are subsisting per se without a subject; as by positing that all qualities are in a subject and not subsisting per se, although in following the ancient writers it may be reasonable to posit that many changes are done there by the divine virtue, which are posited by others to be accomplished by created virtue. Nor do I believe that anyone ought to be condemned because he attributes to God that which can not be ascribed to a creature.

CHAPTER XLI

Concerning the explanation of certain arguments contrary to the previous statement

Contrary to the previous opinion, certain reasons are adduced which, as I have understood them, I now wish to review and refute; others I intend to review and answer more clearly and more fully if they become more fully known to me. But as yet certain writers argue thus: if some substance and some quantity are really the same; then, wherever that substance is, there that quantity will be. Therefore, since the substance of the body of Christ may be in the sacrament of the altar, it follows that the quantity of the body of Christ will be in the sacrament of the altar. Whence, it is thus argued, as I have understood: whenever some are really the same, wherever one of them is, the remainder will be in the same place. But according to the previous opinion the substance of the body of Christ and the quantity of the body of Christ are really the same; therefore, where one is, the rest is; and consequently, as the substance of the body of Christ is in the sacrament of the altar, so the quantity of the body of Christ would be in the sacrament of the altar.

Again, it is argued thus: whenever some are really the same; wherever any one of them is, the remainder of them is in the same place; but the substance of the body of Christ and the quantity of the body of Christ are really the same according to the previous opinions.

But the substance of the body of Christ is in the sacrament of the altar; and, therefore, a quantity is a quantum there by the power of conversion, et ultra; therefore, the substance of the body of Christ is a quantity in the sacrament of the altar, et ultra; therefore, the substance of the body of Christ is a quantum in the sacrament of the altar by the power of conversion, et ultra; therefore, the substance of the body of Christ in the sacrament of the altar is 'having part outside of part and part separate from part,' which is heretical.

As regards the first of these, I concede the last conclusion by which it is deduced; namely, that the quantity of the body of Christ is in the sacrament of the altar.

As regards the second it can be stated variously without prejudice. In one mode, that the proposition assumed, namely, this, whenever some, et cetera, are understood of creatures of which are substance, quantity and quality, is false according to the virtue of language by virtue of a false implication. For it implies that some may be some, and yet that they may really be the same, which is impossible; for some creatures are really never some and one; because of this itself, that there are some, there are many; and if there be many, they are not really the same. Yet of divine persons these must be conceded; that there are more persons and yet that they may be one simple thing. But this can not be conceded of creatures.

I say that, if that proposition is conceded under a good meaning, it becomes in another manner a fallacy of a figure of speech in the form of arguing; from this which is accepted under 'one connotative term,' namely,

244   THE SACRAMENT OF THE ALTAR

'quantity.' Whence, as it does not follow, whenever some are really the same, wherever there is any one of them, the rest of the others is also in the same place. But the 'body of Christ' and 'the body of Christ having part outside of part or part separate from part' are really the same; for 'the body of Christ' is really 'having part separate from part,' and some substance is in the sacrament of the altar the body of Christ; therefore some substance in the sacrament of the altar is the body of Christ 'having part separate from part'; or it may be taken in a narrower sense, thus: 'the body of Christ' and 'existing circumscriptively in a place' are really the same. And it does not similarly follow: whenever some are really the same, wherever there is any one of them, the rest of them is in the same place. 'The body of Christ' in the host and 'existing circumscriptively in a place' are really the same; and some substance in the sacrament of the altar is the body of Christ; therefore, some substance in the sacrament of the altar is 'existing circumscriptively in a place.'

So also it does not follow: whenever some are really the same; wherever there is any one of them, the rest of them is in the same place. But the substance of the body of Christ and some quantity are really the same, and some substance in the sacrament of the altar is the substance of the body of Christ; therefore, some substance in the sacrament of the altar is a quantity. Whence, I say that, although this may be true, 'the quantity of the body of Christ is in the sacrament of the altar'; this is however false, 'the substance of the body of Christ in the sacrament of the altar is a quantity'; as, although this may be true, 'the body of Christ having part separate from part is in

THE SACRAMENT OF THE ALTAR 245

the sacrament of the altar'; yet this is false, 'the body of Christ in the sacrament of the altar is having part separate from part.' Similarly, this is true, 'some substance circumscribed in a place is in the sacrament of the altar'; yet this is false, 'some substance in the sacrament of the altar is circumscribed in a place.' But perhaps you will say that this response is not so valid; for it is not however similar in arguing of abstracts as of concretes. But 'quantity' is a certain abstract having being circumscribed in a place and of this kind are concretes. And, therefore, although such a mode of arguing is not valid in accepting under concretes, yet it is valid in accepting under abstracts; for such however are false, 'the body of Christ' and 'the body of Christ having part separate from part' are really the same. Similarly, the 'body of Christ' and 'circumscribed in a place' are really the same.

But the first of those does not oppose; for the cause, why there is a fallacy of a figure of speech in such a mode of reasoning, is not because it is accepted under the name 'concrete,' but because it is accepted under a 'connotative term.' But now 'quantity' is a 'connotative term,' as 'having' or 'quantum' or any such; and indeed such a mode of arguing fails in accepting under 'quantity,' as in accepting under 'having part distant' et cetera, or 'circumscribed in a place,' or another such concrete.

Whence, neither among the philosophers nor among the Saints it is found that they have made so much distinction between many concretes and abstracts, as some modernists do. Whence, I have never found in any Saint or philosopher that they have made a distinction between 'quantity' and 'quantum,' but they indifferently posit 'quantity' for 'quantum,' and conversely; and sometimes the category, which they have distinguished from the other categories themselves, they have called 'quantum,' and sometimes 'quantity,' not distinguishing between these names.

Moreover, the second does not oppose; for it is manifest that this is true, 'the body of Christ' and 'the body of Christ having part separate from part' are really the same; and similarly is any other, and there is the same proof for all such.

But it is manifestly obvious that this may be true, 'the body of Christ' and 'the body of Christ circumscribed in a place' are really the same; for it follows that the body of Christ is circumscribed in a place; therefore, 'the body of Christ' is really similar to 'some thing which is circumscribed in a place,' et ultra. Therefore, 'something which is really circumscribed in a place,' is really the same as 'the body of Christ,' et ultra; because these are convertible: 'circumscribed in a place' and 'that which is circumscribed in a place'; and it follows that 'something circumscribed in a place' is really the same as 'the body of Christ'; therefore, 'circumscribed in a place' and 'the body of Christ' are really the same. Thus any such proposition can be proved; whence, all such are true, although one term signifies another which is not signified through the rest. Notwithstanding this, however one of those terms can truly be predicated of something with some determination of a 'verb,' of which the rest however is not predicated with the same determination. As this is true, 'risible' and 'man' are really the same; and yet this is true, 'Sortes is a man' per se in the first mode; and this is false, 'Sortes is risible' per se in the first mode. Similarly, this is true, 'man' and 'Son of God' are really the same; for this 'man' in designating the Son of God and 'Son of God' are really the same; and this also is true, 'He was always the Son of God,' and this is false, 'He was always man.'

So is it in the thesis; because this is true, 'some substance of the body of Christ' and 'some quantity' are really the same; and yet this is true, 'this substance is the substance of the body of Christ in the sacrament of the altar'; and this is false, 'this substance is a quantity in the sacrament of the altar.' And as this is false, 'the substance of the body of Christ is a quantity in the sacrament of the altar'; so this is false, 'the substance of the body of Christ is a quantum in the sacrament of the altar by the power of conversion.' And indeed this is false, 'the substance of the body of Christ has part separate from part in the sacrament of the altar'; and so it is obvious that that argument is not valid; as it does not follow, when some are really the same, that wherever any one of them is, the rest of them will be in the same place. 'Some quantum' and 'the body of Christ' are really the same, and the substance of the body of Christ is the body of Christ in the sacrament of the altar; therefore, there is a quantum in the sacrament of the altar. And if you say that arguing in concrete and abstract terms is not similar, I reply that 'quantum' is not more concrete than 'quantity' when for signification; although it may not terminate in 'tas,' as this name 'quantitas,' may terminate in 'tas.' And so the mode of arguing fails in accepting under this name 'quantitas,' as in accepting under this name 'quantum.' And so it is obvious that this does not include a sophism contrary to the previous opinion, although it may fail in the presence of a fallacy of a figure of speech.

But if certain propositions are accepted as true, a conclusion can evidently be deduced contrary to this opinion. Whence, in accepting this proposition, 'when some thing informing another is created to designate this'; wherever that thing has that which is created to designate this, there is such; as wherever something has whiteness, everything there is white; and wherever something informatively has heat, everything there is warm. Therefore, if quantity be another thing distinct from the body of Christ, wherever the substance of the body of Christ has that quantity, there truly is a quantum. But the body of Christ in the sacrament of the altar has quantity, for it is not separated there from quantity; therefore, the body of Christ is really a quantum in the sacrament of the altar, et ultra; therefore, the body of Christ has part separate from part in the sacrament of the altar, which is heretical. If you say that the body of Christ is a quantum there, it is not however there in a quantitative mode.

Then I argue against those writers by preserving their mode of speaking; for I ask about this quantitative mode, whether or not it is a thing distinct from quantity. It can not be said that it is not a thing other than quantity; for the principle of them is that, if one remains and not the rest, they are distinct things; but quantity remains and a quantitative mode does not remain; therefore, they are distinct things. But, that they may not be distinct things, can be proved; for, if they be distinct things, either one is an absolute thing

THE SACRAMENT OF THE ALTAR 249

or the other respective. It is not absolute; for then there would be a quality or a quantity or a substance, any one of which is false; nor is it a relative thing, for neither fundament nor terminus can be assigned to itself; nor can it be classified in any of the others, that is, genera, because not in 'time' nor in 'action' and in 'passion,' nor in the genus 'relation,' nor in 'position,' nor in 'possession,' nor in 'place'; from which it might the more appear that that quantitative mode can be without any 'ubi.' For if God could create some quantum without any other thing, it would truly be a quantitative mode and yet without any 'ubi.'

Besides, it was shown before, that every continuous and permanent quantum has part separate from part, as was obvious before through John of Damascus, or at least these are convertibles: 'quantum continuous and permanent,' and 'having part separate from part.'

From which I argue thus: it is impossible that something may be a 'quantum continuous and permanent' unless it have part separate from part, and conversely; therefore, wherever something is 'a quantum, continuous and permanent,' there it has part separate from part. Therefore, if the body of Christ be a quantum in the sacrament of the altar, the body of Christ will be 'having part separate from part in the sacrament of the altar.' Besides, if the body of Christ be a quantum in the sacrament of the altar, it is, therefore, long, wide and thick; but it is impossible that something may anywhere be long unless it be extended there; and it can not be extended anywhere unless it have there part separate from part. Therefore, if the body of Christ be a quantum in the sacrament of the altar, it will have there part separate from part.

250 THE SACRAMENT OF THE ALTAR

And if you may say that the body of Christ is not a quantum there; on the contrary, that the body of Christ has there quantity inhering in itself; it will, therefore, be a quantum there; as wherever there is something having whiteness inhering in itself, the white is there; therefore, it seems to detract from the reality of the sacrament of the Eucharist to say, that the body of Christ in the sacrament of the altar has one quantity or extension inhering in itself; for then it would be extended there and it would have part separate from part, which is false. And indeed no matter how much this might be conceded, 'the body of Christ is a quantity'; yet this ought to be utterly denied, 'the body of Christ is really a quantity in the sacrament of the altar'; just as this is true, 'the body of Christ is really having part separate from part'; yet this is simply false, 'the body of Christ in the sacrament of the altar is really having part separate from part.'

Therefore, the previous opinion stands on this, that there is no continuous and permanent quantity, unless parts may be placed outside of themselves, whether the parts may be separate in situation or those parts may be parts of a substance or may be parts of qualities. And indeed, as this is true, 'the body of Christ having parts separate in situation is in the sacrament of the altar'; and yet this is false, 'the body of Christ has parts separate in situation in the sacrament of the altar.' So, suppose that this could be conceded, 'a quantity, which is really the body of Christ, is in the sacrament of the altar'; yet this must be absolutely denied, 'the body of Christ is a quantity in the sacrament of the altar'; as this is true, 'some man, who is

THE SACRAMENT OF THE ALTAR 251

the Son of God, always was God'; yet this is simply false, 'the Son of God always was man.'

And so in such it is of much importance to posit something from a part of a subject and from a part of a predicate, which is especially true of connotative names. Such a name is 'quantity'; for this name 'quantity' signifies a thing by signifying that parts of that thing are separate in situation; by virtue of which this is true, 'the quantity of the body of Christ is in the sacrament of the altar'; yet this is simply false, 'the body of Christ is a quantity in the sacrament of the altar.'

It is ended; praise be to God.

COLOPHON

The famous tract concerning the body of Christ, and especially concerning the distinction of point, line, surface, body, quantity, quality, and substance, is ended; edited for all readers on the basis of the Oxonian lecture of the Venerable Inceptor, Master William of Ockham, of England, a most profound investigator of reality, a most learned Professor of Sacred Theology, of the order of Friars Minor; printed at Strassburg, A. D. MCCCCXCI; completed after the Feast of the Epiphany of the Lord.

BIBLIOGRAPHY

ABELARD—Hist. Calamitatum Suarum; Paris, 1616.
ÆGIDIUS, ROMANUS AUGUS.—Quotlibeta; apud Bonetum Locutellum; Venice, 1504. With it the Theoremata eiusdem de sacramento corporis Christi, 1504.
ALEXANDER (NATALIS)—Historia Eccl., VIII; Paris, 1672-86.
ALLIBONE, S. A.—A Critical Dictionary of Eng. Lit. and Br. and Am. Authors; 1854-71.
ALLEN, THOMAS—A History of the County of Surrey, Vol. II., Ockham, 149-151; J. T. Hinton, London, 1831.
ALMAIN, JACQUES—Expositio de suprema Potestate Ecclesiastica et Laica, Monarchia S. Romani Imperii, 1515.
——Libellus de Auctoritate Ecclesiae; Paris, 1526.
——Expositio: circa decisiones quaestionum M. G. Ockam, super postestate summi pontificis; Paris, 1537.
ALVERNUS, GUILIELMUS—Opera Omnia; Paris, 1674, Harvard Lib. (Phil., 1670-71).
AMERICAN CHURCH REVIEW—Vol. XXIV, 1872, pp. 284, 285; on Occam.
ANALECTA FRANCISCANA SIVE CHRONICA ALIAQUE VARIA DOCUMENTA AD HISTORIAM FRATRUM MINORUM SPECTANTIA—Vols. I-II; Ad Claras Aquas (Quaracchi), Vol. I, 1885; Vol. II, 1887.
ANSELM, ST.—Proslogium; Monologium, etc.; trans. by Norton Deane; Chicago, 1926.
AQUINAS, ST. T.—Summa Theol. IIItia, Pars. qu. LXXVIII, Art. 4, Note K; Bampton Lect., 1832.
——Summa Theologica, Part III, No. 3; trans. by the Fathers of the English Dominican Province; pp. 233-468; R. & T. Washburne, London, 1914.
ARISTOTELIAN SOCIETY—Proceedings of; New Series, Vol. XIV; Williams and Norgale, London, 1914.
ARISTOTLE—The Works of Aristotle; Vol. I; trans.; edited by W. D. Ross; Clarendon Press, Oxford, 1928.
——The Works of Aristotle, Metaphysica; 2nd ed.; trans. into English; The Clarendon Press, Oxford, 1928.
——The Works of Aristotle; De Caelo, De Generatione et Corruptione; trans. into English; The Clarendon Press, Oxford, 1922.
——Phisica; Opera Omnia; Basileæ, 1538.

BIBLIOGRAPHY 253

ASCENSIUS, JODOCUS B.—Dialogus magistri Guillermi de Ockham doctoris famosissimi, 1494.
ASSENMACHER, JOHANNES—Die Geschichte des Individuationsprinzips in Der Scholastik; pp. 76-81; Felix Meiner, Leipzig, 1926.
AVERRÖES—Aristotelis' Omnia Opera, 1573-75 (Univ. of Penna.).
AUGUSTINE, ST.—On the Trinity; Vol. VII; edited by T. and T. Clark, Edinburgh, 1873.
——On the Trinity; The Nicene and Post-Nicene Fathers; Vol. III; The Christian Literature Co., Buffalo, 1887.
BACH, JOSEPH—Die Dogmengeschichte des Mittelalters, II; Vienna, 1873-75.
BACON, R.—Opera Quaedam Hactenus Inedita; Vol. I; edited by J. S. Brewer; Longmans, London, 1858.
——Opera Hactenus Inedita Rogeri Baconi Fasc. VIII, IX. Questiones Supra Libros Quatuor Physicorum Aristotelis. Nunc Primum Edidit Ferdinand Delorme Collaborante Robert Steele; Oxonii, 1928.
BAEUMKER, CLEMENS UND HERTLING—Die Europäische Philosophie des Mittelalters; Berlin, 1909.
——Beiträge Zur Geschichte der Philosophie des Mittelalters; Band XXIII., Heft 3-4; pp. 138, 154-165; aschendorffsche Verlagsbuchhandlung, Münster, 1923.
BAIN—Occam's Razor; Oxford, Parker and Co., 1890.
BALDWIN, J. M.—Dictionary of Philosophy and Psychology; 1901.
BALE, JOHN—Acta Romanorum Pontificum; p. 356, 1559.
——Illustrium Maioris Britanniae Scriptorum, hoc est, Angliae, Cambriae ac Scotiae Summarium; Ipswich and Wesel, 1548.
BALTHASAR, KARL—Geschichte des Armutesstreites im Franziskanerorden bis zum Konzil von Vienne; aschendorffsche Verlagsbuchhandlung, Münster, I W., 1911.
BALUZE, STEPHANUS—Miscellanea; ed. J. D. Manse; 4 vols.; Lucca, 1761-64.
BAMPTON LECTURES—Lecture VIII, 1832.
BARACH, C. S.—Zur Geschichte des Nominalismus vor Roscellin; Vienna, 1866.
BARNCKE, F.—Die Deutchen Universitäten im Mittelalter; Leipzig, 1857.
BASCHAB, C. R.—A Manual of Neo-Scholastic Philos.; Herder & Co., St. Louis, 1924.
BASHALL, HENRY ST. JOHN—The Oak Hamlet; The Village of Ockham; Elliot Stock, London, 1900.
BAUCH, BRUNO—Neuere Philosophie bis Kant; Berlin and Leipzig, 1919.

BAUMANN, J. J.—Staatslehre des h. Thomas von Aquino; 1873.
BAUDRY, M. L.—Fragments Inconnus de G. D'Occam: Le Tractatus de Principiis Theologiae; Académie des Inscriptions et Belles-Lettres; pp. 46-55, Comptes Rendus des Séances de L'Année, Janvier-Mars; A. Picard, ed., Paris, 1927.
BAUR, F. C.—Drei Abhandlungen zur Geschichte der alten Philosophie und ihres Verhaltnisses zum Christenthum; hrsg. von Edward Zeller, Leipzig, 1876.
——Die Christliche Kirche des Mittelalters; Zweite Auflage; Fues's Verlag, Tubingen, 1869.
——Dogmengeschichte; II, pp. 233 ff.
——De Divisione philosophiae Beitrage Zur Geschichte der Philosophie des Mittelalters; Vols. I-IV, pt. 2-3.
BAUR, AUGUST—Martin Luther: Ein Lebensbild; VIII, p. 394; Tubingen, 1878.
BAUR, KARL—Luther und der Papst. In: Schriften des Vereins für Reformationsgeschichte; Vol. XXVII, pp. 231-273.
BEESON, C. H.—A Primer of Medieval Latin; Scott, Foresman and Co., New York, 1925.
BENTHEM, H. L.—Engländischer Kirch und Schülen-Staat; P. S. Saurmanns, Bremen, 1732.
BERGMANN, E.—Geschichte der deutschen Philosophie, Die deutsche Mystik; Vol. I; Ferdinand Hirt, Breslau, 1926.
BERNINO, DOMERICO—Historia di Tutte L'Heresie Descritta; Vols. I-III; Nella Stamperia Baglioni, Venezia, 1717.
BERTRANDY—Recherches historiques sur l'origine, l'élection et le couronnement du pope Jean XXII; Paris, 1854.
BETT, H.—Johannes Scotus Erigena; pp. 8-10; Cambridge, 1925.
BIBLIOGRAPHY OF SCHOLASTIC PHILOSOPHY—Archiv. f. Gesch. der Phil.; Vol. X, p. 127 ff., and 247 ff. La Revue Néo-Scholastique; Mai 1902. Revue d'histoire et de littérature religieuses; Sept.-Oct., 1902.
BIEL, G.—Epitoma et Collectorium, circa quattuor Sent. libros; lib. III. Commentarius in tertium librum sententiarum; cum suo indice; Bonzolam, Brixiae, 1574.
——Expositio Missae, Lectio XL A. (Harvard).
——Sermones Gabrielis Biel.; Haguenaw Henry Grau, 1510.
——Gariel Biel super secundo sententiarum; Buxheim, Cartusiae.
BIRCH, A. H.—A Comparison of the Styles of Gaudentius of Brescia; The De Sacramentis, and The Didascalia Apostolorum; Yendall and Co., Risca, Mon., 1924.
BLANC, E.—Traité De Philosophie Scolastique; Tome I, pp. 350-364, 477; II, p. 151; III, pp. 30-32; Librairie Catholique Emmanuel Vitte, Paris, 1909.

BIBLIOGRAPHY 255

BLOUNT, T.—Glossographia, or a Dictionary Interpreting the Hard Words; 3rd ed., London, 1670.
BLUNT, J. H.—Dictionary of Doctrinal and Historical Theology; Edinburgh, 1870.
——The Sacrament of Sacramental Ordinance of the Church; London, 1864.
BLUNTSCHLI—Geschichte des Allgemeinen Straatsrechts und der Politik; 1864.
BÖHMER, H.—Luther in the Light of Recent Research; trans. by Carl F. Huth, Jr.; The Christian Herald, New York, 1916.
——Luther im Lichte der neueren Forschung; 5 Auflage, 1918.
BÖHMER, J. F.—Regesta Imperii: Die Urkunden Kaiser Ludwigs des Baiern, et al Frankfurt am Main, 1839.
BONIFACE VIII—Sextus Liber Decretalium (with glosses); T. Kerver for J. Cabiller & J. Petit, Paris, 1505.
——Sexti Decretalium Compilatio per Bonifacium (with glosses): Lugduni, Fr. Fradin, 1513. Clementinis argumentum Sequentia dare scio. Capita sex supra centum. Leges absque proemio (with glosses). Extravagantes XX. Joannis vigesimisecundi (with glosses).
BONAVENTURA—Opera; Venice, 1756.
BOWEN, F.—The Metaphysics of Sir William Hamilton; John Allyn, Boston, 1887.
BOWER, A.—The History of the Popes; Vol. III, pp. 77-88; Griffith and Simon, Philadelphia, 1845.
BRAMPTON, C. K.—Gulielmi de Ockham Epistola ad Fratres Minores; Blackwell, Oxford, 1929.
——The De Imperatorum et Pontificum Potestate of William of Ockham; The Clarendon Press, Oxford, 1927.
BRANDT, GERARD—History of the Reformation in and about the Low Countries; London, 1720.
BRETT, G. S.—A Hist. of Psychology; Vol. II; Macmillan, New York, 1921.
BREWER, E. C.—The Political, Social and Literary History of France; London, 1863.
——Great Central Points of Mediaeval History; London, 1870.
BREWER, J. S.—Monumenta Franciscana; Longmans, London, 1858.
——Church History of Britain; 1841.
BRODRICK, G. C.—Memorials of Merton College; Oxford, 1885.
——A History of the University of Oxford; London, 1891.

BRUCKER, J. J.—Historia Critica Philosophiae; Vol. III, pp. 846-7, 870, 901-4, 910-11; Vol. VI, pp. 605-08; Impensis Haered, Weidemanni et Reichii, Leipzig, 1742-67.

BUDAEIUS, GULIELMUS PARISIENSIS—Annotationes in Libros Pandectarum; apud Gryphium, Lyons, 1551.

BUDINSKY, ALEXANDER—Die Univ. Paris und Fremde an derselben im Mittelalter; Berlin, 1876.

BULAEUS—Historia Univ. Parisiensis; Vol. IV; Paris, 1665-73.

BURKE, R. B.—The Opus Majus of Roger Bacon; Vol. I, II; trans. by R. B. Burke; Univ. of Penna. Press, Philadelphia, 1928.

BURNS, C. D.—William of Ockham on Continuity; Mind, pp. 506-512; Macmillan, Oct., 1916.

——Occam's Razor; Mind, p. 592; Macmillan, Oct., 1915.

——William of Ockham on Universals; Proceedings of the Aristotelian Society, New Series, Vol. XIV, pp. 76-99; Williams and Norgate, London, 1914.

BURROWS, MONTAGU—Collectanea; Oxford, 1890.

BUSSELL, F. W.—Religious Thought and Heresy in the Middle Ages; Robert Scott, London, 1918.

BZOVIUS, A.—Annales Ecclesiastici Defensio Ludovici IV Imp.; Ann. 1329.

Cambridge Hist. of Eng. Lit., Vol. II; 1908.

CAMDEN, WILLIAM—Britannia, p. 214; Geo. Bishop and J. Norton, London, 1607.

CANISIUS—Refutatio Trium Tractatum, Ingolstadt, by Paul Drew in Vereins für reformations-geschichte; Schriften, V., 1892-93.

CAPELLI, A.—Dizionario Di Abbreviature Latin ed. Italiane; ed. II; Ulrico Hoepli, Milan, Italy, 1912.

CARLYLE, R. W. AND A. J.—History of Mediaeval Politieal Theory in the West; Vols. I.-IV.; Blackwood, London, 1903-1915.

CATHOLIC ENCYCL.—Nominalism.

CAVE, GUILIELMUS—Scriptorum Ecclesiasticorum Historia Literaria, A Christi Nato, usque ad Seculum XIV, etc.; Vols. I, II; apud Gabrielem de Tournes et Filios, Geneva, 1720.

CEILLIER, D.—Hist. Générale des Auteurs sacrés et Eccles., Vol. IX; Vols. I-XXII; Paris, 1729-58.

CHEVALIER, U.—Répertoire Des Sources Historiques Du Moyen Âge, Bio-Bibliographie, Vol. II; Paris, 1907.

CLARK, H. W.—History of English Nonconformity, Vol. I, pp. 25, 39, 75; Chapman & Hall, 1911.

BIBLIOGRAPHY 257

CLARK, V. S.—Studies in the Latin of the Middle Ages and the Renaissance; Schoolmen, pp. 34, 35.
Codex Iuris Canoni Pii X Pontificis Maximi; Romae, 1907.
COFFEY, P.—Epistemology, Vol. I, pp. 284, 312-329; Longmans London, 1917.
COLLIER, J.—An Ecclesiastical History of Great Britain, Chiefly of England; Vol. I; London, 1708; new ed., in 9 vols.; London, 1845.
COPINGER, W. A.—Supplement to Hain's Repertorium Bibliographicum.
COTTON, C.—The Grey Friars of Canterbury; pp. 32-33; The Univ. Press, Manchester, 1924.
COUSIN, V.—Course of the History of Modern Philosophy; trans. by O. W. Wight; Vols. I, II; Vol. II, pp. 31, 37, 89, 296; D. Appleton & Co., New York, 1852.
——Manuel de l'histoire de la Philosophie; Vol. I; Paris, 1829.
CREIGHTON, M.—History of the Papacy during the Period of the Reformation; London, 1882.
CREVIER, J. B. L.—Histoire de l'Université de Paris; Paris, 1761.
CRUMP, C. G. AND J. E. F.—The Legacy of the Middle Ages; The Clarendon Press, Oxford, 1926.
CUDWORTH, R.—The True Intellectual System of the Universe; Richard Royston, London, 1678.
CUTTS, E. L.—Scenes and Characters of the Middle Ages; Virtue & Co., London, 1872.
CYPRIAN, A.—A Treatis Concerning the Trinity; The Anti-Nicene Fathers; Vol. V; The Christian Literature Co., Buffalo, 1886.
D'AILLY, P.—Quaestiones magistri Petri de Alliaco Cardinalis cameracensis super primum tertium et quartum sententiarum. Impressae arte et industria Iohannis barbier expressis honesti viri Iohannis petit. (Univ. of Penna.)
DAMASCUS, JOHN OF—Exposition of the Orthodox Faith; Nicene and Post-Nicene Fathers; Chas. Scribner's, New York, 1899.
——Dialectica (Logica?); Opera Omnia, Patrologiae Cursus Completus, Minge, Tom. XCIV, Paris, 1864.
——Opera; translated into Latin; Basileae, 1559.
DAY, E. H.—Saint Francis and The Grey Friars; A. R. Mowbray & Co., London, 1926.
D'AUBIGNE, J. H.—History of the Great Reformation in Europe; Edinburgh, 1853.
DEAN, AMOS—The History of Civilization; Albany, New York, 1868.

DEAN, D. J.—John Wycliffe, The Morning Star of the Reformation; London, 1882.
DEAN, SIDNEY N.—Proslogium; Monologium; an Appendix in Behalf of the Fool by Gaunilon and Cur Deus Homo; The Open Court Pub. Co., 1926.
DE BURY, RICHARD—Philobiblon; Föreningen för Bokhandtverk, Stockholm, 1922.
DE MARTIGNÉ—La scholastique et les traditions franciscaines; 1888.
DENIFLE, P. H. AND FRANZ EHRLE—Archiv. f. Litteratur u. Kirchengesch. d. Mittelalters; Weidmannische Buchhandlung, Berlin, 1885.
——Die Entstehung der Universitäten des Mittelalters bis 1400; Weidmannische Buchhandlung, Berlin, 1885.
DENIFLE ET CHATELAIN—Chartularium Universitätis Parisiensis; Parisiis. Ex Typis Fratrum Delalain Via a Solone Dicta; Vol. I, 1889; Vol. II, 1891; Vol. III, 1894.
——Die Schriften; 1876-80.
——Quellen zur Gelehrtengeschichte d. Predigerordens in 13 . . . Jahrh. Arch. f. Litt. u. Kirchengesch. d. Mittelalters, II, p. 165 ff.
DESLANDES, M.—Histoire Critique de la Philosophie; Vols. I-IV; Vol. III, pp. 318, 319; Amsterdam, 1756.
DEWULF, M.—History of Medieval Philosophy; trans. by E. C. Messinger; Vol. II; Longmans, New York, 1926.
——History of Medieval Philosophy; trans. by Coffey; pp. 171, 176-191, etc.; Longmans, London, 1909.
——Philosophy and Civilization in the Middle Ages; pp. 1, 3, 73, 110; Princeton Univ. Press, 1922.
——Scholasticism Old and New; trans. by Coffey; Longmans, London, 1910.
——Hist. de la phil. schol. dans les Pays-Bas; Louvain, 1895.
DIECKHOFF, A. W.—Die evangelische Abendmahlslehre in Reformationszeitalter geschichtlich dargestellt.; Bd. I, Göttingen, 1854.
——(Luther's) Lehre von der kirchlichen Gewalt; Berlin, 1865.
DIEFFENBACH, L.—Novum Glossarium Latino-Germanicum Mediae et Infimae Aetatis.
DIETRICH VON NIEM—De scismate; II; 3 ed.; Erler, 1890.
DITTRICH, OTTMAR—Geschichte der Ethik; Vol. III, Mittelalter bis zur Kirchenreformation; Felix Meiner, Leipzig, 1926.
DORÉE, LÉGENDE—Sommaire De l'Histoire des frères Mendicans de l'Ordre de S. Dominique et de S. François; Aux Dépens de La Compagnie, Amsterdam, 1734.

DORNER, D. A.—Das Verhältnis von Kirche und Staat nach Occam; in Th. St. K., 672 ff.; F. A. Perthes, Gotha, 1886.
DORNER, I. A.—History of the Development of the Doctrine of the Person of Christ; Div. II, Vol. I; T. Clark, Edinburgh, 1862.
——Theologische Studien und Kritiken; pp. 672-722; Gotha, 1885.
DOUCOEUR, P.—La théorie de la matière et de la forme chez Guill. Occam; Revue des sciences philosophiques et théologiques; pp. 21-51; Paris, 1921.
DOVE AND FRIEDBERG—Zeitschrift f. Kirchenrecht; Vol. VIII, 69-137.
DRANE, AGUSTA T.—Christian Schools and Scholars; G. E. Steckert & Co., 1910.
DRESSER, H. W.—A History of Ancient and Medieval Philosophy; Thomas Y. Crowell, New York, 1926.
DU BOULAY, C. E.—Historia Universitätis Parisiensis; Vols. I-IV; Paris, 1665-73.
DU CANGE, C.—Glossarium Manuale ad Scriptores Mediae et Infimae Latinitatis; 6 vols.; 1840.
DUGDALE, WM.—Monasticon Anglicanum; R. Harbin, London, 1718.
DUHEM, P.—Mediaeval Contributions to Modern Civilization; London, 1921.
DUNNING, W. A.—A History of Political Theories; Macmillan, New York, 1921.
DU PIN, L. E.—Nouvelle Bibliothèque des Auteurs Ecclésiastiques; Vols. I-XVI, 1693-1710; Vol. XI, pp. 65, 183; A. Pralard, Paris, 1700.
DURANDI PETRI LOMBARDI—Comment. Libri quatuor II, Dist. 3, qu. 7.
DURANDI A ST. PORTIANO—Sent. Theol. Petri Lombardi Comment.; Lib. quatuor I, dist. 19, qu. 5; Venetiis, 1517.
EBERT, F. A.—Allgemeine Geschichte der Literatur des Mittelalters im Abendlande; 2 Vols.; Leipzig, 1874-1887, 1889.
EDWARD, LEROY—The Philosophy of France; The Philosophical Review, May, 1907.
EGBERT, J. C.—Introduction to the Study of Latin Inscriptions; American Book Company, New York, 1896.
EHRLE, F.—Archiv. für Lit. und Kirchengesch. des Mittelalters; I, p. 509 ff.; 1885.
——Der Sentenzenkommentar Peter Von Candia; aschendorffsche Verlagsbuchhandlung, Münster, 1925.

EICKEN, H.—Geschichte der mittelalterlichen Weltanschanung; Stuttgart, 1888.
EISLER, R.—Philosophen-Lexikon; Berlin, 1912.
EICHBERG, WALDEMAR—Untersuchungen uber die Beziehungen der Erkenntnislehre Spinozas zur Scholastik mit besonderer Berücksichtigung der Schule Okkams; Robt. Noske, Borna-Leipzig, 1910.
EMERTON, EPHRAIM—The Defensor Pacis of Marsiglio of Padua; Harvard Theol. Studies, Harvard Univ. Press, 1920.
——Introduction to the Study of the Middle Ages; Ginn & Company, 1896.
ENDRES, J. R.—Geschichte der mittelalterlichen Philosophie; J. Kösel & F. Pusted, München, 1909.
ERDMANN, J. E.—Geschichte d. Philosophie; IV. Vols.; trans. by W. S. Hough; ed. 2nd; New York, 1891.
ERNST, J. E.—The Political Thought of Roger Williams; Univ. of Washington Publications, p. 40, Vol. VI, No. 1, March, 1927.
ERSH AND GRUBER—Dictionary, under Occam.
ENGLISH PRESBYTER—Papers on the Doctrine of the English Church Concerning the Eucharistic Presence; The Church of England Book Soc., London.
FALCKENBERG, RICHARD—History of Modern Philosophy; trans. by A. C. Armstrong, Jr.; Henry Holt & Co., 1897.
FAULKER, J. A.—Ockham, Journal Theol., 9; pp. 359-73; April, 1905.
FEBRE, LUCIEN—Martin Luther; Dutton & Co., 1929.
FEDERHOFER, FRANZ—Ein Beitrag zur Bibliographie und Biographie des Wilhelm von Ockham; Philosophisches Jahrbuch der Görres-Gesellschaft; 38, Band I, Heft, pp. 26-48; Verlag der Fuldaer Achendruckerei, Fulda, 1925.
FELDER, H.—Geschichte d. Wissenschaftl. Studien im Franziskanerorden bis um die Mitte d. 13 Jahrhunderts; Herdersche Verlagshandlung, Freiburg im Breisgau, 1904.
FERET, P.—La faculté de théologie de Paris et ses Docteurs les plus Célèbres; Moyen-Âge, Tome I, 1894; II, 1895; III, 1896; IV, 1897; Paris.
FERNOW, K. S.—Francesco Petrarca nebst dem Leben des Dichters, 1818.
FICKER, JULIUS—Urkunden zur Geschichte des Rœmerzuges Kaiser Ludwig des Baiern; Verlag der Wagner'schen Universitæts-Buchhandlung, Innsbruck, 1865.
FICKER AND HERMELINK—Das Mittelalter (Handbuch der Kirchengeschichte); Zweite Auflage, 1929.

FIFE, R. H.—Young Luther; Macmillan, New York, 1928.
FISCHER, KUNO—History of Modern Philosophy; trans. by J. P. Gordy; Scribners, 1887.
FISCHER, JOS.—Die Erkenntnislehre Anselms von Canterbury; aschendorffsche Verlagsbuchhandlung, Münster, 1911.
FLEMING, W.—The Vocabulary of Philosophy; from 2nd ed. by Chas. Krauth; Smith, English & Co., Philadelphia, 1860.
——The Vocabulary of Philosophy; 3rd ed., by Henry Calderwood; Chas. Griffin & Co., London, 1876.
FLEMING, C. T.—Martin Luther and the Real Presence; Crit. R., II, p. 249.
FLÜGEL, O.—Die Probleme der Philosophie und ihre Lösungen; p. 121; Cöthen, Otto Schulze, 1906.
FORCELLINI—Lexicon, Totius Latinitatis Onomasticon; 1859.
FORSTER, F.—Ueber die Staatslehre des Mittelalters. Allg. Monatsschrift für Wissenshaft und Literatur; 1853.
FOXE, JOHN—The Acts and Monuments; 4th ed., Vol. II, pp. 659, 661, 705-6, 710, 727, 791, 912; Vol. III, p. 189; Vol. IV, p. 260; Religious Tract Society, London, 1684.
——Eccl. Hist.; Vol. II; 1590.
FRANCK, A.—Guillaume Occam et Les Franciscains du XIV⁰ Siècle; Réformateurs et publicistes de l'Europe; Moyen Âge; essay on Ockham; pp. 153-200; Michel Levy, Paris, 1864.
FRIEDBERG, EMIL—Corpus Juris Canonici; 2 vols.; Leipzig, 1879-1881.
——Die mittelalterlichen Lehren über das Verhältnis von Staat und Kirche; 1874.
FULLER, THOM.—The History of the Worthies of English; Thom. Tegg, London, 1840.
GAIRDNER, JAMES—Roll Series, XI, No. Letters and Papers of the Reign of Henry VIII, 1355.
GERFEN, ERNEST—Baptizein and Eucharist; F. J. Heer & Co., Columbus, 1908.
GERSON, JOHANNES—Opera Omnia (Harvard).
GFRÖRER, A. F.—Allgemeine Kirchengeschichte; Stuttgart, 1844.
GIERKE, O.—Political Theories of the Middle Ages; trans. by F. W. Maitland; Cambridge Univ., 1900.
GILSON, E.—La Philosophie au Moyen Âge; pp. 139, 226, 243-303; Payot, Paris, 1925.
GIESELER, J. C. L.—Church History, Vol. III; trans. by J. W. Hull; Harper, New York, 1868.
GLASSBERGER, A.—Chronica, pp. 77, 140, 141, 169; in Analecta Franciscana, Vol. II.

BIBLIOGRAPHY

GOLDAST, MELCHIOR—Collectio constitutionum imperialium (Harvard).
——Politica imperialia.
——Monarchiae S. Romani Imperii; Vols. I, II, III; Francofurti, Zunnerum, 1668.
GOODE, W.—The Nature of Christ's Presence in the Eucharist; Vols. I, II; T. Hatchard, London, 1856.
GOTWALD, W. K.—Ecclesiastical Censure at the End of the 15th Century; The Johns Hopkins Press, Baltimore, 1927.
GRABMANN, MARTIN—Mittelalterliches Geistesleben, Abhandlungen zur Geschichte der Scholastik und Mystik; Max Hueber, München, 1926.
——Thomas Aquinas; His Personality and Thought; Longmans, New York, 1928.
——Geschichte der Philosophie; III, die Philosophie des Mittelalters; De Gruyter & Co., Berlin, 1921.
GRATIANUS, F.—Opus Decretorum; Lucas Antonius de Giunta Florentinus, Venetius impressit; 1514. (Glosses on the text.)
GRASSE, F.—Trésor de Livres rares; 1859-69.
GRAVES, F. P.—A Hist. of Education; Middle Ages; Macmillan, New York, 1914.
GUIZOT, F.—History of the Civilization in Europe; Hurst Co., New York.
HAGENBACH, K. R.—History of Doctrines; Vol. II; trans. by H. B. Smith; Sheldon & Co., New York, 1862.
HAIN—Repertorium Bibliographicum, sub Ockham (No. II, 936), etc.
HALLAM, HENRY—View of the State of Europe during the Middle Ages; Harper & Bros., New York, 1863.
HAMILTON, SIR WILLIAM—Lectures on Metaphysics and Logic; Gould & Lincoln, Boston, 1901.
HAMPDEN, R. D.—The Scholastic Philosophy; Lecture II, p. 74, ff.; Bampton Lectures, Oxford, 1833.
HANCOCK, DR.—The Propitiatory Oblation in the Holy Eucharist; London, 1710.
HARDWICK, C.—A History of the Christian Church, Middle Age; 4th ed.; Macmillan, London, 1874.
HARNACK, A.—Lehrbuch der Dogmengeschichte; Vol. VII, 1894; trans. by Neil Buchanan; Little, Brown & Co., Boston, 1905.
HARNACK, TH.—Luther's Theologie; 1901.
HARRINGTON, K. P.—Mediæval Latin; Allyn & Bacon, New York, 1925.

BIBLIOGRAPHY 263

HARRIS, C. R.—Duns Scotus; Vol. I, The Place of Duns Scotus in Mediæval Thought; Vol. II, The Philosophical Doctrines of Duns Scotus; Oxford, 1927.
HASKINS, C. H.—The Renaissance of the Twelfth Century; Cambridge, Harvard Univ. Press, 1927.
HAUCK, A.—Realencyklopädie für protestantsche Theologie u. Kirche, 3rd ed.
HAURÉAU, B.—Histoire de la Philosophie Scholastique; 2 vols.; Pagnerre, Paris, 1850.
HEFELE, K.—Konciliengeschichte; Vol. VI; 1867.
HENDERSON, B. W.—Merton College; F. E. Robinson, London, 1899.
HICKS, DR.—An Answer to Some Things Contained in Dr. Hicks' Christian Priesthood (Sacrament); Exchange-Ally, London, 1709.
HILARY OF POITIERS—Nicene and Post-Nicene Fathers; Second Series; Vol. IX; New York, 1879.
Historia Di Tutte L'Heresie Deseritta Da Domenico Bernino; Vol. III, pp. 413, 482-485, 498, 501 f., 506, 531 f.; Venezia, 1717.
HÖFER, P. J.—Biographische Studien über Wilhelm Von Ockham O.F.M.; Archivum Franciscanum Historicum; Vol. II, pp. 211-233; Vol. III, pp. 439-465; Vol. IV, pp. 654-669; Typ. Collegii S. Bonaventurae Ad Claras Aquas prope Florentiam (Quaracchi Presso Firinze), 1913.
HÖFLER, H.—Aus Avignon (Aus den Abhandlungen der k. böhm. Gesellsch. der Wissenschaften. VI, Series I, Band.); Druck von Dr. Eduard Grégr, Prag, 1868.
HOFFMAN, C.—Die Lehre der fides implicita; pp. 153 ff; Leipzig, 1903.
HOLBERG, L.—Storia Ecclesiastica; Allgemeine Kirchenhistorie, Vols. I, II; Vol. II, p. 260; in Verlag der Compagniebuchhandlung, Copenhagen und Leipzig, 1749.
HOLZAPFEL, HERIBERT—Handbuch der Geschichte des Franziskanerordens; Herderscher Verlag., Freiburg im Breisgau, 1909.
HOLZER—Mitt. d. Inst. f. öst. Geschichtsforschung; XV; 1521.
HORAWITZ, A.—Sitzungberichte der phil. hist. Klasse d. Kaiserl. Akademie d. Wissenschaften; LXX, 189 ff.; LXXI, 643 ff.; LXXII, 623; Briefwechsel d. Beatus Rhenanus; Leipzig, 1886.
HUBER, V. A.—Dié englischen Universitäten; Vol. I; Cassel, 1839.

BIBLIOGRAPHY

HUGO, DE S. VICTORE—De Sacramento Corporis et Sanguinis Christi; Patrologiae; Vol. CLXXVI, Pars, pp. 402-474; Minge, 1880.

——Speculum de Mysteriis Ecclesiae; Patrologiae; Vol. III, Chapter VII, pp. 355-374; Minge, 1879.

HUNZINGER, A. W.—Lutherstudien; Heft I; A. Deichert'sche Verlagsbuchhandlung Nachf; Leipzig, 1906.

HUSIK, ISAAC—A History of Mediaeval Jewish Philosophy; p. 200; Macmillan, 1916.

HUTTON, EDWARD—The Franciscans in England (1224-1538); Houghton Mifflin Co., New York, 1926.

IRENAEUS—Adv. Haer.; Anti-Nicene Fathers, Vol. I, Book III, Chap. III.

IORGA, N.—Essai De Synthèse De L'Histoire de L'Humanité; Vol. II; Histoire Du Moyen Âge; J. Gamber, Paris, 1927.

JAMES, WM.—Pragmatism; p. 53; pp. 88, 89; Longmans, Green & Co., New York, 1925.

JANET, PAUL—Histoire de la Science Politique; 3rd ed.; Paris, 1887.

JENKS, J. W.—Law and Politics in the Middle Ages; London, 1919.

JOANNIS, DEVOTUS—Institutionum Cononicarum; Liber IV, Vol. I; H. Dessain, Leodii, 1860.

JOURDAIN, C.—Histoire de l'Université de Paris; au XVII° et au XVII° siècle; Paris, 1874.

KAULICH, W.—Geschichte der scholastischen Philosophie; I. Theil, Prague, 1863.

KELLER, LUDWIG—Die Reformation u. d. Älteren Reformparteien; pp. 327, 388; Leipzig, 1885.

KEEVER, E. F.—Ockham, The Man Who Set Luther Thinking; The Lutheran Ch. Rev., Vol. XX, No. 1, Jan., 1901, pp. 49-63; No. 2, April, 1901, pp. 213-232; Vol. XXI, No. 2, April, 1902, pp. 213-232.

——Ockham's Razor; Luth. Ch. Rev., Jan. 1905.

KERN, R.—St. Paul's Conception of the Lord's Supper; p. 239; Luth. Quart., April, 1903.

——On Lord's Supper; trans. by W. A. Snyder; Luth. Quart., July, 1903.

KINGFORD, C. L., et al.—Collectanea Franciscana II; Univ. Press, Manchester, 1922.

KLUGE, F.—Etymologisches Wörterbuch der deutchen Sprache; Strassburg, 1894.

KNEER—Entstehung d. Konzil. Theorie in Röm. Quartalschr.; Supp. I, 56, 57; 1893.

BIBLIOGRAPHY 265

KOESTLIN—Life of Luther; trans.; 1893.
KÖHLER, H. O.—Realismus und Nominalismus; in ihrem Einfluss auf die dogmat. Systeme des Mittelalters; Gotha, 1858.
KROPATSCHECK, F.—Occam und Luther; Beiträge zur Förderung Christl. Theol., IV; 1900.
KROPATSCHECK, F.—Das Schriftprinzip der lutherischen Kirche; Vol. I, pp. 300, 306, 309-326; d. A. Deichertsche Verlag.; Leipzig, 1904.
KRUMBACHER, C.—Geschichte der byzantinischen Litteratur; Munich, 1897.
KUGLER, LOTHAR—Der Begriff der Erkenntnis bei Wilhelm von Ockham; Ein Beitrag zur Geschichte mittelalterlicher Nöetik; H. Fleishmann, Breslau, 1913.
KUHTMANN, ALFRED—Zur Geschichte des Terminismus; Wilhelm v. Occam; pp. 14-37; Quelle and Meyer; Leipzig, 1911.
KURTZ, J. H.—Church History; Vol. II; trans. by John Macpherson; Funk & Wagnalls, 1889.
LANFRANC, B.—De Corpore et Sanguine Domini; Patrologiae; Vol. CL, pp. 407-422; Minge, Paris, 1880.
LAURIE, S. S.—The Rise and Early Constitutions of Universities; D. Appleton & Co., New York, 1907.
LEA, H. C.—A History of the Inquisition of the Middle Ages, Vol. III, p. 134; New York, 1888.
LEACH, A. F.—The Schools of Medieval England; Methuen & Co., London, 1915.
LECHLER, PROF.—Johann Wiclif and His English Precursors; trans. by Prof. Lorimer; The Religious Tract Society, London, 1878.
LECKY, W. E.—Hist. of European Morals; 3rd ed.; Vol. I, p. 17; 1925.
LEE, S.—Dictionary of National Biography; 1885-1900.
LEGRAND—Dictionnaire; Tome VI; Paris, 1747.
LEIGHTON, J. A.—The Field of Philosophy; 2nd ed.; R. G. Adams & Co., Columbus, 1919.
LELAND, J.—Collectanea; Vols. I-VI; B. J. White, London, 1774.
——Commentarii de scriptoribus Britannicis; Oxford, 1709.
LELONG, P. J.—Bibliothèque de la France; I, 475; Paris ed., 1768-78.
LEROY, E.—The Philosophy of France; The Philosophical Rev., May, 1907.
LE ROUX DE LACY ET TISSERAND—Paris et ses Historiens, p. 5; Paris, 1867.
Lexicon Manuale ad Scriptores Mediae et Infimae Latinitatis; apud Garnier Fratres et J.-P. Migne, Paris, 1890.

266 BIBLIOGRAPHY

Liber Chronicarum; Nurembergae, Koberger, 1493.
LITTLE, A. G.—The Grey Friars in Oxford; pp. 224-234, etc.; Clarendon Press, Oxford, 1892.
——Grey Friars of London; Chronicle, edited by J. C. Nichols, XXXV.
LITTLE, A. G., et al.—Collectanea Franciscana; Alberdoniae, Typis Academicis, 1914.
——Studies in English Franciscan History; Univ. Press, Manchester, 1917.
——A Guide to Franciscan Studies; The Macmillan Co., New York, 1920.
LINDSAY, T. M.—A History of the Reformation; Scribner's Sons, New York, 1914.
——William of Occam and His Connection with the Reformation; British Quart. Rev.; Vol. LVI; July, 1872.
——Luther and the Reformation; Good Words, 24; p. 698.
——Luther and the German Reformation; Rev., The Nation, p. 71, p. 153; Aug. 23, 1900.
——Encycl. Britan.; under Occam.
LINDSAY, JAMES—The Logic and Metaphysics of Occam; pp. 521-547; The Monist; The Open Court, Vol. XXX, No. 4, Oct., 1920; Chicago.
——Albertus Magnus as a Philosopher; pp. 620-631; The Hibbert Journal, Vol. XVI, No. 4, July, 1918.
LOOFS, F.—Leitfaden zum Studium der Dogmengeschichte; Halle, 1906.
LOMBARD, PETER—Sententiarum; Lib. IV. Apud Audoenum Paruum, in via ad diuum Iacobum sub insigni Lilii aurei; Paris, 1543.
——Opera Omnia, Patrologiae Cursus Completus Tom. CXCII; J. P. Minge, Paris, 1880.
LORENZ, O.—Deutschlands Geschichtsquellen im Mittelalter von der Mitte des dreizehnten bis zur Mitte des vierzehnten Jahrhunderts; 3rd ed.; Hertz, Berlin, 1887.
LOWE, J. H.—Der Kampf zwischen Realismus und Nominalismus im Mittelalter; Prague, 1876.
LUTHER, MARTIN—The Sacraments; trans. from Walch ed.; Jos. Salyards, Newmarket, 1853.
——The Table-Talk; trans. by William Hazlett; Luth. Pub. Soc., Philadelphia.
——De Captivitate Babylonica Ecclesiae; Opera Latina; Vol. II, p. 263; Jena, 1581; trans. by Wace and Buchheim.
——Bekenntnis vom Abenmahl; Vol. XXX, p. 263; ed. Erlangen, 1841.

BIBLIOGRAPHY 267

LUTHER, MARTIN—Luther's Primary Works; Hodder & Stoughton, London, 1896.
MACKINNON, J.—Luther and the Reformation; Vol. I; Longmans, New York, 1925.
MACKINTOSH, SIR JAMES—History of Philosophy; 3 vols.; Longmans, 1846; The Miscellaneous Works; three volumes in one; A. Hart, Philadelphia, 1850.
MACLEAR, G. F.—Apostles of Mediæval Europe; Macmillan, New York, 1869.
MAITLAND, S. R.—The Dark Ages; London, 1844; 3rd ed.; London, 1889.
MANGAN, J. J.—Life, Character and Influence of Desiderius Erasmus of Rotterdam; Macmillan, New York, 1927.
MANHART, F. P.—The Lord's Supper; Holman Lecture; Luth. Quart., pp. 1-32; Gettysburg, Oct., 1897.
MANSEL, H.—Artis Logicae Rudimenta; Oxford, 1852.
MANSER, M.—Ueber Umfang u. Charakter der mittelalterlichen Scholastik; 1907.
MARCOUR—Antheil der Minoriten am Kampf zwischen Ludwig IV u. P. Johann XXII, b. z. j. 1328. Emmerich, 1874.
MARSILIUS OF PADUA—Defensor Pacis; edited by C. W. Previté Orton, M.A.; Cambridge Univ. Press, 1928.
MARTÈNE AND DURAND—Thesaurus Novus Anecdotorum; II, pp. 692, 719, 829; 1874.
MARTIGNÈ, DA—La Scholastica e le Tradizioni Francescane; Prem. Stab. Poligrafico F. Salvati, Foligno, 1890.
MARTIN, C. F.—The Record Interpretater, Abbreviations; 2nd ed.; Stevens & Sons, London, 1910.
MARVIN, W. T.—The History of European Philosophy; p. 265; Macmillan, 1917.
MAURICE, C. E.—Lives of English Popular Leaders in the Middle Ages; Franciscans; London, 1890.
MAURICE, F. D.—Moral and Metaphysical Philosophy; Vols. I and II; Vol. II, pp. 3-37, 115, 121, 131-133; Macmillan & Co., New York, 1890.
MCCLINTOCK AND STRONG—Encyclopedia of Biblical Theology and Ecc. Lit.; Vol. II; New York, 1883.
MCKEON, R.—Selections from Medieval Philosophers; Scribners, Vol. I, 1929; Vol. II, 1930.
MEGENBERG—Tractatus pro Romana Ecclesia et Pontifice Johanne XXII contra Wilhelmum Occam.
MELANCHTHON, P.—Historia de vita et actis Lutheri; Vitenberg, p. 5; 1549. (Univ. of Penna.)
Merton Muniments; The Clarendon Press, Oxford, 1928.

MICHALSKI, KONSTANTY—Les courants philosophiques à Oxford et à Paris pendant le XIV° siècle; pp. 59-88; Bulletin International de L'Académie Polonaise des Sciences et des Lettres; I. Partie; Cracovie, 1922.
MICHELET, M.—The Life of Martin Luther; trans. by G. H. Smith; D. Appleton & Co., New York, 1846.
MILL, J. S.—System of Logic; Harper & Bros., New York, 1858.
MILLMAN, H. H.—History of Latin Christianity; Vols. VII, VIII; J. Murray, New York, 1881.
MINERVA—Jahrbuch; under Occam.
MINGES, P. PARTHENIUS—Geschichte der Franziskaner in Bayern; Verlag der J. J. Lentner'schen Buchhandlung, München, 1896.
MORELL, J.—View of Philosophy in Europe; Pickering, 1846.
MUENSCHER, W.—Elements of Dogmatic History; trans. by Jas. Murdock, New Haven, 1830.
MÜLLER, KARL—Kirchengeschichte II.; Tubigen, 1911.
——Der Kampf Ludwigs des Baiern mit der römischen Curie, Vol. I-II; Verlag der H. Laupp'schen Buchhandlung, Tubigen, 1879, 1880.
MULDER, W.—Een Deventersch Ockham-Handschrift; Het Boek; pp. 96-101; Martinus Nijhoff, Lange Voorhout 9 Den Haag; 12 Jaargang No. 3, Maart, 1923.
MURATORI, L.—Annali D'Italia; 15 vols.; XXIX, pp. 165, 195, 201, 209, 210-212, 221, 249; Presso Gli Eredi Barbiellini Mercanti di libri, e Stampatori a Pasquino, Roma, 1753.
NEANDER, A.—Church History; 9 vols.; T. Clark, 1847.
——History of Dogma; 2 vols.; Bohn, 1858.
NICOLSON, R.—De Guilielmo de Ockham; a MS. written between the years 1559 and 1664. Also a poem, a MS., De celeberrimo Guilelmo de Ockam. The MS. is found in a book given to Harvard Univ. by Thomas Hollis, between the years 1664 and 1667; for there are the words written: accepto 15 Aug., c. 1767.
NOACK, LUDWIG—Die christliche Mystik nach ihrem geschichtlichen Entwickelungsgange im Mittelalter und in der neuern Zeit dargestellt; Königsberg, 1853.
OGG, F. A.—A Source Book of Mediæval Hist.; American Book Co., New York, 1907.
O'LEARY, DELACY—Arabic Thought and Its Place in History; Dutton & Co., London, 1922.
OLGIATI, F.—The Key to the Study of St. Thomas; trans. by J. S. Zybura; B. Herder Book Co., St. Louis, 1925.

BIBLIOGRAPHY 269

PACKARD, S. R.—Europe and the Church Under Innocent III; Henry Holt, New York, 1927.
PAETOW, L. J.—Guide to the Study of Mediæval History; Univ. of California, 1917.
PARKINSON, A.—Collectanea Anglo-Minoritica (Grey Friars); Thomas Smith, London, 1726.
PATTON, J.—British History of Papal Claims, Vol. I; 1666-1763.
PELZER, A.—Les 51 articles de Guillaume Occam censurés; pp. 240-270; en Avignon, en 1326; Revue D'Histoire Ecclésiastique, Avril-Juillet, 1922; Pierre Smeesters, 1922.
PERRY, A. J.—J. Trevisa's Dialogus inter Militem et Clericum; Oxford Univ. Press, London, 1925.
PETZHOLD, J.—Bibliotheca bibliog.; Leipzig, 1866.
PHILOLOGUS—Zeitschrift für das klassische Alterthum, Vol. I-LXIII; Vol. LIII in two parts; Supplement V, 1-9; 72 vols.; 1846-1904; edited by Sentsch; Schneidewin, Crusins and Hess.
PICAVET, F.—Esquisse D'une Histoire Générale et Comparée des Philosophies Médiévales; Félix Alcan, Paris, 1907.
——Essais sur L'Histoire Générale et Comparée des Théologies et des Philosophies Médiévales; Félix Alcan, Paris, 1913.
PLOTINUS—Annead; IV, 21; 1835.
POOLE, R. L.—Index Britanniae Scriptorum; The Clarendon Press, Oxford, 1902.
——Wycliffe and Movements for Reform; Epochs of Church History; London, 1889.
——On Ockham; Dict. Nat. Biogr.; Vol. XLI, p. 359 sq.; 1895.
——Illustrations of the History of Mediæval Thought and Learning; 2nd ed.; Soc. for Promoting Christian Knowledge, London, 1920.
——Chronicles and Annals; The Clarendon Press, Oxford, 1926.
POTTHAST—Wegweiser durch die Geschichtewerke des europäischen Mittelalters; Bibliography and List of Ockam's Controversial Writings; p. 871.
PRANTL, C.—Geschichte der Logik im Abendlande; I-IV; Vol. II, pp. 327-420; Leipzig, 1855-1867; Gustav Fock, Leipzig, 1927.
——Der Universalienstreit im dreizehnten und vierzehnten Jahrhundert; Sitz.-Ber. der Münchener Akad., 1874.
——Michael Psellus und Petrus Hispanus, eine Rechtfertigung; Hirzel, Leipzig, 1867.
PREGER, W.—In Schriften des Vereins für Reformationsgeschichte; Vol. V; 1892-3.

PREGER, W.—Ueber die Anfänge des kirchenpolitischen Kampfes unter Ludwig dem Baier; (Aus den Abhandlungen der k. bayer. Akademie der Wiss. III, CI, XVI. Bd. II, Abth.); Verlag der k. Akademie, München, 1882.
——Der kirchenpolitische Kampf unter Ludwig dem Baier und sein Einfluss auf die öffentliche Meinung in Deutschland. (Aus den Abhandlungen der k. bayer. Akademie der Wiss. III, CI, XIV. Bd. I, Abth.); München, 1877.
——Geschichte des deut. Mystik im Mittelalter; 3 vols., 1874, 1881, 1893, Vols. I, II. In der ersten Halfte des XIV Jahrhunderts.
Presbyter, an English; Papers on the Doctrine of the English Church, concerning the Eucharistic Presence; The Church of England Book Society, London.
PREVITÉ-ORTON, C. W.—The Defensor Pacis of Marsilius of Padua; Cambridge, 1928.
RADBERTUS, PASCHASIUS—Liber de Corpore et Sanguine Dimini; Patrologiae, Minge.
RABUS—Logik und Metaphysik, Occam; p. 169 (U. P.).
RAND, E. K.—Founders of the Middle Ages; Harvard Univ. Press, Cambridge, 1928.
RASHDALL, H.—The Universities of Europe in the Middle Ages; Vols. I and II; Clarendon Press, Oxford, 1895.
——Friar's Preachers; Oxford.
RAYNALDUS, ORDORICUS—Annales ecclesiastici ab anno quo desinit Card. C. Baronius, 1198, usque ad annum 1534-1565, etc., continuati. Coloniae Agrippinae, 1864; Lucae, 1750. (Episcopal Divinity School, Philadelphia.)
REINWALD, F. H.—Epitome theologiae Christianae; Berlin, 1835.
RETTBERG, F. W.—Occam und Luther; Theologische Studien und Kritiken; pp. 69-136; F. Perthes, Hamburg, 1839.
REUSCH, F.—Index librorum prohibitorum; 1886.
REUTHER, H.—Geschichte der religiösen Aufklärung in Mittelalter, 2 vols.; Berlin, 1875-77.
RIEZLER, S.—Vatikansiche Akten. z. deut. Ges. in der Zeit Ludwigs des Bayern, pp. 5, 66; Innsbruck, 1891.
——Die literarischen Widersacher der Päpste zur Zeit Ludwigs des Baiers; Duncker and Humbolt, Leipzig, 1874.
RIFFEL—Geschichte, Darstellung der Verhältnisse zwischen Kirche und Staat; 1836.
RITSCHL, ALBRECHT—Die christliche Lehre von der Rechtfertigung und Versöhnung, I, p., ed. 2; Jahrbücher fur deutsche Theologie, 1868.
——Fides Implicata; Bonn, 1890.

RITTER, HEINRICH—Geschichte der christlichen Philosophie; Vol. VIII, pp. 574-604; F. Perthes, Hamberg, 1845.
ROBERTS, W. D.—Metaphysica of Aristotle; Oxford, 1908.
ROBERTSON, J. C.—History of Christian Church; 3 vols.; J. Murry, 1868.
ROBINSON, J. H.—The Pre-Reformation Period; Original Sources of European History; Vol. III, pp. 1-34, No. 6; Univ. of Penna., 1912.
ROSS, W. D.—Metaphysica of Aristotle; Oxford, 1908.
——The Works of Aristotle; Oxford, 1928.
ROUSSELAT—Études sur la Philosophie dans le Moyen Âge; Paris, 1840-42.
RUTER, MARTIN—A Concise History of the Christian Church; Carlton & Porter, New York, 1834.
SAGITTARIUS, CASPAR—Introductio in Historiam Ecclesiasticam; Vols. I, II; J. F. Bielckius, Jena, 1718.
SAVIGNY, F. C. VON—Gesch. d. rom. Rechts im Mittelalter; Heidelberg, 1816.
SCHAFF, P.—History of the Christian Church; Vols. I-VII; Vol. I, pp. 691, 719; II, p. 188, ff.; 1858-1890.
——Schaff-Herzog Encyclopedia of Relig. Knowledge; 1884; 3rd ed., 1918.
SCHJELDERUP, H. K.—Hauptlinien der Entwicklung der Philosophie von Mitte des 19. Jahrh. bis zur Gegenwart; Kristiania, 1920.
SCHMALENBACH, H.—Das Mittelalter Sein Begriff und Wesen; Quelle & Meyer, Leipzig, 1926.
SCHREIBER, W.—IV, Wilhelm von Ockkam; Die politischen und religiösen Doctrinen unter Ludwig dem Baiern, pp. 59-82; Druck und Verlag der Jos. Thomann'schen Buckhandlung, Landshut, 1858.
SCHWAB—Johannes Gerson; Würzburg, 1858.
SCOTUS, IOANNIS DUNS—Super Quarto Sententiarum; Lugdunique excusum in edibus Jacobi Myt: sumptu honesti viri Jacobi. q. Francisci de Giunta, etc.; Lyons, 1520.
——Opera Omnia XII, edito nova junxta editionem; Wadding, Minges, P.P.
SEEBERG, R.—Dogmensgeschichte; Vols. I and II; pp. 144-197; trans. by C. A. Hay; Luth. Pub. Soc., 1905.
——William of Occam. The New Schaff-Herzog Encyclopedia of Religious Knowledge; Vol. VIII, pp. 215, 220; New York, 1920.
——In Herzog-Haucks Realencyklopädie; Vol. XIV, under Ockam.

SEEBERG, R.—On the Lord's Supper; Luth. Quart., Oct., 1906.
——Das Schriftprinzip der luth. Kirche; I, p. 309, ff.; Leipzig, 1904.
——Luther und Luthertum in der neuesten katholischen Beleuchtung; Leipzig, 1904.
——Die Theologie des Iohannes Duns Scotus; Leipzig, 1900.
SEIDENBERG—Die kirchenpolitische Litteratur unter dem Kaiser Ludwig dem Bayern und die Zunftkämpfe vornehmlich in Mainz; in: Westdeutsche Zeitschrift für Gesch. u. Kunst; VIII, p. 101.
SETON, W.—Nicholas Glassberger and His Works (1200-1310); The Univ. Press, Manchester, 1923.
SEYBOLT, R. F.—The Manuale Scholarium; Nominalism at Heidelberg; pp. 40-43; Harvard Univ. Press, Cambridge, 1921.
SHALLO, M. W.—Lessons in Scholastic Philosophy; The Peter Reilly Co., Philadelphia, 1923.
SHELDON, H. C.—History of Christian Doctrine; Vol. I; Harper & Brother, New York, 1886.
SIEBECK, R.—Geschichte der Psychologie; Gotha, 1884.
——Die Anfänge der neueren Psychol. in d. Scholast., Ztschr. f. Philos. u. Phil.; Vol. 94, p. 161 ff.; Vol. XCV, p. 245 ff.
——Occams Erkenntnislehre in ihrer historischen Stellung, im Archiv. fur Gesch. der Philosophie, Bd. X, p. 317 ff.; Berlin, 1897.
——Das Unmittelbare in unserer Bestimmung; F. E. B. Mohr, Tübigen, 1917.
SIGNORILLO, N.—Lexicon Peripateticum, Philosophico-Theologicum; Naples, 1893.
SILBERNAGEL, J.—Wilhelm von Ockam Ansichten über Kirche und Staat; pp. 423-433; Historisches Jahrbuch; VII, Band. 3. Heft; Herder & Co., München, 1886,
SMITH, A. L.—Church and State in the Middle Ages; Oxford, 1913.
SMITH, P.—Erasmus, A Study of his Life, Ideals and Place in History; Harper & Bros., New York, 1923.
SMITH, P. AND GALLINGER, W. P.—Conversations with Luther (Selections from Table-Talk); Pilgrim Press, New York, 1915. Luther's Correspondence and Other Contemporary Letters; The Luth. Pub. Soc., Philadelphia, 1913.
SMITH AND WACE—Dictionary of Christian Biography, 1877.
SORLEY, W. R.—A History of English Philosophy; G. P. Putnam's Sons, New York, 1921.
STÄHELIN—Huldreich Zwingli u. sein Reformationswerk; 1884.

BIBLIOGRAPHY 273

STEVENS, L.—Dict. of Biography; 1703.
——Essays in Ecclestiastical Biography; 2 vols.; London, 1850.
STÖCKL, A.—Geschichte der Phil. des Mittelalters; Vol. I; trans. by T. A. Finlay; Longmans, New York, 1914.
STANGE AND DITTRICH—Vox Latina, lateinisches Lesebuch III; Dieterich'scher Verlag., Leipzig, 1926.
SULLIVAN, J.—Marsigilo of Padua and William of Ockam; The American Hist. Rev.; Vol. II, No. 3, pp. 409-426; April, 1897; Vol. II, No. 4, pp. 593-610; July, 1897; New York.
——Ann. Rep. Amer. Hist. Assoc., 1902, Vol. I, pp. 65-81.
——Eng. Hist. Rev., The Manuscripts and Date of Marsiglio of Padua's "Defensor Pacis"; Vol. XX, 1905, pp. 293-307.
TAYLOR, H. O.—The Mediæval Mind; Vol. II; Macmillan, New York, 1911.
——Thought and Expression in the Sixteenth Century; Vol. I, pp. 73, 77, 200; n. 16, 213, 214; II, 5, 24; n. 5, 42, 268 f.; New York, 1920.
TENNEMANN, W. G.—Geschichte der Philosophie; Vol. VIII, p. 866; Paris, 3rd ed.; Barth, Leipzig, 1820.
——Manuel de L'Histoire de la Philosophie; (trans. by V. Cousin; Vols. I and II; Vol. I, pp. 382-388; 1829).
——Manuel of Philosophy; trans. by Arthur Johnson; London, 1870.
THILLY, F.—A History of Philosophy; p. 215 ff.; Henry Holt & Co., New York, 1914.
THOMAS, A.—Extraits des Archives du Vatican pour servir à l'Histoire du Moyen Âge in Mélanges d'Archéologie et d'Histoire de l'École de Rome; pp. 446-452; 1882.
THOMASIUS—Historia Contentionis inter Imperium et Sacerdotium; 1722.
THOMPSON, E. M.—Handbook of Greek and Latin Paleography; D. Appleton & Co., New York, 1892.
THOMSON, J. R.—A Dictionary of Philosophy; 2nd ed.; R. F. Dickinson, London, 1892.
THORBURN, W. M.—Occam's Razor; Mind; pp. 287, 288; Macmillan, April, 1915.
——The Myth of Occam's Razor; Mind; pp. 345-353; Macmillan & Co., New York, July, 1918.
THORNDIKE, L.—History of Medieval Europe; Houghton, New York, 1917.
THUROT, C.—L'Enseignement dans l'Université de Paris au Moyen Âge; Paris, 1850.

274 BIBLIOGRAPHY

TOWNSEND, W. J.—The Great Schoolman of the Middle Ages; pp. 267-287; G. E. Stechert, 1920.
TRITHEMIUS, JOHANNIS—Primae Partis Opera Historica, Quotquot hactenus reperiri potuerunt omnia; Typis Wechelianis apud Claudium, Francofurti, 1601.
TURNER, S.—History of the Middle Ages; Vols. I-III; Longmans, 1917.
TURNER, W.—History of Philosophy; Ginn & Co., New York, 1903.
TSCHACKERT, P.—Peter von Ailli; Vorwort ix, p. 43; F. A. Perthes, Gotha, 1877.
TYTZ, JOANNIS—Lexicon Theologicum; Cologne, 1619.
UEBERWEG, F.—History of Philosophy; trans. by G. S. Morris; Vol. I, pp. 460-467; Scribner, Armstrong & Co., New York, 1875.
UEBERWEG-BAUMGARTNER—Grundriss der Geschichte der Philosophie; Vol. II, pp. 589-607; E. S. Mittler & Son, Berlin, 1915.
ULLMAN, C.—Reformers before the Reformation; trans. by Robert Menzies; 2 vols.; T. & T. Clark, Edinburgh, 1863.
VAUGHAN, R. A.—Hours with the Mystics; 2 vols.; Strahan, 1880.
VAUGHN, E. V.—The Origin and Early Development of the English Universities to the Close of the Thirteenth Century; Social Science Series (The Univ. of Missouri Studies); Vol. II, No. 2; University of Missouri, August, 1908.
VICTOR, ST. HUGO—Opera Omnia De Sacramentis; Vol. II, p. 314f.; Minge, Paris, 1880.
VILLANI, GIOVANNI—Historia; Venice, 1562.
VOGEL, A.—Überblick über die Geschichte der Philosophie; Teil. I, II; F. Brandstetter, Leipzig, 1905.
WACE, HENRY, AND BUCHHEIM—Luther's Primary Works; Hodder & Stoughton, London, 1896.
WADDING, L.—Annales Minorum Fratrum; 8 vols.; Lugd., 1625-1654; Fonseca, Vol. VII, VIII; continued to 1622; Rome, 1731-1886. (Congressional Library.)
——Annales Ordinis Praedicatorum; Rome, 1746.
WADDINGTON, G.—History of the Church from the Earliest Ages to the Reformation; Harper & Bros., New York, 1875.
WAGENMANN, B.—Under Occam; Real. Encyl., Vol. IV; Leipzig, 1882.
WALCOTT, G. D.—Kantian and Lutheran Elements in Ritschl's Conception of God; XII, p. 121; New York, N.P., 1904.
WALKER, L. J.—Theories of Knowledge; p. 14; Longmans, Green & Co., London, 1910.

WATTENBACH, W.—Deutschlands Geschichtsquellen im Mittelalter bis zur Mitte. d. 13 Jahrh.; 1904.
WENNER, G. U.—New Light on Luther; The Bible Record; Vol. IX, No. 8, pp. 339-346; October, 1912.
Western Philos. and Theol. in the Thirteenth Century; Harvard Theol. Rev., 1918, p. 409; 1923, p. 143.
WERNER, K.—Die Scholastik des späteren Mittelalters; 4 vols.; 1883.
——I, John Dunn Scotus.
——Die nachscotistische Scholastik; Wilhelm Braumüller, Vienna, 1883.
——IV, Der Endausgang d. mittelalt. Scholastik: W. Braumüller, Vienna, 1883.
——D. Entwicklungsgang des mittelalters; Psychol.; 1876.
——Gesch. d. Philos.; VIII; 1845.
WINDELBAND, W.—A History of Philosophy; trans. by J. H. Tufts; Macmillan, New York, 1895.
WILLMANN—Geschichte des Idealismus; Vol. II, Fathers of the Church and the Middle Ages; 2nd ed; Brunswick, 1907.
WOLF, G.—Quellenkunde der deutschen Reformationsgeschichte; I, 74 f.; 1915.
WOOD, A.—Historia et Antiquitates Universitätis Oxoniensis; Vol. I, pp. 160, 169; Vol. II, p. 5 ff., p. 87; Univ. Oxn., Oxford, 1674.
——History and Antiquities of the University of Oxford; Oxford, Gutch, 1792-1796.
——Life and Times of Anthony Wood; Antiquary of Oxford; Clarendon Press, Oxford, 1891-1900.
WOODWARD, G. R.—The Political Theories of Martin Luther; Putman, 1910.
WORKMAN, H. B.—John Wyclif; Vol. I-II; The Clarendon Press, Oxford, 1926.
WRIGHT, C. H. C.—A History of French Literature, p. 94; 1912.
ZARNCKE, F.—Die deutschen Universitäten im Mittelalter; Weigel, Leipzig, 1857.
ZYBURA, J. S.—Present-Day Thinkers and The New Scholasticism; B. Herder Book Co., St. Louis, 1926.

www.ingramcontent.com/pod-product-compliance
Lightning Source LLC
Chambersburg PA
CBHW071956220426
43662CB00009B/1159